The Olympic Arts Festival is pleased to co-sponsor The Museum of Contemporary Art's "Automobile and Culture" exhibition, which offers the unique opportunity to view the automobile as an aesthetic design object and to examine the ways in which the automobile has, since its invention in the late nineteenth century, served artists as a powerful metaphoric icon.

Visitors will find it fascinating to discover that, in 1487, Leonardo da Vinci had already drafted the prototype of an ingenious spring-driven car, and that as early as the turn of this century, Toulouse-Lautrec was drawing illustrations of aesthetically dazzling, if mechanically elementary, automobiles. It will prove a particular pleasure to come nearer to our own time and view the Surrealist canvases, in which the image of the automobile has been transformed into the stuff of fantastic dreams. As the automobile became an indispensable part of modern life, it was increasingly integrated into works of art, both as image in, for example, works of Pop art, and as physical sculptural material. The Los Angeles Olympic Organizing Committee is gratified that The Museum of Contemporary Art is sharing these and other discoveries with residents of California and thousands of visitors from throughout the world.

The Olympic Arts Festival established its relationship with the museum soon after the festival was created. At that time, the museum was little more than promises and architectural sketches, but it did have the prestige and persuasive skills of its Founding Director, Pontus Hulten, and its Director, Richard Koshalek. The Los Angeles Olympic Organizing Committee shared a common bond with the museum in that when the 1984 Olympic Games were awarded to Los Angeles in 1978, the Olympic Organizing Committee consisted of little money and seven people in temporary offices. Today, with the help of its official sponsor, the Times Mirror Company, the Olympic Arts Festival stands as a reminder of Los Angeles's commitment to fostering cultural development that will reaffirm the city as a vital international center for the arts. The "Automobile and Culture" exhibition exists as one of the many cultural events supported by the Los Angeles Olympic Organizing Committee and is presented under the auspices of the Olympic Arts Festival, which has endeavored to bring together the best of the arts during a special period in Los Angeles's history.

—Robert J. Fitzpatrick, *Director*, Olympic Arts Festival

AUTOMOBILE

GERALD SILK

Angelo Tito Anselmi
Henry Flood Robert, Jr.
Strother MacMinn

AND CULTURE

*Original Photography
by Henry Wolf*

Harry N. Abrams, Inc., Publishers, New York

The Museum of Contemporary Art, Los Angeles

Museum Editor: Bridget Johnson
Editorial Assistants: Jacqueline Crist,
Elizabeth A.T. Smith

Abrams Editor: Joan E. Fisher
Designer: Samuel N. Antupit

*Library of Congress Cataloging in
Publication Data*
Main entry under title:
Automobile and culture.
    Published in conjunction with an ex-
hibition organized by the Museum of
Contemporary Art in Los Angeles.
    Bibliography: p.
    Includes index.
    1. Automobiles in art—Exhibitions.
2. Automobiles—Designs and
construction—Exhibitions.
3. Automobiles—Social aspects
—Exhibitions. I. Silk, Gerald.
II. Museum of Contemporary Art
(Los Angeles, Calif.)
N8217.A94A97   1984
704.9′496292222074019494 83-22164
ISBN 0-8109-1815-3 (Abrams)
ISBN 0-8109-2283-5 (pbk)
Illustrations © 1984 The Museum of
Contemporary Art, Los Angeles
Published in 1984 by Harry N. Abrams,
Incorporated, New York.

The Los Angeles Olympic Organizing Committee, Ford Motor
Company, Fiat S.p.A., and Renault have provided major funding to "Automobile and Culture,"
an Olympic Arts Festival exhibition, Times Mirror, official festival sponsor.

This exhibition is part of The
Temporary Contemporary, the
Museum's inaugural series of
exhibitions and related events.
Development of The Temporary
Contemporary was funded in
part by a major grant from Citi-
corp/Citibank.

TITLE PAGE: 1981 *Lamborghini Coun-
tach.* Model S. PAGES 4–5: 1902 *Olds-
mobile Curved Dash Runabout.* OP-
POSITE: steering wheel of a 1910 *Ford
Model T.* PAGES 8–9: headlight of a 1910
Ford Model T. CONTENTS PAGE: taillight
of a 1933 *Pierce Arrow, Silver Arrow,*
Model 1234.

Printed and bound in Japan

CONTENTS

FOREWORDS

One cannot say that in general our relation to the automobile is very graceful. It is more like a passionate liaison that has its elements of love and hate, where one often tends to blame the other for one's own defects.

We do not deal with the car as we do with other man-made contraptions—the car has become too much a part of our unconscious. This is not surprising, considering the number of hours that many people spend behind the steering wheels of their darlings. Although this relation is superficially graceless, it has an underlying and very robust wild dignity.

There are a few objects that we assume to be extensions of our bodies: a car, a motorcycle, a boat, a gun, for example, but when these objects do not function, we get as angry as if a friend had deceived us. In Hollywood, there is no greater star than the car. The car is virtually omnipresent—no other technical invention has altered life as radically as has the automobile: it has changed our cities, the landscape and the way we see it, the environment, architecture, our lifestyles. As is often the case, when something is very important, we have trouble appreciating its true dimensions and value. On one hand, we take the car for granted until we have a motor failure or a flat tire; on the other, it enters our dream world, the unconscious, to a great degree. When the gigantic mass of a ten-ton truck passes ten feet in front of us at, let us say, sixty miles an hour, we find it quite normal.

What then is the car? It is, I think, the flesh given to that old phantom: personal freedom, individual liberty. It is the twentieth-century realization of the great romantic nineteenth-century dream: personal independence. What James Joyce calls HCE: Here Comes Everybody.

One might object here, for example, to say personal freedom while driving is restricted by many written rules and regulations. But in reality, this is not so. The rules are actually few, and easy to learn. They are also, to a great extent, international. One might argue that there exists an even greater number of unwritten rules that one had better obey. Yet for all its complexity, modern car driving is the most amazing social phenomenon ever seen. Almost everybody—all classes, ages, men, and women— is free to take his powerful machine on the road. In some countries, such as Belgium, one does not even need a driver's license.

Theories have been formulated about individual freedom and its consequences within a social pattern. In the nineteenth century, anarchist theory was an important component in political and philosophical discussions. The anarchist ideas were represented by men like Proudhon, Bakunin, and Kropotkin, who then played roles as large as Marx did. History and its evolution has run them over. What they—all of them—said was this: people would be better off with fewer rules to live by rather than with more. A few common agreements would be sufficient. Left to themselves, people are competent and capable. Confusion is sometimes as valuable as order.

Headlight of a 1931 *Duesenberg Boattail "French" Speedster,* Model J

There is a peculiar and amusing resemblance between these theories and the phenomenon of automobile traffic. The a priori, totally impossible postulate—liberty for more or less everybody to use a very powerful, even deadly machine, in an extremely difficult context—is rather happily resolved in a system of thousands of little adjustments, agreements, common habits, eye contacts, and signals. Although sometimes one feels the need to use insults or fly into a rage, the number of accidents is actually quite small, if one takes into account the amount of traffic, and what could go wrong, if everyone did not use a certain equilibrium of confidence and mistrust in the other drivers' skills.

Law and order play a rather small part in all this. In Paris, the police refuse to have anything to do with accidents that involve only damage to the car. Some cities are less governed than others, where traffic runs faster (and smoother?). It is more intriguing to drive in Tokyo, Paris, or Rome, than in Los Angeles, New York, or Stockholm. The big star-shaped places like the "Etoile" (around the Arch of Triumph) in Paris, are the most interesting situations to watch. In that specific case, traffic feeds in and out of thirteen different streets and avenues, and the drivers have to sort it out among themselves, something no system of traffic lights and policemen could ever do. Taking into account the size of the problem and the way it is resolved, it is an amazing achievement, constantly repeating itself around the clock, through the decades.

Since the invention of the automobile, artists have been fascinated by it, commenting on the world of cars in their works with love and in despair. Great photographers have registered automobile shapes, the mystery of speed, the magic of the lacquer finish or the chrome detail, the virile or feminine forms. Architects have sometimes lovingly designed automobile dwellings, the garage; urban planners and highway specialists continue to cope with the ever-growing numbers of cars. These comments and considerations, given to what is for most of us an everyday companion, is the subject of this book and the exhibition "Automobile and Culture." This is the first retrospective of automobile design.

Pontus Hulten
Founding Director

I t is hard to realize that eighty-five-years ago there were virtually no automobiles. In 1898, the entire United States registered only eight hundred cars—and while this statistic undoubtedly errs somewhat on the side of pessimism, it is a very far cry from the latest statistic of 124 million odd, or approximately one vehicle per 1.9 inhabitants.

From a temperamental plaything of the eccentric and philistine rich, the automobile has become an integral part of modern living. It is the accepted form of short-range transportation for business and pleasure alike. It governs urban planning, and must rate as the prime factor in the American swing-away from a "downtown" philosophy. Whole areas of countryside have had to be remodeled to create new highways.

Taken even more widely, the internal combustion engine has become an essential of war and peace, powering (at some time) all forms of land, sea, and air transportation, and supplanting the horse in agriculture. It has created employment, directly and indirectly. Looking beyond those employed in the manufacture, assembly, and servicing of automobiles, one must consider those who drive them for a living, and those whose work is dependent upon them. Add those engaged in the building, maintenance, and policing of highways, and others who administer the automobile fiscally to governmental profit, and one recognizes that few Americans—indeed, few Western citizens—are not among the vehicle's dependents.

Nor is the automobile simply transportation. Though Ransom Olds and Henry Ford evolved cheap mass-produced cars between 1900 and 1914, the automobile has since become an object of pride and affection. Success in life is reflected in the automobile one drives, be it sporting, luxurious, or merely individual. Anonymous black four-door sedans have been among the first casualties of prosperity, and the last thirty years, especially, have added a new dimension to automobilism—the collection of antique cars.

How far this relates to an artistic concept is questionable. Duesenbergs, Rolls-Royces, and Bugattis are handmade: the same cannot be said of either a Cast Iron Wonder Chevrolet or a contemporary Renault or Morris. Yet these are preserved as landmarks of social history, vehicles devoid of the modern way of in-car living. Extra clothes provided what heating there was, defective elements were repaired, not replaced, and we thought in terms of double-clutching and tire-changing. Say what you like, 1920s automobiles may have been dependable, but living with them was by no means painless.

The automobile has conferred freedom of movement upon the masses, but there is a dark side to the coin. With so many people's livelihood geared to transportation, recessions hit harder and more comprehensively. Rapid movement from A to B saves lives: it also takes them, in terrifying numbers. Too much horsepower—and too little audible or visual sensation of it—can be perilous in the hands of the unskilled. Too many cars spell urban congestion and pollution of the air, and the explosion in automobile ownership since World War II has imperiled supplies of oil.

Nobody, however, wants to be the first to relinquish the so newly won freedom, to return to crowded buses and railroads. One wonders how many citizens will have reacted positively to the car-sharing propaganda seen on all the freeways of Los Angeles. As a Briton, I can recall the almost carless decade of the forties, but at that time the automobile was not yet fully a part of our way of life, and one thought essentially in terms of railroads for transportation. It was not until 1956 and the Suez Crisis that it was brought home to us that two hundred miles of motoring per month did not suffice for our needs, even in a small island with inadequate highways.

This publication and exhibition celebrating the automobile and culture can serve to educate the public to the automobile's basic social impact, and perhaps inspire more intelligent future use of the motorized vehicle. Let us hope that it will guide us to accept the automobile—but as the community's servant rather than its menacing master.

Lord Montagu of Beaulieu

Right: 1913 *Mercer Raceabout.*
Model Type 35-J
Far right: 1931 *Bugatti Berline de Voyage.* Model Type 41
(Royale)
Preceding pages:
1936 *Mercedes-Benz Special Roadster.* Model 500K

Right: 1925 *Rolls-Royce Boat-tail Speedster.* Model Phantom I
Far right: 1948 *M.G. Midget.* Model MG TC
Following pages: Engine of a 1936 *Mercedes-Benz Special Roadster.* Model 500K

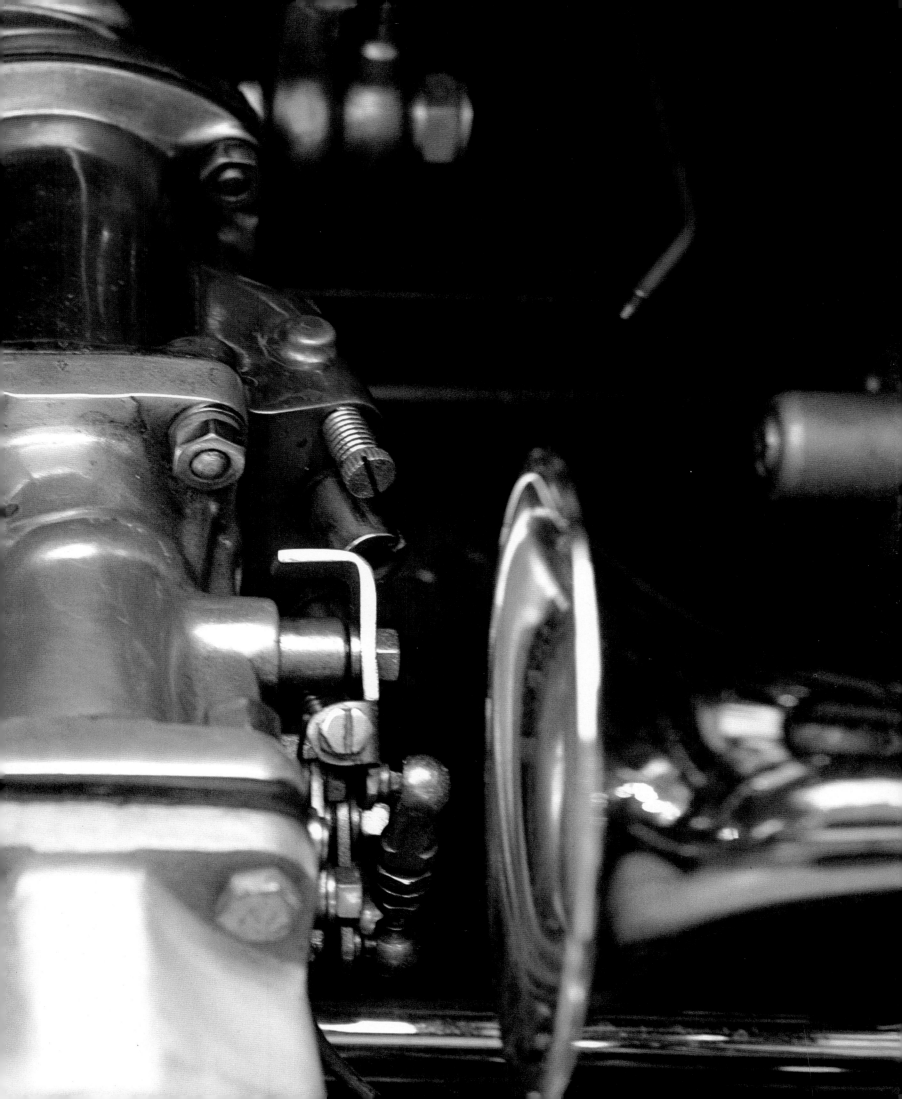

THE AUTOMOBILE IN ART

Hood ornament on a 1933
Pierce Arrow, Silver Arrow,
Model 1234

FIRST VISIONS

Almost as soon as it was invented, the automobile began to make its way into the art world. The automobile, one of the great modern inventions, has become a major attraction in museums of history, technology, and transportation; as objects of potential beauty and aesthetic significance, motorcars are exhibited in the design sections of art museums. But as imagery and subject matter in works of art, the automobile appeared in museums and galleries long before the cars themselves were put on display.

Throughout their histories, art and the automobile have engaged in a rich and fruitful relationship. Many modern artists and illustrators have used the image of the automobile in their work as an expression of ideas and sensations associated with the automobile or simply as a representation of itself. Compared with the horse-drawn carriage or even the train and the bicycle, the car produced intoxicating feelings of personal freedom, power, and liberation, which frequently captured the artist's imagination. In order to express these new experiences and feelings, artists were forced to develop new visual languages. So the car began to influence not only the content of art, but also its form.

The automobile was introduced during a time of tremendous technological progress, when developments in transportation and communication intensified the vitality of the urban revolution, altered man's conception of space and time and his perception of the environment, bombarded him with stimuli, and extended his geographic horizons. The automobile initially functioned as an optimistic symbol of change and progress, but as the potential dangers and abuses of technology became more evident, the wholehearted approval and celebration of the motorcar gave way to more sober, critical, and negative assessments of its impact.

The various ways artists incorporated the car into their work reveal something about general social attitudes toward the automobile and the emergence of modern industrialized society. Art, however, does not merely reflect culture, but is part of culture itself. A work of art that contains auto imagery can mirror a society's feelings about the car, but it also can ar-

The inventor of the automobile has had more influence on society than the combined exploits of Napoleon, Genghis Khan, and Julius Caesar.

—William Ogburn, *Machines and Tomorrow's World*, Public Affairs Pamphlet, No. 25, 1938

Full twenty tripods for his hall he framed,/ That placed on living wheels of massy gold,/ (Wondrous to tell,) instinct with spirit roll'd/From place to place, around the bless'd abodes/ Self-moved, obedient to the beck of gods.

—Homer, *The Iliad*

School of Albrecht Dürer. The Triumphal Procession of Maximilian I, *Plate 95,* The Austrian War. *Original blocks before 1526, reprint, Vienna, 1883–84. Woodcut. The Metropolitan Museum of Art, New York City. Harris Brisbane Dick Fund*

Leonardo da Vinci. Design for a scythed vehicle or war machine. Facsimile of original drawing in Turin Collection. c. 1483. Elmer Belt Library of Vinciana, University of California at Los Angeles

ticulate ideas, and criticize and interpret existing values. Art can thus promulgate, record, analyze, and perpetuate the myths and rituals associated with the automobile. While the artist's view is one of many possible records of history and culture, it provides evocative, penetrating means and dimensions through which culture and its artifacts may be better understood.

Artists were among the first to project visions of self-propelled vehicles centuries before the car was actually invented and produced. Leonardo da Vinci's celebrated proposals for spring-driven cars and horseless wagons were developed as part of a series of studies for devices related to locomotion. In much the same way as a wind-up toy, Leonardo's car was designed to operate with uninterrupted forward motion, powered by two springs. The coils were to be tightened manually; as one coil unwinds and releases energy necessary to propel the vehicle forward, its companion is rewound. The springs are linked to the car's wheels by pulleys; a steering shaft, attached to a single rear wheel, functions like a boat's tiller. Leonardo's prototypes for self-propelled vehicles, several of which had potential military application, are a testimony to the Renaissance faith in man's ability to order and control the universe, and can be interpreted as an attempt to overcome limitations imposed by nature. His proposed inventions stem from the same impulse that spurred the development of perspective, the greatest of all Renaissance artistic inventions. Just as artists, employing mathematics and geometry, developed perspective to order and control the pictorial world, so Renaissance inventors and engineers, many of whom were themselves artists and architects, enlisted science to regulate and organize the actual environment. Leonardo was obsessed with perspective and shared with his contemporaries the belief that the roles of artist and engineer were not separate and distinct. Because of his wide-ranging genius, Leonardo was much sought after by the patrons of Italy, and his approach to the relationship between art and technology anticipates that of more recent art movements, in which the practice of art is joined to the practice of invention and design.

Taking his cue from the Italian Renaissance tradition of the artist-engineer, the German artist Albrecht Dürer mixed art and mechanical invention freely. Dürer was the most renowned printmaker of his time, and used mechanical techniques, such as engraving and woodcutting, to produce multiple works of art. He even invented an apparatus for making perspectival images in which connecting threads, anchored from a single spot to the contours of an object, would record the points where the strings intersected a frame. Like light rays striking the surface of film, these filaments passing through a frame represent, in principle, the elements of a primitive forerunner to the modern camera.

Dürer's artistic and intellectual abilities were put to the services of the Holy Roman Emperor and German King Maximilian I. One of the products of this liaison was an extraordinary series of more than one hundred and thirty woodcuts entitled *The Triumph of Maximilian I*. An elaborate conception coordinated by counselors, historians, philosophers, poets, and a battery of artists, artisans, and laborers, these works celebrated Maximilian's achievements and fantasies. One group of the woodcuts depicts concepts for mechanically propelled vehicles that commemorate war victories. Most of the woodcuts were probably executed by Dürer's contemporary, Hans Burgkmair, although it is not certain who designed this series of moving chariots.

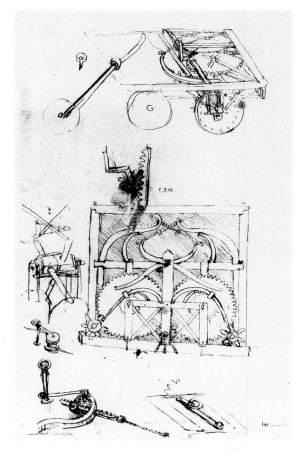

Leonardo da Vinci. Design for a spring-driven car or horseless wagon. Facsimile of original drawing from Codex Atlanticus, *folio 296, verso A. c. 1478. Elmer Belt Library of Vinciana, University of California at Los Angeles*

G. B. SELDEN.
ROAD ENGINE.

No. 549,160.   Patented Nov. 5, 1895.

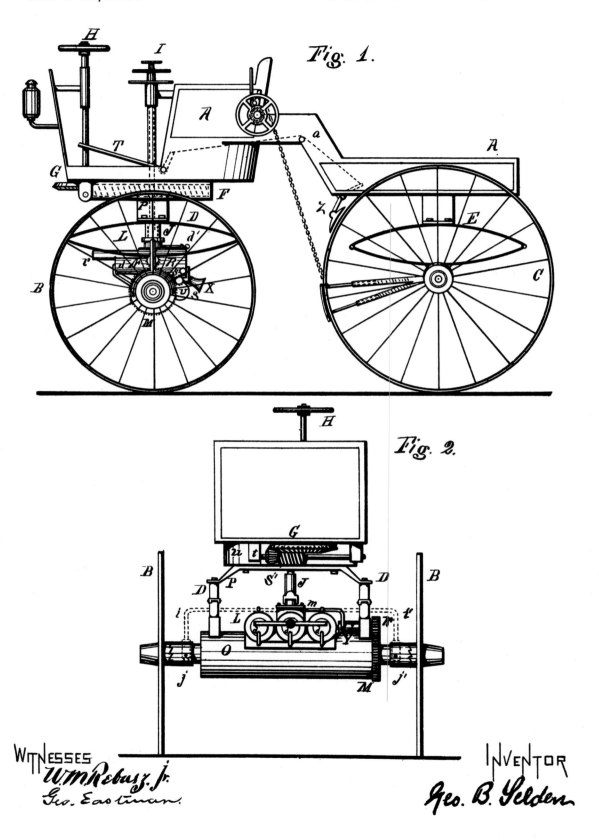

Fig. 1.

Fig. 2.

WITNESSES
W. M. Rebasz Jr.
Geo. Eastman.

INVENTOR
Geo. B. Selden

Each chariot is powered in a different manner; the entire grouping presents strange visions of mechanical propulsion devices, including treadmills and an assortment of hand- or foot-operated cogs, spokes, and gears. While the hand-driven cogwheels of the wagon depicted in *The Triumphal Procession of Maximilian I: The Austrian War* may be the most sophisticated contrivance, the device remains highly impractical. These vehicles were never intended to be built, and they should be regarded as symbols that fused the past and the present. The ancient concept of victory, incarnated in the elaborate chariot bedecked with allegorical and contemporary figures, was combined with fantastical modern invention.

These early schemes for automobiles demonstrate the Renaissance union of art and technology, an idea originating in ancient Greece, where *technē* was the root word for both art and science. Although modern engineers argue that Leonardo's designs could have worked, these early proposals remain visionary. The generation of inventors who, at the end of the nineteeth century, pioneered the modern automobile, were engineers and machinists, not artists.

The road leading from the dreams of self-propelled vehicles to operable automobiles was not always smooth. Major breakthroughs occurred when less feasible sources of energy—springs, clockworks, gunpowder, fire, wind, water, and pedals—were replaced by more practical forms of power—first, steam; later, internal combustion. Among the more intriguing early schemes for automobiles are the vehicles produced by the French engineer Nicholas Joseph Cugnot, and by the American inventor and engineer Oliver Evans. Constructed in the late 1760s and early 1770s, Cugnot's cumbersome car is generally regarded as the grandfather of the modern auto. Stoked by a huge steam boiler, it was built to carry artillery, but its mammoth size, slow speed, and poor maneuverability made it less effective than horse-drawn conveyances. It is rumored that Cugnot's vehicle went out of control on an early test run and demolished a wall; this mishap has earned the dubious distinction of being the first auto accident. In 1805, Evans, utilizing a high-pressure steam engine, manufactured his "Amphibious Digger," a dredging device meant to move on land and in the water. This awkward twenty-ton contraption astonished and amused the residents of Philadelphia, where it was built, as it lumbered down the city streets at a top speed of four miles per hour.

Experimentation in self-propelled vehicles stretched from Europe to the United States, and some controversy exists as to whom should be considered the true inventor of the automobile. Many automotive historians divide the honor between two German engineers, Karl Benz and Gottlieb Daimler. When Benz successfully assembled his prototype two-cycle gas engine in 1879, he was building on foundations established by the Frenchman Jean-Joseph-Etienne Lenoir, and the German Nickolaus August Otto. Having labored unsuccessfully on a motor, Benz, urged on by his wife, decided to try again on New Year's Eve. He dramatically recounted the details: "We were, back again, standing in front of the engine as if it were a great mystery that was impossible to solve. My heart was pounding. I turned the crank. The engine started to go 'put-put-put' and music of the future sounded with regular rhythm. . . . Suddenly the bells began to ring—New Year's Eve bells. We felt they were not only ringing in a new year, but a new era." When Otto's

Above and opposite: G.B. Selden. Patent application drawing for a road engine, No. 549, 160. Granted November 5, 1895. Ink on paper, 10 × 15¼". The Smithsonian Institution, Washington D.C.

engine patent lapsed, Benz borrowed from it to develop a four-stroke motor, installing it in a somewhat unstable three-wheeled vehicle that owed much to bicycle construction. In 1885, he unveiled this vehicle, and while its maiden voyage resulted in a crash, the modern automobile age was under way.

  In 1886, Gottlieb Daimler, separated from Benz by a mere sixty miles, launched his independent version of the automobile. Designing a gift for his wife, Daimler started with a four-wheel carriage, originally intended to be horse drawn, to which he attached an engine and steering gear: the first genuine "horseless carriage." Achieving speeds of up to eleven miles per hour, Daimler's car possessed some remarkably sophisticated features—fan cooling, an engine mounted on rubber shocks, and a system to preheat oil and gas using engine exhaust. Over the next few years, Benz and Daimler revised and refined their models; by the late 1880s the automobile was being sold commercially, and Germany had become the first manufacturing and marketing center of the motorcar. Its lead did not last long. In the 1890s, Emile Levassor, a Frenchman, having obtained the patent on the Daimler motor, rethought the basic design of the car and converted the "horseless carriage" into a true mechanically propelled vehicle with a more powerful engine and a sleeker design. Levassor was eventually honored in one of the major artistic monuments to the automobile after his extraordinary victory in 1895 at the Paris–Bordeaux–Paris motor race. Levassor's nearly forty-eight hours of uninterrupted driving, an amazing feat of skill and endurance, has yet to be surpassed. The reliability of his internal combustion engine vehicle, built with and named for René Panhard, catapulted France into the automotive vanguard.

In the same year that Karl Benz constructed his gas engine, George B. Selden, an American inventor and patent attorney, submitted a patent for an internal combustion car, though an operable Selden vehicle was not built until 1904. In early automotive history, this particular patent was less important as a blueprint for an actual car than as the center of a controversy, in which a group of auto manufacturers tried to use it to monopolize the young industry. Throughout the 1880s, many experimental automobiles were developed in the United States, but the first successful American car was assembled in 1893–94 by two bicycle mechanics, Charles E. and J. Frank Duryea. Working out of Springfield, Massachusetts, the Duryea brothers put the first American automobile on the road. Not long after the Duryeas's invention, Elwood Haynes produced a motorcar in Indiana in 1893–94, and Henry Ford built his first model, a quadricycle, in Detroit in 1896, seven years before the Ford Motor Company came into existence.

In the early decades of automotive invention, Europe was in the forefront until the outcome of a car race rearranged the positions of superiority in the fledgling automobile industry. Just as Levassor's victory in the Paris–Bordeaux–Paris rally of 1895 made France a front-runner in the auto culture, so a Duryea car put the United States on the automobile map later that year, after winning the first official American race sponsored by the *Chicago Times-Herald* on Thanksgiving Day. Beating out a Benz, the only other finisher, the Duryea demonstrated that American cars could compete with European makes. These early auto rallies emphasized endurance more than speed and were intended to publicize the dependability of the car in an effort to convince potential owners that automobiles were practical and reliable.

During this initial era of experimentation and invention, the relationship between the car and art was not as direct as when Renaissance artists had produced visionary designs for self-propelled vehicles. Some of the early patent drawings, though, might be thought of as worthy of aesthetic appreciation, especially because of their affinity with certain developments in recent art. With the emergence of earthworks and site-specific sculpture, artforms sometimes best comprehended through elaborate sketches, models, and diagrams, early automotive patent drawings can be viewed as forerunners to contemporary movements. Still, the aesthetic potential of patents remains secondary to their role in the actual invention of the automobile.

The construction of the motorcar in the late nineteenth century established a new dialogue between artist and automobile, one that typifies the subsequent history of auto art. With few exceptions, the artist no longer participates directly in the design of cars, but rather includes its image in his work. In his depiction of the motorcar and its associated sensations, the artist attempted to grasp the meaning of this innovation, from its impact on daily life to its implications for culture in general.

Opposite: W.H. James. Patent application drawing for a self-propelled land vehicle, British Patent No. 6297, August 15, 1832. Ink on paper, 18¼ × 26". Comptroller General, United Kingdom Patent Office, London and The New York Public Library

INVENTION AND CELEBRATION

The invention of the automobile was part of a sweeping scientific and technological revolution at the turn of the century that brought forth the telephone, the airplane, the wireless telegraph, the electric light, "talking machines," moving pictures, synthetic fibers and plastics, and major theories in physics, mathematics, and psychology. Essential advances in auto design and production were also closely connected to the development of the internal combustion engine, pneumatic tires, and refinements in the coordinated moving assembly line.

  The transformations wrought by these numerous innovations and discoveries were undoubtedly radical, such that one contemporary observer claimed in 1913 that "the world has changed less since the time of Christ than it has in the last thirty years." Moved by this sense of change, artists sought motifs capable of symbolizing this modern metamorphosis, this feeling of transition from the old to the new. As a prime contributor to this sense of change, the automobile became one such symbol.

  In its role as emblem of an age in transition, the car was represented in various ways. It became a symbol of the dawn of the modern era, often compared with the great figures and achievements of the classical world, which not only stressed the magnitude of the accomplishments of the modern era, but also provided it with a certain legitimacy and pedigree.

  This pairing of the automobile with a classical figure or artifact was symptomatic of the turn-of-the-century notion of the myth of the machine. Since myths often arise to help explain complex and sometimes unintelligible phenomena, it was inevitable that a mythology developed around objects felt to possess such extraordinary powers, objects that were altering the environment and man's perception of the world.

  Henri de Toulouse-Lautrec's 1896 lithograph *The Automobilist* is perhaps the earliest example of the image of the automobile in the work of a major modern artist. Fascinated with the kinetics and rhythms of modern life, particularly that of dance halls and cafés, Lautrec expressed the tempo of modernity in a portrayal of his cousin as a supercharged extension

I love my automobile... she is my life, my artistic and spiritual life... full of riches... she is more dear, more useful, more full of education than my library, where the closed books sleep on their spines, than my paintings, which hang dead on my walls all around me, with their immobile sky, tree, water and figures....
—Octave Mirbeau, *La 628-E8*, 1908

Henri de Toulouse-Lautrec. The Automobilist. *1896. Lithograph, 14³⁄₄ × 10¹⁄₂". The Art Institute of Chicago. Gift of Charles F. Glore*

Georges Rochegrosse. Automobile Club of France; Fourth International Exhibition; Motor, Cycle, and Sports Show. *1901. Color lithograph, 76 × 50″. Posters Please, Inc., New York City*

of a fuming vehicle. In the diagonally divided composition, the vibrantly delineated, forward-surging explosive form of the car and its possessed driver are contrasted with the somewhat sketchy background figures of a promenader and her dog. The centuries confront one another: the tranquil nineteenth-century world of Impressionist imagery is pitted against the tumultuous vision of twentieth-century technological invention.

With some exceptions, Lautrec's lithograph is one of the rare examples of automobile art done by a major artist before 1910. Technological subject matter was not high on the list of academic artists, who preferred the more accepted themes of history, ancient mythology, and religion. It is curious that many of the more modern artists were unsympathetic to technological subjects, and devoted their efforts toward the development of a new pictorial language, initially applying it to traditional themes of still life, landscape, and the figure. Moreover, the automobile was not the most common fixture of the world's streets by 1910, although its popularity was growing, especially in the United States.

Around the turn of the century, the automobile was most often represented in advertising posters and in illustrations for books and magazines. (Lautrec himself was greatly responsible for legitimizing poster making as a medium capable of aesthetic expression.) The emergence of the poster as a sophisticated artform was linked to some of the same developments instrumental to the birth of the modern automobile. Improved techniques of mechanical reproduction made the poster a visually arresting marketing device, and more economically viable, just as refinements in the mass production of the motorcar made it a marketable product appropriate to mass advertising.

Many of the posters of the period commemorate car races. Most of these pioneering competitions were not held at racetracks, but, like modern rallies, ran from city to city, often covering vast distances. Initiated in France in 1895 with the famous 732-mile Paris–Bordeaux–Paris run, racing spread throughout Europe and America. As an event, the early auto race tested the skill and daring of the driver and the speed and reliability of the automobile. While the accomplishments of the race car drivers made many of them modern-day heroes, the success of an automobile carried commercial value. Competition on actual roads brought the automobile closer to the daily lives of people, demonstrating the viability of the car as a means of transportation. Racing itself was thus a form of car advertising; posters, in turn, dispersed its commercial messages in two-dimensional form.

In 1904, H. Belléry Desfontaines designed an advertising poster for the French auto manufacturer Automobiles Richard-Brasier, whose racer had recently won the famous Gordon Bennett competition, an international rally sponsored by the American newspaper baron James Gordon Bennett. Although the piece embodies references to the classical themes of triumph, the windswept mythological figure preceding the speeding race car makes an allusion to Aurora, the classical harbinger of the dawn, here leading the way for an internal combustion version of Apollo's sun-carrying chariot. Fueled by contemporary millennial sentiments, the car became the symbol of the dawning of a new age, the incarnation of a technological energy akin to the power of the sun.

An 1898 poster by Georges Gaudy announces the Course

Jules Chéret. Benzo-Moteur, Special Petrol for Automobiles. *c. 1900. Color lithograph, 48¼ × 33½". Posters Please, Inc., New York City*

P. Montanya. Catalunya Cup. *1909. Color lithograph, 57¼ × 40¼". Park South Gallery at Carnegie Hall, New York City*

Camille Lefèbvre. Monument to Emile Levassor. *1907.*
Marble relief after Aimée-Jules Dalou at Porte Maillot,
Paris

Bruxelles, an auto race sponsored by the Automobile Club of Belgium. Painter, magazine illustrator, accomplished cyclist, and race car driver, Gaudy put Father Time behind the wheel of a fast-moving auto, his cloak, snowy hair, and beard whipped by the wind. Gaudy emphasized speed, the characteristic of the car that most captured the public imagination. Swirling lines spin off the car's tires. These spirals, derived from sinuous Art Nouveau arabesques, are shapes rooted in the organic world, which, at the time, was understood as the antithesis of industry and technology. But in Belgium the style of Art Nouveau was placed at the service of La Belle Epoque, and celebrated the vibrant aspects of modern life, including the car and the auto race. By placing Father Time in the driver's seat of a zooming motorcar, Gaudy seems to be suggesting that modern speed alters the traditional notion of time. Done two years before the turn of the century, the poster may also be using Father Time, a customary symbol of the end of an old year, to represent the end of an old century, its demise accelerated by the arrival of new technology.

These early automobile races provided the modern age with a hero, the race car driver, a new man for the new world, whose driving set records of speed and endurance. Subject of novels, poems, and works of art, the race car driver as modern idol became a theme appropriate to monumental sculpture. The *Monument to Emile Levassor*, erected in 1907 at the Porte Maillot in Paris, stands out as one of the most grandiose tributes ever paid to an automobilist. Levassor, a pioneering car inventor, racer, and victor of the Paris–Bordeaux–Paris course in 1895, was ennobled in a manner normally accorded only to war heroes and political leaders, and in the liberal atmosphere of late nineteenth-century France, to laborers. Levassor, a hero in reality, traveled over seven hundred miles, averaging close to fifteen miles per hour, and endured nearly forty-eight hours of virtually nonstop driving, a feat yet to be equaled. Scoring victory in an internal combustion car, he helped to build with René Panhard, Levassor also helped to propel France into a prominent position in early automotive history.

A year after Levassor's death in 1897, the Automobile Club of France commissioned the monument, and selected the realist sculptor Aimée-Jules Dalou, known for his monuments to labor, to execute it. Working from contemporary photographs, Dalou made two studies for the piece, from which bronze models were cast. Sometimes called "Monument to the Automobile," these bronzes, of which there is no precise record of the number made, were sold commercially.

Following Dalou's death, the project was entrusted to his pupil Camille Lefèbvre, who elaborated on Dalou's design. The final monument resembles a Greco-Roman triumphal arch, except that the arch itself is occupied by the sculptural portrayal of Levassor's triumph. Movement is implied by forms that emerge from the stone. Levassor leans forward as if to encourage the car onward; the ground plane of the relief becomes the finish line, which was the Porte Maillot itself and across which burst the victorious driver and his racer, greeted by the cheers of the spectators.

Such early automotive adventures as races, long-distance journeys, and schemes for motorcars, also became popular in the literature of the day. In fact, around the time of the car's invention, science fiction writers fantasized and fabricated machinery capable of sensational alterations in

Pierre Bonnard. Margin drawings for La 628-E8 *by Octave Mirbeau. 1907 edition (An accounting of the oftentimes humorous travel experiences made possible by the automobile.)*

Aimée-Jules Dalou. Monument to the Automobile. *1911. Bronze, 8" high. Private collection, Providence, Rhode Island*

H. Belléry Desfontaines. Automobiles Richard-Brasier, Winners of the Gordon Bennett Cup. *1904. Color lithograph, 34¾ × 56¾". Musée de la Publicité, Paris*

Opposite: Georges Gaudy. Automobile Club of Belgium, Brussels to Spa Race. *1898. Color lithograph, 51¼ × 38¼". Musée de la Publicité, Paris*

space and time. Since fantasy has foundation in fact, the speculations within science fiction were often sparked by the recent advances in science and technology.

In 1880, one year after Karl Benz proclaimed a "new era" with the invention of an internal combustion engine, Jules Verne, French novelist and the father of modern science fiction, wrote *La Maison à Vapeur* (The Steam House), which introduced a strange hybrid of car and mobile home that the aviator Alberto Santos-Dumont would later classify as "an automobilism that, in these days, had not as yet a name." Verne's vehicle may have been inspired by an actual steam car invented by Dr. Conseil, his friend. In this peculiar version of car travel, Verne recognized the potential for a freedom unavailable in other forms of transport, especially in the railroad, by which one is tied to both timetable and track: "...the modern car.... What a dream! To stop when one wishes, leave when one pleases, to walk, to stroll, or gallop, if one likes, to carry not only one's bedroom but also one's salon, dining room, smoking room, and of course, one's kitchen and cook—there's progress." The vehicle of progress becomes a tool of diabolical power in his work of 1904, *Maître du Monde* (Master of the World). Combining all the best features of the latest advances in transport, Verne creates "the *ne plus ultra* of automobilism," called the "Epouvante"—part car, submarine, and airplane. The Epouvante may have been inspired by Leonardo's drawings of locomotion, which were much admired by Verne. With Epouvante in hand, Verne's protagonist declares "...with it I have undisputed power over the whole world and there is no human power which can resist me under any circumstances." Verne addresses a dilemma characteristic of new technology: is it an instrument of liberation or enslavement; should it be embraced or feared?

Many of the early automobile books contained illustrations that comprise one of the more prolific early genres of auto art. For instance, *La 628-E8,* a text describing the motoring adventures of its author, Octave Mirbeau, was accompanied by delightful pen and ink marginal sketches of cars, drivers, and roads by the French artist Pierre Bonnard. Mirbeau was a member of *anarchisme,* a literary school that stressed freedom and individuality. He envisioned the automobile as an object capable of providing actual personal liberation, and of symbolically expressing cultural and artistic emancipation. In *La 628-E8,* named after Mirbeau's auto registration number, he appealed to artists, writers, and critics to devote their efforts to the depiction, description, and analysis of the automobile. Bonnard, though generally noted for his sensuous and sensitively colored paintings of intimate interiors and genteel Parisian life, was a car buff himself, fascinated by the rapidly changing modern world. His whimsical drawings for Mirbeau's text hardly prepare us for the author's breathless description of the sensations produced while riding in a zooming motorcar: "...all is moving, teeming, passing, changing, vertiginous, boundless, and infinite... [one's] brain becomes a race-course without end, where thoughts, images, and sensations boom and roll at the rate of a hundred kilometers an hour... Life rushes upon you, is thrown into disorder, becomes animated with frenzied movement like a cavalry charge, which vanishes cinematographically like the trees, hedges, walls, and silhouettes which line the road."

The disparity existing between the verbal and visual representations of automobiles illustrates the difficulties of devising artistic

Paul Gervais. Fright. *Frontispiece to* The Complete Motorist *by A.B. Filson Young, 1904 (after a lost painting). The Detroit Public Library*

means appropriate to a new and changing reality. The modern world demanded a new and more appropriate language in art. There is, for example, a jarring anomaly in the *Monument to Emile Levassor* between the subject matter of new technology and its very traditional sculptural portrayal. In this instance, innovation in art lagged behind innovation in technology. It was not until Cubism and its pictorial vocabulary of fragmentation, transparency, overlapping and simultaneity that a visual idiom more evocative of sensations of speed and dynamism developed, and it was the Italian Futurists who first applied Cubist vocabulary to modern phenomena, especially to the image of the motorcar.

Until that time, artists and illustrators around the turn of the century, particularly in their drawings for auto magazines, books, clubs, and individual enthusiasts, adopted similar formulas for depicting fast-moving cars and racers. Georges Gaudy, E. Montaut, Gamy, Henry Meunier, André Névil, and Umberto Boccioni all attacked the problem of illustrating speed and motion. With little variation, they indicated velocity and movement through smoke and dust-shrouded cars that seemed to lurch ahead, threatening the picture plane, coaxed onward by their forward-hunching, determined-looking drivers, whose racing garb of flowing black cloaks, tight-fitting caps, and dark goggles gave them a fanatic and dangerous appearance. Madly spinning wheels, barely making contact with the ground, streaks of windblown lines, and careening car bodies literally bending with the contours of hairpin curves, were exaggerated and foreshortened by a bird's eye perspective.

Many illustrators suggested the dynamism and modernity of the car by contrasting it with the world it was destined to overtake. In Umberto Boccioni's early series of untitled tempera sketches for the Automobile Club of Italy in Rome, automobiles outdistance the horse and the bicycle, invade rural settings, startling and confusing the inhabitants, and compete with aristocratic leisure activities such as riding and hunting.

The best known of these illustrations opposes the race car against the horses and dogs of a foxhunt, as the fox, unable to outrun his pursuers, hitches a ride with a racing car. The car's superiority over the horse, as an object of both speed and sport, was Boccioni's message—one that was fairly common in the art, the literature, and even the films of the day.

In the actual evolution of transportation, the car was required to demonstrate its advantages over other forms of locomotion, and the horse-drawn wagon was a prime competitor. Especially in the United States, where the car was an affordable convenience, the automobile was thought of as safer, more dependable, sanitary, and economical than the horse. Exhausts were pleasanter than excreta, and cars were more controllable and maneuverable than the sometimes unpredictable horse. Autos were faster and easier to operate; mechanical problems were generally quicker and simpler to remedy than a sick or tired animal.

Motoring was also seen as providing pleasures and thrills comparable to that of horseback riding. One such assessment can be found in *The Complete Motorist,* written in 1904 by the Briton A.B. Filson Young. Something of an auto manual, travelogue, and anthology of car lore and anecdotes, *The Complete Motorist* contains a section of letters composed by such

John Sloan. Gray and Brass. *1907. Oil on canvas, 21½ × 26¾". Collection Arthur G. Altschul, New York City*

Henri Gervex. Dinner at the Pré Catelan. *1908–9. Oil on canvas, 78¾ × 118¼". Collection Francois Gérard Seligmann, Paris*

Gamy. Grand Prix of America. *1913. Hand-colored lithograph, 16 × 32". L'Art et L'Automobile Gallery, New York City*

Umberto Boccioni. Postcard of Automobile and Fox Hunt. *1901. Original: Tempera on board, 31 × 52¾". Automobile Club d'Italia, Rome*

Opposite: Anonymous. Michelin Tire, the One Adjusted to the Wheel of Fortune. *c. 1905. Color lithograph, 58 × 42½". Posters Please, Inc., New York City*

writers as Rudyard Kipling and John St. Loe Strachey, who were asked to contribute their feelings about the car. One respondent, Lady M. Jeune, wrote:

> There is a monster in the stable who has to be exercised, and from time to time you hear his brothers hooting to him as they rush past along the road.... There is no sensation so enjoyable—except that of riding a good horse in a fast run—as driving in a fast motor. The endless variety of scenery; the keen whistle of the wind in one's face; the perpetual changing sunshine and shadow, create an indescribable feeling of exhilaration and excitement; while the almost human consciousness of the machine; the patient, ready response which it makes to any call on its powers; the snort with which it breasts the hill, and the soft sob which dies away when it has reached the summit, make it as companionable as any living being.

In her fairly passionate description of the motorcar, Lady Jeune imbues the auto with human and animal traits, establishing a sense of communion with it that is somewhat erotic in nature. This feeling of intimacy between man and machine runs throughout the history of auto iconography.

Like so many of the auto books of that period, *The Complete Motorist* contains exquisite technical drawings, and a depiction of a speeding auto. Paul Gervais's *L'Effroi* (Fright), a painting exhibited at the Paris Salon in 1904, was reproduced as the book's frontispiece. A roadster tears along a country lane, frightening a group of cavorting nymphs and satyrs, who flee into the woods. This odd and beguiling theme summarizes a host of attitudes about the automobile, from car as a symbol of destruction of the rural, idyllic world, to car as an object that helps men to attract women, producing sensations of a nearly orgasmic nature, and providing a means of escape to or actual setting for sexual encounters. Man and car become a new centaur.

Birthplace of the modern auto, Europe was at first nearly a decade ahead of America in auto technology. Most automobile historians, however, now argue that by the early 1900s the gap between the European and American auto culture had narrowed considerably.

The artistic climate in Europe was not terribly congenial to the inclusion of technological subjects in art. Academic disapproval of such themes was equally as strong in America, and modernism had yet to really penetrate the American artistic scene. As in Europe, auto art was most common in advertising posters and illustrations, but since the Ashcan School, one of the major early twentieth-century American art movements, was made up of artists who were often also illustrators, images of cars occasionally appeared in their more serious work.

The label "Ashcan" was coined by hostile critics who were contemptuous of the raw, vernacular nature of the art that explored the vitality of the developing American metropolis, particularly New York City. These artists were fascinated with human interactions in urban settings, and, for the most part, technological subjects played a minor role in their pieces. Generally, when the car does appear, as in George Bellows's *Upper Broadway* (1910) and William Glackens's *Washington Square* (1912), it functions as an incidental part of the urban scene.

In these early years, the motorcar remained a plaything of the rich. Even in the United States, where car ownership was democratized earliest, the automobile was commonly considered and depicted in terms of its upper-class associations. In *Gray and Brass* (1907), John Sloan, an Ashcan artist with socialist affiliations, caricatured the strivings of the new moneyed class, parodying its passion for fashionable material possessions. Completed just a year before Henry Ford's mass production of the Model T contributed enormously to universalizing car ownership, *Gray and Brass* belongs to the world in which the car lay principally within the grasp of the rich. An overfed, plumed, primped, and dull-witted bunch chug along in an auto barely capable of supporting their overweight. In his journal, Sloan recalled the scene that ignited the painting: "...the pomp and circumstance that marked the wealthy group in their motorcar...a brass-trimmed, snob, cheap, 'nouveau-riche' laden automobile passing the park."

While Sloan, a progressive artist by American standards, satirized the car's connections with the leisure class, most conservative and academic artists, especially in Europe, treated the car as a chic and desirable accoutrement of the wealthy. Henri Gervex's *Dîner au Pré-Catelan* (Dinner at the Pré-Catelan) portrays French high society arriving at and departing from the fashionable Pré-Catelan restaurant in luxurious motorcars. Gervex, an artist with solid academic credentials who frequently addressed themes from modern life, here drenched the scene with a Proustian, almost suffocating elegance, and stocked the work with a cast of identifiable figures, including the Marquis de Dion of the early auto manufacturing family, the pioneering aviator Alberto Santos-Dumont, and Madame Gervex herself.

On both sides of the Atlantic, advertisements for cars capitalized on the upper-class connotations as a selling point. Ads featured elegantly tailored figures, with elite breeds of dogs in tow. Footmen hold open the car door; chauffeurs take riders for a leisurely spin. Sometimes chic and wealth are joined by sex appeal as advertising ploys. Handsome, well-dressed men behind the wheel of a motorcar are often the focus of admiring feminine glances. As George Dupuy commented in "The Conquering Automobile," an article published in 1906 by the American magazine *Independent*: "the automobile is the idol of the modern age.... The man who owns a motorcar gets for himself, besides the joys of touring, the adulation of the walking crowd, and the daring driver of a racing machine that bounds and rushes and disappears...in a thunder of explosions is a god to the women." Beautiful and elegant women, and partially draped classical gods, regularly adorned these early advertisements, the first examples of an unsevered chain of sexy car-sexy women images that link the entire history of auto art and auto advertising. Typical of the era's conservatism, these alluring, seminude figures were cast in classical roles, a device that only slightly veils the potential prurience of the images.

It seems fitting that the trophies awarded to the winners of auto races, an exclusively male domain, frequently portray the most explicit car-women motifs. One example is the Coppa della Velocita, sometimes called the "Coppa Florio" after its sponsor Cavaliere Vincenzo Florio. Designed by Polak, a little-known sculptor, the prize, presented at the annual Brescia Motor Week, borders on the outrageous. A bare-breasted female figure, arms outstretched and hair waving in ideal Art Nouveau arabesques, elides with the form of the race car.

Sir Herbert von Herkomer. The Future. *1905. Colored photogravure on menu card, 10 × 8". Yale Center for British Art, New Haven, Connecticut. Gift of Haus and Agnes Platenius*

Jacques-Henri Lartigue. Peugeot 22 HP: Maman, Papa, Yves, Zissou, M. Laroze. *Gelatin silver print, 12×16". Association des Amis de Jacques-Henri Lartigue, Paris*

The trophy awarded in the Gordon Bennett competition was designed by a little-known jeweler, Aucoc. As in the Coppa Florio, speed is suggested by the sinuous mounds on and behind the wheels of an auto. Boxier and stodgier than the Coppa Florio, the Gordon Bennett trophy reverses the position of male and female: a young boy perched on the car's hood holds aloft a torch in one hand, and grasps the steering wheel behind him with the other; a winged female Victory stands on the car's seat.

Sir Hubert von Herkomer, Royal Academician, filmmaker, and early motorist, sponsored his own motor rally in Germany in 1905, the Herkomerkonkurrenz, for which he designed a trophy and other regalia. Like so many of the awards of the day, his prize portrays beautiful, partly nude classical male and female figures. But for the first time they are identified; Herkomer named the young boy holding a garland "The Spirit of the Motorcar," and the woman, nearly swooning in ecstasy, "The Joy of Speed." In his design for a menu card for a banquet at the conclusion of the course, Herkomer depicted a gauzily cloaked, languid female, strapped to the front end of a motorcar, and draped with a banner reading "Die Zukunft" (*The Future*).

Jacques-Henri Lartigue. The Marquis de Soriano in a Gregoire Automobile in the Bois de Boulogne. *1911. Gelatin silver print, 12×16". Association des Amis de Jacques-Henri Lartigue, Paris*

In 1903 Herkomer created his own greeting card for the holidays, showing Father Time as a passenger in an automobile. It was inscribed "Compliments of the Season." The Herkomer memorabilia thus summarize several sentiments expressed in automobile art at the turn of the century: a scantily garbed, classical nude female reaffirms the connection between speed, and intoxicating sensual experiences. Father Time's ride in a motorcar perhaps inplies that since speed alters the sense of time, the motorcar speeds up the arrival of a new era, an interpretation suggested in Herkomer's allegory of the automobile as the future.

Many of the examples of automobile-related art at the turn of the century are found in what might be called the "minor" arts—book and magazine illustrations, posters, and trophies. Often, these works were associated with the world of auto racing that in turn was tied to the commercial marketing of the car. The medium of photography was also used as a promotional device. Photographs chronicled auto racing and contests, automobile manufacture and repair, inventors posing ceremoniously in their recently built cars, as well as stunts and exotica, such as cars climbing stairs, cars

Jacques-Henri Lartigue. Grand Prix of the Automobile Club of France. *1912. Gelatin silver print, 11¾ × 15¾". Association des Amis de Jacques-Henri Lartigue, Paris*

Robert Demachy. Speed. *1904. Photogravure, 4¾ × 7". Collection James Sheldon, Andover, Massachusetts*

50

attached to balloons floating through the sky, and American Indians driving or riding in automobiles. Many early photographic images reveal the obvious and subtle ways in which the automobile infiltrated and altered culture and society in the early twentieth century. They documented the changes in urban settings as cars began to clog the streets, and recorded the increasing presence of the motorcar in a now more accessible rural world. Many of these photographers remain anonymous, but the subject of the automobile did attract four important early twentieth-century photographers, whose distinct interpretations and approaches spell out some of the basic issues confronting this medium.

The French photographer Jacques-Henri Lartigue was enamored of the automobile. He was born in 1894 into a creative, wealthy, stylish, bourgeois family. His grandfather helped to invent an early form of monorail transportation; his brother tinkered with automobiles and airplanes and was a pioneering aviator. Surrounded by this atmosphere of invention, Lartigue began taking photographs at the precocious age of seven. Many of his early shots record his family's automobile outings and adventures—repairing a tire or waiting for a herd of goats to cross the road. He also photographed motorcars on Parisian streets and in parks and documented several major auto-racing events such as the 1905 Gordon Bennett Cup race and the 1912 Grand Prix of the Automobile Club of France.

His photographic vision was that of a spectator quickly seizing the moment. Saddled at first with a large tripod camera unsuitable to his snapshot sensibility, Lartigue eventually acquired a hand camera. Its fast lens and shutter speed were able to arrest unique, visual moments, converting fugitive and elusive events into permanent records. Lartigue's youth and naiveté encouraged him to experiment freely. Breaking with photographic convention, he often produced intentionally blurred and cropped shots, using the edge cutting off the image to capture the spirit of flux characteristic of the modern world. For example, one of a series of photographs taken of the Grand Prix of the Automobile Club of France in 1912 emphasizes speed and motion by slicing the image of the race car and counterposing it and its blurred wheels with the strange leftward tilt of spectators and poles. In its contrast between speeding car in the foreground and pedestrians in the background, *Grand Prix* compositionally recalls Toulouse-Lautrec's *The Automobilist*.

In the history of photography, Lartigue is often credited with initiating one of its basic approaches—the snapshot aesthetic, the instantaneous recording of actual events. Lartigue intuited that the most effective way to grasp and express the spirit of certain modern phenomena, including the speed of the automobile, was through this snapshot approach. Thus the car can be understood as indirectly influencing the development of one of the important visions in modern photography.

Lartigue's sensibility ran counter to pictorialism, one of the prevailing currents in contemporaneous photography, which is exemplified by another car-related image, Robert Demachy's *Speed* of 1904. Since photography was not always considered to be a legitimate artform, pictorialist photographers tried to make their shots resemble images from more allegedly respectable mediums, especially painting and engraving. They borrowed techniques from these mediums and attempted to vary texture,

Eugène Atget. Courtyard of Rue de Valence. *1922. Modern silver print by Berenice Abbott, 7 × 9½". Collection Walter Hopps. Photograph on deposit with Menil Foundation, Houston*

incorporate subtle gradations of light and shade, and carefully organize composition. Demachy's *Speed*, first published in Alfred Stieglitz's photographic magazine *Camera Work*, was manipulated in various ways. He employed a gum-bichromate process in which sensitized salts applied to photographic prints permit the artist to work almost as a painter does with pigment. In *Speed*, Demachy uses this process to soften focus, to alter tone, and to add grain and texture to the surface of the print. As a result, areas of light and dark rhythmically contrast, and the exhaust and dust seem almost palpable. In comparison to Lartigue's shots of fast-moving cars, Demachy's *Speed* feels posed, and appears to freeze and immobilize rather than capture and evoke the sense of rapid movement. Demachy was an avid motorist, but his image of a speeding automobile, a subject rare in his oeuvre, demonstrates the difficulties confronting turn-of-the-century artists in depictions of such themes. Lartigue's solution, without question, was more effective.

Eugène Atget's "documentary" sensibility was another major photographic approach of the period. Atget's photographs, which he tried to sell to museums, libraries, and artists, were intended to record and preserve particular aspects of Paris and its environs. Like Lartigue, he was a somewhat idiosyncratic figure. Lartigue came to photography at an extremely early age, eventually abandoning it as he matured, but Atget began his career as a stage actor, briefly tried his hand at painting, and finally decided on photography when he was in his early forties. Youthful vitality informs Lartigue's shots: he impetuously embraced novelty and was intoxicated by speed. Atget's images suggest that he resisted change: born in 1857, he lived through the time when the look of Paris was radically altering. His photography seemed to be a way to preserve the architecture that was slowly abandoned, neglected, and destroyed by progress. He used his camera as a conservator's tool, and painstakingly recorded his view of premodern Paris. Lugging around a heavy tripod-mounted plate camera, Atget combed the city and its surroundings, often settling on particular streets or quarters, where he scrupulously recorded the most representative and evocative housefronts, doors, courtyards, alleyways, and local inhabitants.

In *Cour Rue de Valence* (Courtyard of Rue de Valence), a car and some cycles appear to be posed in a dilapidated courtyard, a neat foil between old and new. The image has none of the snapshot qualities of a Lartigue, nor any of the pictorialized manipulations of a Demachy: Atget lets the visuals of the scene speak for themselves. But his use of a wide-angle lens and a view camera blurs, shrinks, and distorts the forms at the edges of his photographs. As a result, the central objects are most prominent and in sharpest focus, and they seem to occupy what resembles a scoop of space. Atget's involvement in the theater seems to have influenced his photographic vision: the objects at the center of his images are the main actors, and the surrounding space, often with its entrances and exits of doorways and alleys, a scenic backdrop.

Since *Cour Rue de Valence* was part of a series of photographs of courtyards, it may seem to include a car almost by accident. But Atget had a particular interest in automobiles. His father and grandfather built carts and wagons, and undoubtedly Atget sensed that modernization would eventually make his family's means of livelihood obsolete.

Alfred Stieglitz. Old and New New York. *1910. Photogravure, 8 × 6". Fraenkel Gallery, San Francisco*

Photographer, editor, and publisher of *Camera Work,* Alfred Stieglitz shaped and influenced the debate surrounding the major issues of modern art and photography in the early part of the century. As the director of the Little Galleries of the Photo-Secession, a New York space devoted to modern art and photography known as 291, Stieglitz helped to secure for photography a legitimate place within the fine arts. The early numbers of *Camera Work* provided a forum for discussion of the proper approach to photography, from the pictorialism practiced by Demachy, to straight, unmanipulated photography. Stieglitz's own work evolved from suffused, atmospheric, even moody images toward more sharply focused photographs of scenes that contained strong formal elements.

It was not until somewhat later in his career that Stieglitz became expressly concerned with the automobile as subject matter. But because he was intrigued by the urban landscape early on, the image of the automobile found its way into his work. In 1910, Stieglitz published a now famous photo, *Old and New New York.* It is typical of his pieces of this period in that it recognizes a formal power in the urban landscape, particularly by means of the relationships between the diagonals and right angles and the alternations between light and shade. The structure and chiaroscuro of the New York cityscape were enough to make a solidly composed photograph, but Stieglitz never divorced form from content. There is a syncopation of darks and lights in the photo: the dark-toned, older cast-iron buildings at the right and left edges frame the light-colored sky. In turn, the sky frames the central grays defining the ascending skeleton of the new building in construction. As the smaller houses recede diagonally into space, they move from darkness into light, again ending in the building under construction. The entire image suggests a progression from old to new. As part of the new New York, automobiles line the streets of Stieglitz's photo, but he focuses far more on the exposed edifice in progress, drawing attention to the structural honesty associated with modern architecture. He undoubtedly felt this building to be a more dramatic symbol of transition to the modern. Stieglitz's photograph suggests that by 1910 the automobile, at least in New York City, was becoming less of a novelty and more of an accepted part of the urban landscape.

These four photographers used the automobile to varying degrees and in distinct ways to symbolize a society in transition, and to represent the birth of the modern age. The juxtaposition between the old and the new is explicit in Atget's sense of loss for the past and in Stieglitz's celebration of the future; it is less overt in Lartigue's oppositions between walkers and racers, and most veiled in Demachy's manner of casting aspects of contemporary life in terms of traditional pictorial conventions. Despite these differences of approach, the automobile remains the symbol of modernity. These photographers operated on the cutting edge of a new sensibility, and their work reflects this position in terms of an attachment to the old or an embrace of the new.

The art of this early period, much of it commercial, feels exploratory, sometimes tentative, unsure of how to come to grips, both stylistically and conceptually, with a world undergoing radical change. The next generation of artists, especially the Futurists, began to investigate this modern world, to use it as potential subject matter, and to develop styles of expression for this new age.

A.M.CASSAN

TRIPLEX

PROLIFERATION
AND
ASSIMILATION

In 1909, the Italian poet and propagandist Filippo Tommaso Marinetti founded Futurism, an art movement that extolled modern technology. True to their name, the Futurists believed that technology represented the wave of the future. An embrace of the most modern phenomena was a necessary antidote to Italy's devotion to its past because this devotion, especially to its Classical and Renaissance heritage, was impeding cultural development. In the mid-nineteenth century, Italy had achieved political unification, which the nation hoped would lead to a general Italian *risorgimento,* or rebirth. By the early twentieth century, this new renaissance had yet to materialize. Futurism was in part tied to Italian nationalism, and Marinetti co-opted the political device of the manifesto to announce a cultural program designed to rejuvenate Italian society.

Working in various mediums—painting, sculpture, architecture, design, literature, music, and theater—the Futurists used the automobile as an important symbol and favored subject matter. Inspired by the revolutionary effects of developing technology, the Futurists regarded the auto as a paradigmatic innovation that was physically altering the environment and changing man's perception of the world; it thus symbolized Futurist ideas about modernity and technological progress. Capable of rapid movement that intensified a rider's experiences of urban environments, the automobile could induce a sense of power, exhilaration, and emancipation.

Certain tenets in Futurist thought were determined by actual experiences related to the automobile; the artists did not simply arrive at an ideology and then seek objects to symbolize its principles. Observing or riding in a speeding car confirmed the Futurist belief that dynamic, simultaneous sensations were among the basic forces of reality. The Futurists promoted the physical and emotional experiences of potency, intoxication, and liberation produced by car travel, and the automobile helped to shape the violent, frenetic, and anarchistic nature of much Futurist art.

The Futurist artist Giacomo Balla executed over one hundred works using as primary subject matter either the image of a speed-

Within myself I sensed new beings full of
  dexterity
Building up and organising a new universe
A shopkeeper of untold wealth and prodigious size
Was arranging an extraordinary display-window
And gigantic shepherds were leading
Great dumb herds that browsed on words
And around whom all the dogs in the road were
  barking
And passing that afternoon by Fontainebleau
We arrived in Paris
At the moment when the mobilisation posters
  were going up
And my comrade and I understood then
That the little motor-car had brought us into a
  new Epoch
And though we were both mature men
We had just been born.

—Guillaume Apollinaire, *The Little Motorcar*

A.M. Cassandre. Triplex. *1931. Color lithograph, 47⅛ × 31⅝". Charles Hack Fine Arts, New York City*

Above and opposite: Giacomo Balla. Study of a moving automobile. 1912–14. Pencil drawing in Balla's notebook no. 5. Collection Signorina Luce Balla, Rome

ing automobile or a visual record of its effects. Images of motorized vehicles, including automobiles, electric trams, and motorcycles, are also present in the works of the other major Futurist artists Luigi Russolo, Gino Severini, Umberto Boccioni, and Carlo Carrà, and in the works of the lesser-known Futurists Mario Sironi, Achille Funi, and Gino Galli. The image of the automobile recurs throughout Futurist literature and poetry, especially in the manifestos and verse of F. T. Marinetti. Attempting to distinguish Vorticism, a technological British art movement, from Futurism, the artist and writer Wyndham Lewis somewhat derogatorily labeled the Italian movement mere "automobilism." Nonetheless, he was acknowledging the fact that Italian Futurism was the first major modern art movement to adopt the automobile and to explore car-related experiences as suitable subject matter.

The automobile first appeared as a symbol of the Futurist movement in F. T. Marinetti's "Founding and Manifesto of Futurism" of 1909. The often-cited broadside proclaimed that "the world's magnificence has been enriched by a new beauty; the beauty of speed. A racing car whose hood is adorned with great pipes, like serpents of explosive breath— a roaring car that seems to run on grapeshot—is more beautiful than the *Victory of Samothrace*." Marinetti's aesthetic analogy between a contemporary technological object and the museum-enshrined classical masterpiece boldly and belligerently announced the rejection of the past and its artifacts in favor of the objects and ideas of the modern world. Marinetti selected the

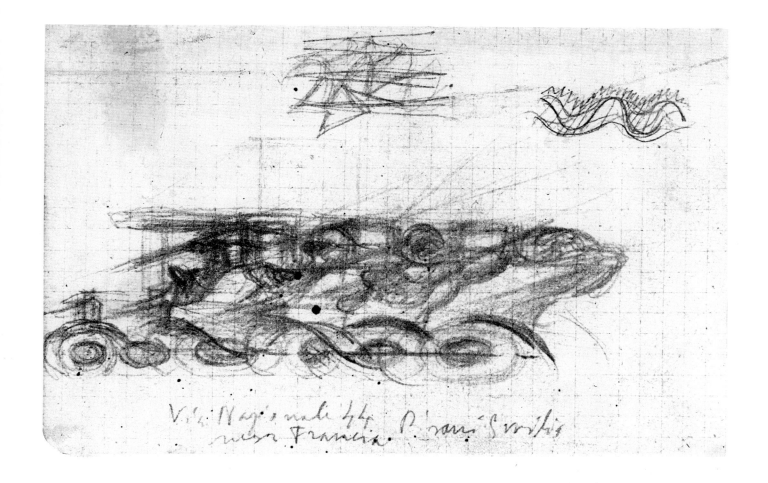

automobile as the object most representative of the contemporary world because he felt that it best expressed the concept of dynamism. In a world animated by the principle of dynamism, all objects are thought to be in a state of motion—even those appearing to be at rest are in motion by virtue of their own internal movements. All things, either mobile or immobile, constantly interact with one another and with their surroundings. Speed amplifies dynamism, and together they change experiences of time and space.

Influenced by the contemporary French philosopher Henri Bergson, who theorized that reality is in constant flux, the Futurists intuited that speed and dynamism, manifestations of new technology and the new urban environment, constituted the essence of reality. In their analysis of speed and motion, the Futurists believed that they had discovered insights into the underlying nature of existence. "Speed," Severini stated, "has transformed our sensibility... has led to the majority of our Futurist truths... has given us a new conception of space and time itself." "Dynamism," claimed Boccioni, "constitutes reality.... There is no such thing as rest, only motion." The concepts of rapidity and flux were ideally suited to Futurist ideology because they embody parallel notions of forward motion and continual change. The concept of dynamism is also conveniently antithetical to the classical canons of stability and order, against which the Futurists rebelled.

Futurist art invariably depicted the automobile in motion. In a series of images of swiftly moving motorcars, Giacomo Balla concentrated on the speed and dynamism rather than the form or design of the auto.

Luigi Russolo. Dynamism of an Automobile. *1911. Oil on canvas, 41¾ × 55¼". Musée National d'Art Moderne, Centre de Pompidou, Paris*

Giacomo Balla. Abstract Speed. *1913. Oil on canvas, 79½ × 129¼". Private collection, Turin*

Done mostly between 1911 and 1915, the titles of these works indicate Balla's focus: *Speeding Automobile, Abstract Speed, Dynamism of an Automobile, Wake of a Speeding Automobile.* By superimposing a repeating, diminishing image of the car from right to left and overlaying a network of lines and forms, Balla was able to emphasize the appearance of directional energy and activate the space surrounding the car. The technique nearly obliterates the shape of the auto, creating an impression of velocity and mobility.

These converging vectors and churning whirlpools suggest violent struggle. The phalanx of V-shaped forms alludes to what the Futurists called "force-lines"—basic units of force that constitute the dynamic core of all objects. The coils of spiraling shapes also signify kinetic qualities and symbolize dynamic forces that penetrate and scatter the static environment. Balla's work represents the battle between Futurism and the past: the automobile, incarnation of speed and dynamic forward movement, becomes symbolic of Futurism itself; the inert environment, now fragmented, is symbolic of the vanquished past.

Balla's sketches and preliminary drawings reveal that he began with the image of a single immobile car, working from the Fiat Types I and II of 1909–12, and overlapped additional images slightly ahead of the original vehicle. As the image multiplies, abstract patterns materialize. By inserting force-lines and whorls, and by flattening the car's form, Balla was able to metamorphose his stodgy prototype into something sleekly suggestive of intense movement.

Balla's methodology was closely connected to experimentation in the photography of locomotion, to the studies of phases of movement by Eadweard Muybridge, and particularly to the chronophotography of Etienne-Jules Marey and the Futurist photodynamism of his friend and colleague Anton Giulio Bragaglia. Muybridge arranged a series of cameras along a path to be followed by moving animals or people; as the figures moved forward, they tripped the shutters of the successive cameras, each of which captured a phase of the figure's motion. Employing a single camera and a strip of film loaded in a mechanism similar to the revolving chamber of a pistol, Marey recorded the sequential and overlapping positions of moving objects. Bragaglia's photodynamism represented an attempt to register the continuity of an action in space, but he did not shoot images at different moments. Instead, he exposed single plates that recorded movement over a longer period of time, ending up with blurred, smeared, nearly apparitional forms.

Dynamism of an Automobile, a painting executed by fellow Futurist Luigi Russolo between 1911 and 1912, parallels Balla's formula of a fast-moving car as symbolic of the dynamic present disrupting the static past. Russolo portrays the image of an automobile moving from right to left. The car seems to slice through space; motion is expressed by a progression of crimson force-lines that overlay the indigo-colored auto, and become closer, blunter, and more vertical as they move from right to left. Bits of architecture, noticeable at the top of the composition, seem bent and warped by the force and pressure of the force-lines. *Dynamism of an Automobile* suggests formal similarities to Russolo's painting of 1912, *Rebellion.* In *Rebellion,* a wave of recurring blood-red wedges, representing a mass of humanity, dominates the composition. The work was exhibited at the Sackville Gallery in London with an accompanying description: *"Rebellion:* The collision of two forces, that of the revolutionary element made up of enthusiasm and red lyricism against the force of inertia and reactionary resistance of tradition. The angles are the vibratory waves of the former force in motion. (The perspective of the houses is destroyed just as a boxer is bent double by receiving a blow in the wind.)" The compositional similarities between *Rebellion* and *Dynamism of an Automobile* suggest that the automobile, like the surging marchers in *Rebellion,* functions within the painting to symbolize a dynamic destruction of the past.

Speeding along in a fast-moving car produced a feeling of physical liberation and power that the Futurists wished to transfer, ideologically, to the movement as a whole. Marinetti panegyrized: "The intoxication of great speeds in cars is nothing but the joy of feeling oneself fused with the only *divinity."* The automobile's ability to provide a sense of physical freedom made it an ideal symbol for a movement that promoted the emancipating capabilities of new technology. The car's association with power, force, and *machismo* was ideally suited to a movement bent on destruction of the established order. The car became a cultural "getaway" vehicle, commandeered by artists who, in their assault on the status quo, functioned as cultural race car drivers.

Identification of the automobile with the technological revolution directly influenced the style of Futurist art. In Balla's later works, such as *Abstract Speed* and *Lines of Speed,* he removed the car's image from the composition but retained the abstract patterns that resulted from a pictorial analysis of the speeding auto. Balla attempted to present a pure and abstract signification of speed and dynamism that was more suggestive of inner, absolute, and universal forces. As Futurist colleague Fortunato Depero explained in 1915, "By studying the speed of automobiles and in so doing discovering the laws and essential force-lines of speed," Balla was encouraged to develop and adopt an abstract visual language. These first abstract compositions inspired a group of three-dimensional constructions called "plastic complexes" by Balla and Depero in their joint manifesto entitled "The Futurist Reconstruction of the Universe" (1915). The plastic complexes were to serve as models for restructuring the environment. The automobile became the source, and art the intermediary for the discovery, analysis, and distillation of universal and abstract dynamic principles that could be applied to create a better world.

Futurist art was affected by other automobile-related phenomena, especially by the experiences of simultaneous sensations. The concept of simultaneity was formulated and widely discussed during the first two decades of the twentieth century, particularly in France and Italy. As Marinetti defined the term, simultaneity implied that to a perceiver, a multitude of events seemed to be happening at once, or simultaneously. Simultaneity was a function of the increasing speed and motion characterizing contemporary existence, as the Futurist Ardengo Soffici remarked: "External velocity, by intensifying our mental action, has modified our perception of space and time. As a result, we have the contiguousness and contemporaneity of things and events, or the simultaneity of sight and emotions."

The automobile and other motorized forms of transportation provided ideal opportunities to experience these sensations. The car significantly heightened the general bustle and confusion of rapidly developing urban centers, and automobile travel intensified the impression that contemporary life was characterized by overwhelming amounts of fragmented, imbricated stimuli.

Several Futurists portrayed the automobile as a component of urban pandemonium. Many of the works in Balla's automobile series depict the car interacting with the environment and include pictorial signs representing speed, light, and noise—an attempt at suggesting simultaneous sensory impressions. In *Speeding automobile + lights* (c. 1913), *Rhythm + noise + speed of an automobile* (1913–14), and *Speeding automobile + lightnoise* (c. 1913), Balla created a vocabulary of abstract ciphers: meander patterns for sound, and luminous circles and arcs for light, almost completely disintegrating the form of the motorcar itself.

Futurist art also expressed the notion of simultaneity as something produced by actual auto travel. In Gino Severini's painting *Autobus* (1912), translucent figures are seated in a moving bus. A series of intersecting diagonals, punctuated by fragments of architecture, store signs, and billposters, conveys a sense of movement and of inundation by a kaleidoscopic mélange of sensory information. As the artist described it, *Autobus* was "...an endeavor to produce by means of lines and planes the rhythmic sensation of speed, of spasmodic motion and of deafening noise. The heavy vehicle pursues its headlong career from Montmartre to Montrouge along the crowded streets of Paris, dashing across the path of other motors, grazing their very wheels and hurling itself in the direction of the houses so that 'the houses seem to enter the motorbus and the motorbus the houses.'" Severini implied that the physical and psychic sensations of motorized travel had a direct effect on artistic style; the tumultuous nature of contemporary experience could not be portrayed in a conventional manner and thus led the artist to adopt a new visual idiom of expression.

The vocabulary of French Cubism played an important role in the Futurist effort to develop a style appropriate to the modern world. The Futurist debt to Cubism varied from artist to artist. Balla, for example, was probably influenced least by the French movement. As the oldest Futurist artist, he had already developed a coherent style before the advent of both Futurism and Cubism. Severini, who had settled in Paris in 1906, was affected more strongly by Cubism. In 1911, Severini urged his Futurist colleagues to visit Paris in order to encounter Cubism firsthand; Russolo, Boccioni, and probably Carrà made the trip, while Balla remained in Italy.

Cubist devices—fragmentation and dematerialization of form, solidification of space, use of transparency and overlapping—were adopted by the Futurists to express speed, dynamism, aggression, and simultaneity. According to the Futurists, the Cubists were squandering a radical and potentially dynamic style on staid, traditional subjects. The Futurist assertion about Cubism was not completely accurate; although the best-known Cubists, Pablo Picasso and Georges Braque, showed little interest in modern technological motifs, others such as Robert Delaunay, Fernand Léger, and Marcel Duchamp dealt with technological and mechanical themes. The Futurists, borrowing Cubist formal innovation and adding vibrant colors, were more outspoken and programmatic in connecting the most revolutionary aspects of modern art to the most revolutionary aspects of modern life.

Futurist poetry endeavored to re-create experiences that

had been affected by the automobile. Poets tried to convey a sense of simultaneity, for instance, by evoking the excitement of the rapidly changing metropolis in which the automobile was a critical factor. In Luciano Folgore's "Automobile Quasi Te," disparate images and abrupt shifts of place and time are strung together:

> All around me the world is in motion
> All around me the city—no longer immobile
> my trip
>   moving
>   headlong
> of leaveshousesparapetsstreetlamps
> of tired men traveling on foot
> and of dust
> from the tires
> flurrying.

As in most of these works, the automobile is represented as one of many discrete yet interconnected elements within a composition.

Futurist writers and poets were compelled to abandon traditional approaches and discover or invent languages more appropriate to the expression of the transformations in contemporary society. Marinetti, recognizing the need for a new literary form, created what he called "words-in-freedom," intermingling words, letters, and images, replacing customary punctuation with mathematical symbols, and using compositionally arranged, diverse, and expressive typography. "My reformed typesetting," exclaimed Marinetti, "allows me to treat words like torpedos and to hurl them forth at all speeds." He chopped, elongated, and twisted words and letters, producing frenetic and fluid arrangements. In one of his best-known "words-in-freedom," *After the Marne, Joffre Visited the Front in an Automobile*, written in French in 1915, Marinetti enlarges and distorts the letters "M" and "S," converting them into shapes suggestive of mountains and winding roads. These and other letters, along with mathematical symbols, dismembered and onomatopeic words, dance wildly across the page. The "ta ta ta ta ..." of artillery is mixed with the "dynamic verbalization of the route," "xx = spirals 5 spirals spiral pneumatic" and "vitessssssssssxxxxxxssssssss."

In *Respiration of the Earth* (c. 1915), Marinetti sketched the image of a speeding car whose back wheels trail off into repeating letters suggestive of the car's noise. *Speeding Automobile* (1915) spells out its contents as "the sum of colors, forms, analogical psychic impressions of a fast landscape," and exploits unconventional typography and words, rather than an unusual layout, to convey these sensations. In *Zang Tumb Tumb* (1914), the section "Correction of proofs + desires in speeds" compares and interweaves revised manuscript with a variety of modern phenomena: electricity, and boat, train, and car travel. In the account of the "speeding cars," each stanza is embraced by words indicating the car's velocity. At "70 km. per hr. trrrrrrrrrrrr," the driver is half-thrown back beneath the enormous wheel that "spins like a planet"; as the car accelerates to "85," "95," and then "100" kilometers per hour, the "trrr's" of the text grow physically larger. A final "stop" issued in bold, black letters brings "(instinctive braking tremors of the driver) ⅛ of the car 3 wheels nibbling tranquil fodder blondness ironies of a village 306 years old."

The automobile thus encouraged the formulation of novel aesthetic vocabularies in both art and literature. As Umberto Boccioni argued: "The means of artistic expression handed down to us by the culture

Giacomo Balla. Speeding Automobile + Lights. *c. 1913. Oil on cardboard, 19 × 26¾". Collection Mr. and Mrs. Morton G. Neumann, Chicago*

Gino Severini. The Autobus. *1912. Oil on canvas, 22¼ × 24¼". Pinacoteca di Brera, Milan*

are worn out and no longer capable of receiving and interpreting the emotions that have come to us from a world that has been completely transformed by Science. The new conditions of life have created an infinity of completely new, natural elements, which therefore had never entered previously into the domain of art, and for which the Futurists intend to discover a new means of expression at any price."

Despite the Futurist movement's disavowal of the past, many of its attitudes toward the automobile were borrowed from earlier sources. Futurist ideology held that the vital aspects of modern life, the true origin of artistic inspiration, superseded the power of traditional works of art. This idea had already been expounded by Octave Mirbeau in *La 628-E8:*

> Machines appear to me, more than books, statues, paintings, to be works of the imagination. When I look at, when I hear the life of the admirable organism that is the motor of my automobile, with its steel lungs and heart, its rubber and copper vascular system, its electrical nervous system, don't I have a more moving idea of the imaginative and creative human genius than when I consider the banal, infinitely useless books of M. Paul Bourget, the statues, if one can call them that, of M. Denys Puech, the paintings—a euphemism— of M. Detaille?

Mirbeau believed that a good motorist proudly loves his car as one does a beautiful woman, and that "a car-driver, always speeding across space, like a tempest or a cyclone, is something of a superman." The infatuation with the automobile, and the belief that the car enhanced man's power, encouraged interpretations of the relationship between man and machine as intimate and often sexual. Consequently, the car was invested with human or animal qualities, and in this union between man and motor, the two joined forces to create a supernatural being, what might be called a "mechanical centaur." This concept of "mechanomorphism" circulated widely in the literature of the day.

Alfred Jarry wrote for Marinetti's periodical *Poesia;* his proto-Dada play *Ubu Roi* (*King Ubu*) was the model for Marinetti's own drama *Le Roi Bombance.* In *Le Surmâle* (*The Supermale*), Jarry introduced an extraordinary creature capable of surpassing all known limits of lovemaking and locomotion. Jarry attributed a variety of animal associations to the automobile, ranging from the erotic description of its "immodest organs of propulsion" to instinctual characterization—"metallic beast, like a huge beetle [that] flattened its wingsheath, scratched the ground, trembled, agitated its feelers and departed." Jarry's expressions of mechanomorphism and ideas on violence, anarchism, and deformation all infiltrated the Futurist program.

In *The New Weapon—The Machine* of 1905, Mario Morasso, Italian nationalist thinker and writer, prefigured many of Marinetti's ideas. Morasso described the car as "an iron monster, awed by the heartbeat of its motor...breaking loose a repressed vibration and trembling." To Morasso, the machine "lives in continuous communion with man, so that unavoidably he becomes accustomed to considering it a living part of himself," resulting in an "amazingly strong being, a strange species, a centaur of flesh and metal and of wheels and limbs." Marinetti would later develop the notion of synergy between man and machine in the "Founding and Manifesto of Futurism," as artist and auto undertake an erotic and aggressive joyride.

Even before the manifesto, Marinetti developed a similar theme in his 1905 poem "To the Automobile," also called "To My Pegasus" and "To the Racing Automobile." Since Pegasus is sometimes regarded as a symbol of poetry itself, Marinetti, in his identification of Pegasus with the automobile, seems to be casting the car in the role of modern muse for the modern world. The poem, a bizarre mixture of symbolist analogy, anarchic violence, and proto-Futurist technological exaltation, describes a car journey in which man and machine achieve an intimate and sensual union in a battle against the forces of nature. The driver erotically entreats his auto: "I am at your mercy... Take me!/ .../ I become inflamed with the fever and desire/ of the steely breaths from your full nostrils!" While urging it onward, "I finally unleash your metallic bridle... You launch yourself,/ intoxicatingly, into the liberating Infinite!" The car, "a vehement God of a race of steel," becomes a modern-day Pegasus, possessing mechanical power analogous to the supernatural forces of the mythological winged horse, "an automobile drunk with space,/ pawing the ground with anguish, strident teeth biting at the bit." In concert with man, the car transcends the conventional bounds of nature: "Hurrah! No longer contact with the impure earth!.../ Finally, I am unleashed and I supplely fly/ on the intoxicating plentitude/ of the streaming stars in the great bed of the sky!"

Adventures of man and motorcar continue in Marinetti's "Founding and Manifesto of Futurism." The first part of the manifesto, "The Founding," is the story of a turbulent car ride in which artist and auto share energy: "We went up to the three snorting beasts to lay amorous hands on their torrid breasts. I stretched out on my car like a corpse on its bier, but revived at once under the steering wheel, a guillotine blade that threatened my stomach." When the journey falters and the car dives into a ditch, the car must inspire man: "When I came up—torn, filthy, and stinking—from under the capsized car, I felt the white-hot iron of joy deliciously pass through my heart!" In turn, man must rejuvenate the auto: "They thought it was dead, my beautiful shark, but a caress from me was enough to revive it; and there it was, alive again, running on its own powerful fins!" This joyride serves as a metaphor for the inspiration and predicted development of Italian Futurism. The opening passages of "The Founding" captures the sense of Italy's cultural deterioration: "the old canal muttering its feeble prayers and the creaking bones of sickly palaces." Technology's role as guide and means of emancipation is personified by the motorcar: upon hearing "the famished roar of automobiles," artist and auto embark on a violent and sensual "journey," fleeing the past ("Let's go! Mythology and the Mystic Ideal are defeated at last") and forging into the future ("We're about to see the Centaur's birth and, soon after, the first flight of Angels!"). In Futurist symbology, the Centaur represented a hybrid of artist and machine that was to become the basis of a new cultural order fusing art and technology. To accomplish this union, the artist would investigate and learn to understand the machine, as Marinetti argued in a later manifesto: "Through intuition we will conquer the seemingly unconquerable hostility that separates our human flesh from the metal of motors."

According to Marinetti, interaction between man and machine would culminate in a new species. This strange evolutionary fantasy is elaborated in his manifesto "Multiplied Man and the Reign of the Machine":

> ...if we grant the truth of Lamarck's transformational hypothesis we must admit that we look for the creation of a non-human type in whom moral suffering, goodness of heart, affection and love, those sole corrosive poisons of inexhaustible vital energy, sole interrupter of our powerful bodily electricity, will be abolished. We believe in the possibility of an incalculable number of human transformations, and without a smile we declare that wings are asleep in the flesh of man.... Man... will master and reign over space and time.

This theory reflects the Futurist's naively utopian belief in technological progress and its potential to transmute the psychology and physiology of the human race.

Expressions of mechanomorphism in the first decades of the twentieth century are far more frequent and convincing in literature, poetry, and even theater and performance than in painting and sculpture. Undoubtedly, the difficulty posed by representing organicized machines and mechanized men accounts for their relative rarity in the visual arts. There are, however, some examples: Balla's automobile series, Russolo's *Dynamism of an Automobile* (1911–12), Severini's *Speeding Automobile* (1913), Achille Funi's *The Motorcyclist* (1914), and Gino Galli's *Mechanical and Animal Dynamism* (1914). All attempt to express a bond between man and machine by intermingling figures with their automobiles. Marinetti's eugenic fantasies may have had a visual counterpart in Boccioni's famous sculpture *Unique Forms of Continuity in Space* (1912), which in its resemblance to the *Victory of Samothrace,* to Etienne-Jules Marey's models of birds in flight, and to Marinetti's neo-Lamarckian "non-human" type, unites the development and progress of technology, biology, and aesthetics.

The relationships between man and machine found their richest expression in Futurist poetry. Mario de Leone's *Fornication of Automobiles* anthropomorphizes the car, likening a car crash to an act of copulation:

> tra...ta...ra...ta...mbu
> Involuntary collision,
> furious fornication
> of two automobiles—energy,
> embrace of two warriors
> bold of movement
> syncopation of two "heart-motors,"
> spilling of "blood-gas."
> Stopping of the coming and going
> stagnation immobile of curiosity,
> moaning. Moaning of the wounded.
> Coagulation of business.
> Cumbersome remainder
> of the two dead machines,
> rapidly swept
> from a heat of hands,
> sweeping of the enormous misshapen skeletons.

In *Heartbeats of an Automobile,* Auro d'Alba animalizes a car in imagery reminiscent of work by Jarry, Morasso, and Marinetti:

Saturated with red gas
        pawing
                trembling
I break loose
I open up columns of atmosphere
doors of liberty
The streets—intoxicated bloodsuckers
they suck me   suck me
              at the heels
the cadavers of miles
devoured by the cannibal motor.

In performances of Futurist theater and music, machines occupy a particularly important position. The technology that was imitated or evoked in Futurist art and literature could play an actual role in Futurist theater and music. As projections of the artists' visions of the world, Futurist theater, much of it designed by architects, included functioning machines and architectural sets, often based on unrealized proposals for objects and architecture. Enrico Prampolini's *Magnetic Theatre,* though never performed, was not meant to include actors; the movements of an elaborate machine constituted the performance. When actors did participate in Futurist theater, they often mimicked machines. Giacomo Balla's performance entitled *Printing Press* (1914) consisted of twelve performers. Two pairs of two players jerked to and fro like surging pistons. Connected to each pair was a third player whose arms spun like a cog wheel, and the two arms of the human cogs, in turn, meshed like gears. Futurist music—everyday sounds, sometimes mixed with more conventional music—comprised the production. In 1914, during the most famous of his *intonarumori* (noise machine) concerts, Luigi Russolo performed *Meeting of Airplanes and Automobile,* regaling his audience with the sounds of backfiring motors, droning engines, and other noise from the world of machines.

In all these works of Futurist art, literature, and performance, representations of a communion between man and machine, organicized machines, and mechanized men, symbolized the belief that intuition of the internal workings of machines would provide a more profound understanding of the forces characterizing contemporary existence. This theme, combined with the introduction into art of images and devices from the technological world and the urban environment, embodied the Futurist ideal of a total integration of art and life. By bringing their art into closer, more direct contact with the revolutionary advances of contemporary civilization, the Futurists wished to invigorate and stimulate their artistic production. Believing that technological growth would inevitably affect every aspect of society, the Futurists hoped that their art, as technology's major aesthetic proponent, would achieve parallel significance. The Futurist introduction of mechanical subject matter into art, especially the inclusion of machinery and mechanical noises into theater and performance, was part of a general assault on traditional artforms, and an attempt to bridge the actual dichotomy between art and life.

John Sloan. Hill, Main Street, Gloucester. *c. 1916. Oil on canvas mounted on masonite, 25¾ × 31¾". The Parrish Art Museum, Southampton, New York. Littlejohn collection*

John Sloan. Indian Detour. *1927. Etching, 6 × 7¼". Kraushaar Galleries, New York City*

The Futurist artists, operating in many mediums, gathered and concentrated a variety of sentiments about the automobile. In selecting it as the symbol of the movement, the Futurists chose well. As the iconography of the automobile developed in modern art, nearly all later themes concerning it had origins in Italian Futurism. Outside Futurism, most European artists who utilized automobile imagery eschewed the Italian movement's "autolatry" and its euphoric, somewhat naive faith in the total beneficence of new technology. These other artists demonstrated a more critical, less romantic attitude, diverging from Futurist principles and expanding upon ways in which mechanical imagery could be used in art.

Early in the century, American artists were much less involved with the theme of the automobile than were their European counterparts. The American painter John Sloan was the major exception; while the Futurists were ecstatically embracing the automobile as a symbol of cultural liberation, Sloan was exploiting it to satirize certain American values. With the eye of a muckraking reporter and social critic, Sloan used the car to expose the foibles of society, though as the automobile became more accessible to the general population, he abandoned some of his prejudice toward it.

Sloan's change in attitude marked the growing acceptance and commercialization of the automobile during the first decades of the twentieth century, when the histories of the car in America and Europe diverge. The motorcar was initially regarded as a plaything for the rich, and ownership conferred status. But the motorcar shed its association with the monied class earliest in the United States. America's high standard of living and wider distribution of income produced a larger potential car market, and mass production of the automobile made more economic sense. Rich in raw material, lean in labor, the United States turned to mechanization as a solution. With mechanization came standardization, which boosted production methods and facilitated automotive repair. While it is generally agreed that European-made cars were better crafted, the American models were lighter, cheaper, less controlled by government regulation, and simpler to operate. Thus, the car was democratized earliest in America: "The automobile is European by birth, American by adoption," as automotive historian John B. Rae phrased it.

John Sloan became more ardent about the car as it gained wider public acceptance. The portrayals of his friend Randall Davey, a car fanatic, and his autos became highly enthusiastic, and Sloan began to chronicle several automobile adventures in his work. In the painting *Hill, Main Street, Gloucester* (c. 1916), Sloan adapted a by then common motif, contrasting the excitement and thrill of whipping along in Davey's open roadster with the lethargic pace of a horse-drawn cart. In the brisk ink sketch *Davey's Simplex Touring Car* (1919), he conveyed the sense of speed and liberation he experienced on several cross-country jaunts to the American Southwest. The product of one of these trips, the etching *Indian Detour* (1927), gives history a twist: tourist buses and well-to-do travelers encircle a group of Santa Fe Indians performing a ritual dance, an ironic reversal of the nineteenth-century image of a ring of Conestoga wagons protecting pioneers from Indian onslaughts. In the late etching *Movie Troupe* (1920), Sloan captured the collective public desire that yearned for the glamour and wealth of screen stars. The limousine, swarmed by a crowd, is both a symbol of wealth and a symbol of the American dream. As film historian Julian Smith wrote in

John Marin. Street Movement, New York City. *1934. Watercolor, 17½ × 21½". Collection Holly and Arthur Magill, Greenville, South Carolina*

"A Runaway Match: The Automobile in the American Film, 1900–1920," published in "The Automobile and American Culture," a special 1980–1981 number of *Michigan Quarterly Review*: "America fell in love with both movies and cars, while Hollywood and Detroit fell in love with each other. The star-in-the-car soon became a staple of publicity within both industries."

Several American artists working in the teens and twenties were attracted to themes related to the automobile, though no single style or approach characterizes these pieces. These American artists, working during a time when the automobile was becoming a common fixture, were mesmerized by the overall dynamics of the metropolis. Through artists' eyes, gigantic and distinctively American artifacts such as skyscrapers and bridges functioned as symbols evocative of the grand energies of the burgeoning cityscape. John Marin's series of paintings and watercolors of New York City incorporate images of the car as but one of many fragmented, interpenetrating, sometimes clashing images of bridges, skyscrapers, people, and sunlight. All combine to satisfy Marin's philosophy, that "the whole city is alive; buildings, people, all are alive." Louis Lozowick's *Doorway into Street* (1930), and many of his lithographs of the twenties and thirties *Checkerboard* (1926), *Hanover Square* (1929), *57th Street* (1930), and *Traffic* (1930), treat the automobile with the dynamic dignity characteristic of his depictions of urban artifacts. Marin interpreted the urban world as energetic and tumultuous; Lozowick, a Precisionist artist, argued that "beneath all the apparent chaos and confusion, is... order and organization which find their outward sign and symbol in... the American city." Against a geometric armature of checkerboard tiles and rectangular panes of glass, Lozowick frames the cropped image of the lower half of an automobile. As in nearly all his works incorporating representations of the car, Lozowick places it within an overall patterned grid of the architecture, streets, light, and shadow of the city. The car is part of a new, efficient, rational, urban world, which Lozowick saw as "an expression of optimism."

As early as 1916 Stuart Davis addressed the subject of "the dynamic American scene," as he put it, "the brilliant colors on gasoline stations, chain-store fronts, and taxi-cabs; ... fast travel by train, auto, and aeroplane which brought new and multiple perspectives." Davis was fascinated by the American roadside, which, to him, teemed with energy, variety, and excitement. He emphasized the dynamic qualities and multiple perspectives of contemporary life, and in his early attempts to portray the American roadside environment he borrowed from Futurist ideology. With its flattened forms and distorted bird's-eye perspective, Davis's *Gloucester Street* (1916) merely hints at the unification of several disparate scenes, evincing his struggle to create a sense of dynamism and simultaneity. What he hinted at in *Gloucester Street* was realized two years later in a painting entitled *Multiple Views,* in which discrete scenes from the roadside culture are packed side by side and on top of one another.

Cars, gasoline pumps, and garages continued to appear in his work and announce one of his basic intentions: to evoke dynamic energies and simultaneous sensations of the environment through juxtaposition of various aspects of the landscape. Davis wrestled with the problem of pictorially representing synchronous events, as he remarked: "What is required is that all areas be simultaneously perceived by the spectator. You see things

Louis Lozowick. Doorway into Street. *1930. Lithograph, 14 × 7".* Collection Mrs. Adele Lozowick, New York City

73

Stuart Davis. Windshield Mirror. *c. 1932. Gouache, 15¼ × 25". Philadelphia Museum of Art. Gift of Mrs. Edith Halpert*

Stuart Davis. Garage Lights. *1931. Oil on canvas, 32 × 42". Memorial Art Gallery of the University of Rochester, New York. Marion Stratton Gould Fund*

as a unity at the same time. What there is, *all* at the same time." Davis best captured these feelings and forces in his paintings from the 1930s, such as *Garage Lights* (1931), *New York–Paris No. 3* (1931), *Windshield Mirror* (1932), and *Gas Pumps* (1938), in which the interaction of vibrantly colored, jigsaw puzzle–like forms create jazzy syncopations and vivid pulsations.

The success of these works is due primarily to Davis's receptiveness to the style of the American roadside culture. His ability to sustain a dialogue between high art and vernacular forms imparted tremendous vitality to his work. He combined high art influences, such as the synthetic Cubist interwedging of flattened, dismembered forms, and the Fauvist use of intense color, with the abrasive shapes and colors of billboards and neon signs. The work of Fernand Léger, who also painted gas pumps, auto junkyards, motors, and mechanics; of Joan Miró and Henri Matisse, whose painting *Through the Windshield* prefigured Davis's own *Windshield Mirror,* were especially inspirational.

Although separated by a span of fifteen years and developed on different continents, Matisse's *Through the Windshield* and Davis's *Windshield Mirror* bear provocative similarities. The Matisse depicts a vista seen through a car windshield; the Davis, a scene through a windshield and its rear-view mirror. Both contain perspectives unique to the automobile and found in works by artists John Vachon, Edward Hopper, Hans Hofmann, William Copley, Allan D'Arcangelo, Alex Katz, and Howard Kanovitz. The Royal Academician Hubert von Herkomer, painter, motorist, sponsor of the Herkomer rally, and designer of car trophies, was among the first artists to be attracted to this point of view. He wrote in 1905: "The pleasure [of motoring] ...is seeing Nature as I could in no other way see it; my car having 'tops,' I get Nature framed—and one picture after another delights my artistic eye."

For Davis and Matisse, the vantage point through a car windshield extended their repertoire of subjects and compositions. The decorative unification of different spatial levels onto the flat canvas surface in *Through the Windshield* reveals Matisse's realization that the car windshield could provide a valid variation on his theme of interior-exterior juxtapositions, which he usually explored through windows, doors, balconies, and mirrors. Matisse often used the balcony or window to frame, structure, and in certain respects to mediate and domesticate the inherent entropic disorder of nature. He found in the automobile a "mobile" balcony that permitted him to expand his pictorial horizons: the car windshield functioned as visual and psychological filter. *Through the Windshield* was inspired by an actual auto journey that Matisse took in 1916, an event chronicled by the painting. The sketchbook or drawing board propped on the seat of the motorcar, echoing the shape of the windscreen, might well refer to Matisse's preliminary drawings for *Through the Windshield,* or for other paintings such as *Route à Clamart* (1916–17), which was derived from sketches done from the interior of the automobile on this long motor trip.

Less decorative and more dynamic, Davis's *Windshield Mirror* displays an overall pattern or structure that best approximates his goal "to see things as a unity at the same time." In Davis's art, Fauvist and Cubist vocabularies are used to produce an essentially Futurist sensibility, with the most invigorating influences being the forms and sensations of the environment itself.

Henri Matisse. Through the Windshield. *1917. Oil on canvas, 15¼ × 22". The Cleveland Museum of Art. Bequest of Lucia McCurdy McBride in memory of John Harris McBride II*

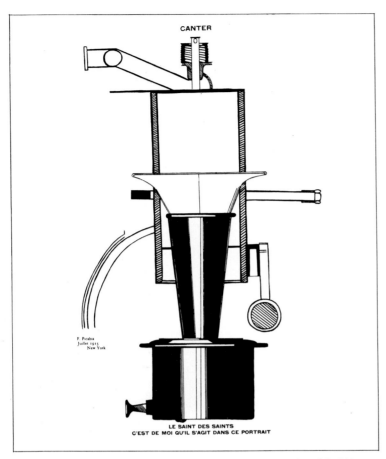

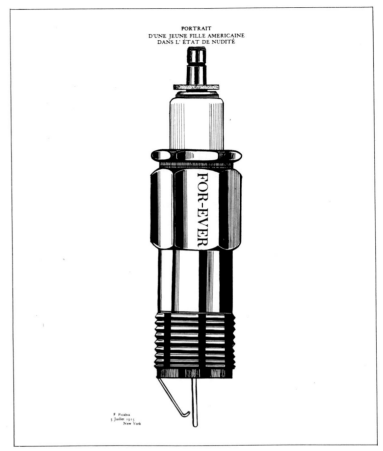

Francis Picabia. Le Saint des Saints. *Lithograph reproduced in 291, nos. 5 and 6, July/August 1915. Art Library, University of California at Los Angeles*

Francis Picabia. Portrait of a Young American Woman in a State of Nudity. *Lithograph reproduced in 291, nos. 5 and 6, July/August 1915. Art Library, University of California at Los Angeles*

Francis Picabia. Portrait of Marie Laurencin—Four in Hand. *c. 1917. Ink and watercolor on board, 22 × 18". Collection Mrs. Barnett Malbin (The Lydia and Harry Lewis Winston Collection), New York City*

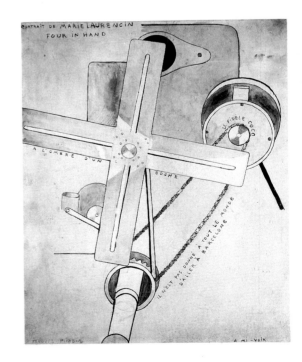

The most significant contribution to the iconography of the automobile in American art during the first few decades of the twentieth century resulted from the European artist Francis Picabia's contact with the American environment. In the years immediately preceding several visits to the States in the early and mid-teens, Picabia was associated with the French Puteaux and the *Section d'Or* groups, two related circles of Cubist artists who were enthralled with science, mathematics, geometry, and motion. Throughout Picabia's career, his art underwent frequent changes and, in his own words, his stay in America "brought about a complete revolution in my methods of work.... Almost immediately upon coming to America it flashed on me that the genius of the modern world is in machinery and that through machinery art ought to find a most vivid expression." Soon after arriving in the United States, Picabia executed a series of five object-portraits for Alfred Stieglitz's new periodical *291;* each of the five drawings depicts an object or group of objects related to the machine world, and four out of the five are connected with automobile imagery. The objects bear no actual physical likeness to the individuals they are intended to represent, yet they do correspond to their subjects, and the drawings are inscribed with the subject's name or with other clues to his or her identity. Those portrayed, Alfred Stieglitz, Marius de Zayas, Paul Haviland, perhaps Agnes Ernst Meyer, and Picabia himself, were instrumental in the production and publication of the new *291* journal, which was a successor to Stieglitz's *Camera Work.*

In his self-portrait, *Le Saints des Saints,* Picabia represented himself by means of an automobile horn, which he copied from an advertisement. Various scholars have suggested that the horn refers to Picabia's notoriously clamorous personality, and to his role as a mouthpiece for modern art. The drawing also contains sexual innuendo alluding to his infamous promiscuous behavior: a phallic automobile horn and a tongue-in-cheek inscription "Le Saints des Saints." The horn surmounts what can be identified as the cross-section of a car cylinder, a large rectangle to which a valve spring connects at the center top, and a camshaft at the bottom right. Within the cylinder walls of the combustion chamber, the region where the mechanical explosion erupts, Picabia superimposed and visually interlocked the tooting end of his horn, replacing the pistons and connecting rod assembly. By locating the phallic horn where pistons pump and combustion occurs, Picabia might have been suggesting a mechanical analogy for sexual activity. As he was known for mingling the mechanical, the erotic, and verbal-visual puns, Picabia projected a self-image appropriate to his reputation as a womanizer and adulterer.

The *Portrait of a Young American Woman in a State of Nudity,* an image of a spark plug borrowed from an automobile magazine advertisement, has been traditionally interpreted as referring to Picabia's judgment that American women were wanton—the spark plug is an obvious symbol of a "hot woman" able to ignite flames of passion. It has been speculated that the plug must represent a woman active in *291* who was also an auto enthusiast. This is the only object-portrait not specifically identifying the subject, so the original generic association with American women, whose beauty, boldness, and directness impressed Picabia, should probably be retained.

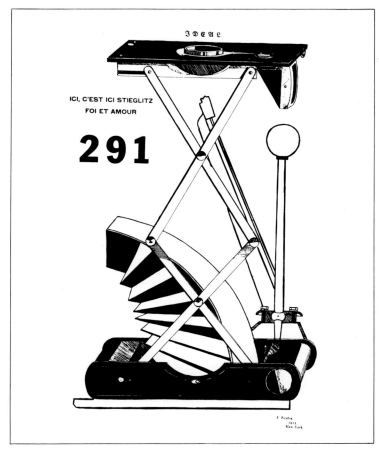

Francis Picabia. Portrait of Alfred Stieglitz. *Lithograph reproduced in* 291, *nos. 5 and 6, July/August 1915. Art Library, University of California at Los Angeles*

Portrait of Alfred Stieglitz is, logically, a camera, taken from an advertisement in Stieglitz's own publication *Camera Work*. It is accompanied by two shafts, a car's gearshift, and hand brake. Because the gearshift appears to be in neutral, the brake lever at stop, and the camera's limp bellows unattached to its lens, the image has been interpreted as a symbol representing Stieglitz's feelings of failure about his attempts to promote modernism in America. The interpretation requires qualification, since Stieglitz was reportedly enthusiastic about *291*. The configuration of the camera may allude to his actual camera, "simple, almost primitive...its sagging bellows held up by pieces of string and adhesive tape," as artist Konrad Cramer remembers it.

The components of the portrait of Marius de Zayas, the Mexican-born caricaturist, theorist, primitive-art collector, and gallery director, are generally considered the most enigmatic of the five. A series of wires connects a woman's corset and two superimposed automotive systems—one electrical, the other lubrication. By representing de Zayas with a diagram of a mechanical system, something that joins several different components into an interdependent scheme, Picabia may have been referring to de Zayas's position as the central organizer of *291*. The generator, the object that fires the entire electrical system, and the part-connecting rod, which joins together several parts of the lubrication system, are appropriate symbols for an editor, the individual who "generates" ideas and organizes the operation into a smooth "well-oiled machine."

The object-portraits pay homage to the individuals most responsible for the *291* publication. Picabia unifies them on a mechanical and personal level; not only are they all represented by machines, but nearly all have some connection with the automobile, an object of paramount importance in Picabia's life.

These drawings were derived from advertisements and commercial illustrations, and they comment on the pervasive commercialism of American culture as described by de Zayas in the same issue of *291*: "Any effort, any tendency, which does not possess the radiation of advertising remains practically ignored." The drawings, faithful copies of the ads, were "depicted with the precision and relief of a mail order catalogue, with no attempt at aesthetic expression," as Picabia's first wife, Gabrielle Buffet-Picabia, analyzed them. They ironically point out the imitative character of much American art of the early twentieth century.

Similar to many of his compatriots working in America at the time, Picabia believed that the United States, especially New York City, was the most fertile soil for the pursuit of modernism; he was baffled by the American artists who continued to travel to Europe to learn about art. "Your New York," he proclaimed in 1913, "is the cubist, the futurist city. You have passed through all the old schools. You are futurists in word, deed, and thought." European artists Albert Gleizes and Marcel Duchamp would echo his sentiment in the twenties. "Your New York is the place—there are the modern ideas," they instructed American artist Charles Demuth, "Europe is finished."

Picabia's object-portraits were audaciously novel in terms of straightforward presentations; these precise linear executions of mechanical forms were nearly indistinguishable from blueprints or mechanical drafts.

Picabia's exploitation of mechanical forms in portraiture was undoubtedly influenced by the work of Marius de Zayas and by his close friend Marcel Duchamp. In 1913, de Zayas executed a series of extraordinary drawings called *Caricature: Absolute and Relative.* Although each work is titled and refers to a specific individual or pair of individuals, many of the pieces combine abstract lines, shapes, and mathematical formulas, and do not resemble their human subjects.

In the object-portraits, Picabia substituted precise mechanical forms for de Zayas's numerical symbols, a strategy explored earlier in Marcel Duchamp's inclusion of nearly verbatim translations of mechanical objects in his works, such as in his *Coffee Grinder* (1911) and his *Chocolate Grinder No. 2* (1914). Picabia's mechanical portraits differ somewhat from the Duchamp pieces. The clarity of form in Picabia's art, unlike the painterliness in Duchamp's, aligns the work more closely with the world of crisp mechanical illustration. Picabia's machines, especially his object-portraits, allude to twentieth-century technology, using, for example, images of automobile parts, a new model camera, and an electric lamp. Duchamp's subjects are nostalgic pre-twentieth-century objects—a coffee mill and the chocolate grinder with rococo Louis XV legs.

In Picabia's object-portraits, the machine becomes an analogical device to represent human psychology and behavior in art. As Picabia wrote:

> The machine has become more than a mere adjunct of life. It is really a part of human life... perhaps the very soul. In seeking forms through which to interpret ideas or by which to expose human characteristics I have come at length upon the form which appears most brilliantly plastic and fraught with symbolism. I have enlisted the machinery of the modern world, and introduced it into my studio. ... I mean ... to work simply on and on until I attain the pinnacle of mechanical symbolism.

Picabia believed that machines were worthy of aesthetic interpretation and representative of the spirit of the modern world. Since machines are designed to extend human capabilities, they can mirror our existence. By employing mechanical imagery in his art, Picabia held up the mirror of the machine and reflected its image back at man. As Paul Haviland explained in an issue of *291*:

> We are living in an age of the machine. Man made the machine in his own image. She has limbs which act; lungs which breathe; a heart which beats; a nervous system through which runs electricity. The phonograph is the image of his voice; the camera the image of his eye. The machine is his "daughter born without a mother." That is why he loves her.... Having made her superior to himself, he endows the superior beings which he conceives in his poetry and in his plastique with the qualities of machines. After making the machine in his own image, he has made his human ideal machinomorphic.... Without him she remains a wonderful being, but without mind or anatomy. Through their mating they complete one another. She brings forth according to his conceptions.

Joan Miró. Portrait of Heribérto Casany (The Chauffeur). *1918. Oil on canvas, 27½ × 24½". The Bragaline Collection, New York City*

Haviland points to man's creation of machines that ape his actions. The concept of the machine as a "daughter born without a mother"—words Picabia used as titles for a drawing published in the issue of *291* that contained object-portraits and later for a painting—equated man's creation of the machine with God's creation of man. Throughout history and mythology, heroes, saviors, and messiahs have been the offspring of unusual circumstances of birth. In creating the machine, man could perform without a partner, and play the role of a god. Endowing the machine with feminine gender reaffirmed the masculine desire to display potency; both machines and women were seen as objects to be manipulated, accoutrements to man's existence that were, paradoxically, both superior and dependent upon him. Picabia was a great lover of women and cars, owned over a hundred vehicles in his lifetime, and was dominating and manipulative in his treatment of both. Picabia's often autobiographical art frequently explores a visual idiom in which the automobile is portrayed as the object, and sexuality as the subject. His object-portraits serve as an ideal example of his philosophy of the relationship existing among man, artist, and the machine.

New York had a strong impact on Picabia, and was instrumental to his adoption of mechanical subject matter. After returning to Europe in 1916, Picabia continued to explore mechanical themes related to the automobile. He first settled in Barcelona and launched the magazine *391,* an ironic successor to *291.* In *391,* he published several object-portrait drawings, including depictions of his friends the artists Marie Laurencin and Albert Gleizes, who had both come to Barcelona. Laurencin, who did promotional art for Renault, was represented as a motor-generator. *Cones,* a sketch of automobile cylinders and plugs, represents Gleizes, the French Cubist painter and theorist associated with the *Section d'Or* group and an enthusiast of American technology and urbanism.

During this time, Joaquin Torres-Garcia and Joan Miró were working in Barcelona. It is uncertain whether or not either was aware of the Picabia circle and its activities. In 1917, however, Torres-Garcia's art changed greatly, as he adopted a more modernist vocabulary and content, evidenced in his oil of that year *Barcelona Street Scene.* Robustly painted interlocking slices of urban life fill the canvas. Cars, trams, and pedestrians clog the street; fragments of signs announce lamp stores and the cinema, products of the modern world. Miró's art, gradually evolving throughout the teens, did not undergo a radical change at this moment. But in 1918, he completed a piece related directly to the automobile and indirectly to Picabia's object-portraits. In *Portrait of Heribérto Casany (The Chauffeur),* Miró indicates his friend's relationship to cars by the picture of a motorcar that hangs near the seated figure.

Over the next few years, Picabia lived in Switzerland and Paris. In 1920, in Paris, Picabia launched another magazine, *Cannibale,* which contained a photograph of Picabia at the wheel of an auto and Tristan Tzara, the leader of Zurich Dada, in the front seat. Entitled *Mercer 85 h.p.,* after the name and horsepower of the car, the photo is captioned: "Two exhibitionists intoxicated by the abuse of the automobile." Both title and caption are *entendres* playing on analogies between high speed and high living, and between exhibitors of art and exhibitors of outrageous behavior.

The relationship between Francis Picabia and Marcel

Duchamp was particularly fruitful: they were close friends, shared artistic ideas, and influenced each other throughout their careers. Duchamp was not as fanatic about cars as was Picabia, though he did make a sketch called *Two People and an Automobile* during a motoring journey in 1912. The journey along the Paris–Jura road with Picabia and the French avant-garde poet and art critic Guillaume Apollinaire provided the initial impetus to Duchamp's *The Bride Stripped Bare by Her Bachelors, Even (the Large Glass)*. One of the most notorious works in the history of art, the *Large Glass* was constructed between 1915 and 1923 in New York, where the artist continued to explore a general interest in the machine. Related to Picabia's painting *Child Carburetor* (c. 1919), in which the operation of a carburetor serves as a metaphor for the sexual act, Duchamp's *Large Glass* contains mechanical imagery suggestive of a sexual encounter. Much of the pseudo-scientific operation of the *Large Glass,* elucidated by the notes in the *Green Box,* is described or perhaps veiled in automotive terms. The bride is a "motor … with quite feeble cylinders, in contact with the sparks of her constant life (desire-magneto).…At her base, is a reservoir of love-gasoline," which Duchamp called "a sort of automobiline." Among the bride's other parts are "desire-gears" and cogs, and her blossoming is explained as "the image of a motor car climbing a slope in low gear. (The car wants more and more to reach the top, and while slowly accelerating, as if exhausted by hope, the motor of the car turns over faster and faster, until it roars triumphantly.)"

Duchamp had originally intended to incorporate the experience of the Paris–Jura journey in a separate work of art. The piece, to be constructed out of wood, as Duchamp said, "which seems…like the affective translation of powdered silex" (the material used for making road beds), was to have as its leading characters nine nudes (corresponding to the nine malic molds of the *Large Glass*) and a "headlight-child" (corresponding to the Bride).

The *Large Glass* remains a basically enigmatic work, despite the appearance of certain explicit human-mechanical correspondences such as "love-gasoline," "desire-magneto," and "desire-gears." Duchamp's forms go through abstruse and convoluted processes, a parallel to the human intermingling of the psychological and the physiological, the internal and the external, the chemical and the emotional. Produced on a transparent support, the *Large Glass* is opaque in its meaning. Duchamp thought of it as an apparition, a three-dimensional shadow of a four-dimensional object; as he described, "It is like the hood of a car, the part that covers the motor."

Obliqueness and subtlety differentiate Duchamp's piece from Picabia's generally more direct work. For Picabia, a piston surging into a cylinder becomes the obvious means of describing sexual intercourse, with perhaps a hint of human folly defined by his sometimes absurd mechanisms. On the other hand, Duchamp's language, visual and verbal, is so strangely evocative that the mysteries of his machines partake of the mysteries of life.

Picabia's initial object-portraits and Duchamp's *Large Glass* were executed in New York City. Because their vision and approach were so unconventional, Picabia and Duchamp were considered to be the nucleus of New York Dada, a geographically and stylistically diverse group of artists operating in the teens and twenties. Officially founded in Zurich in 1916, Dada was intended to be a state of mind rather than a unified school or

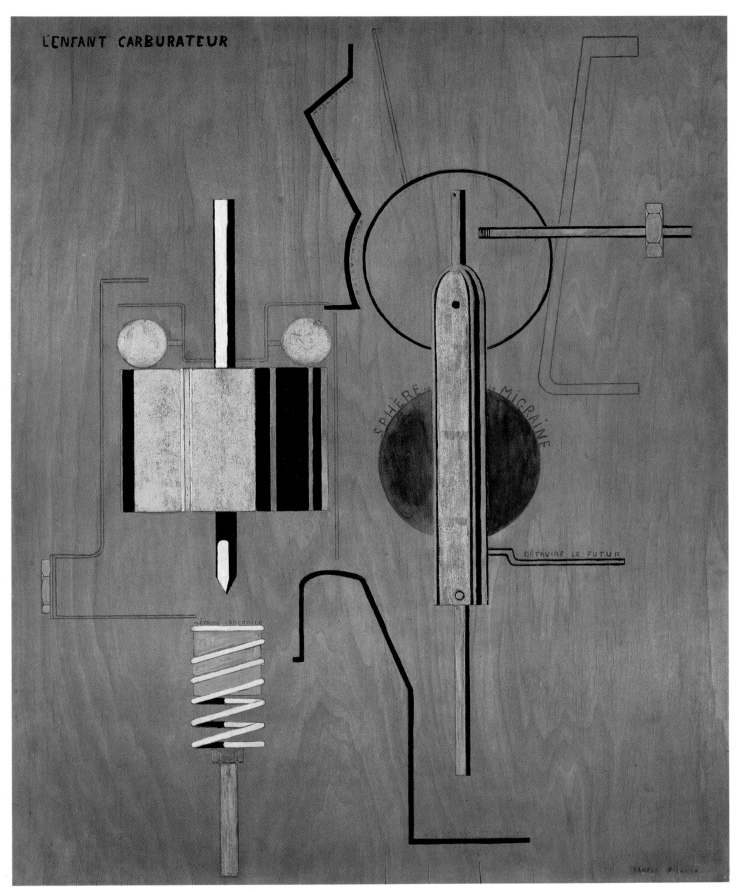

Francis Picabia. The Child Carburetor. *1919. Oil, enamel, metallic paint, gold leaf, pencil, and crayon on stained plywood, 49¾ × 40".*
The Solomon R. Guggenheim Museum, New York City

Marcel Duchamp. Two People and a Car (Study). *1912. Charcoal on paper, 13¾ × 11½". Collection Mme. Marcel Duchamp, Villiers-sous-Grez, France*

style; it was argued that the sensibility of Dada existed before the movement was ever christened. Dada intentionally reflected the irrationality and immorality of a war-torn world and bourgeois conventions. Dada art employed anarchy, shock, destruction, and nihilism, or playfulness and chance, but it did express hope for a new aesthetic and social order. Although World War I awakened artists to the destructive potential of technological advance, there existed no clear-cut and consistent Dada attitude toward modern technology. The object-portraits and the *Large Glass* might suggest dehumanization because of their translation of human activities into mechanical terms, but at the same time this equation of man and machine had tremendous aesthetic and psychological potential. The object-portraits, in particular, opened artists' eyes to the intrinsic beauty of mechanical forms, while they reflected Picabia's personal infatuation with aspects of modern technology. Picabia and Duchamp, in their treatments of automobile imagery, suggested a wide range of sometimes paradoxical possibilities for the use of machine forms in art.

Several artists associated with Berlin Dada, the most politically revolutionary of the Dada groups, used imagery related to the automobile. In his photocollage *Tatlin at Home,* Raoul Hausmann portrayed the Russian Constructivist artist Vladimir Tatlin as a "man who had nothing in his head but machines, automobile cylinders, brakes and steering wheels." In his portrait, Hausmann used a profusion of automotive images, snipped directly from magazines and newspapers, to illustrate Tatlin's philosophy of uniting art, technology, and politics. Hannah Höch, another member of Berlin Dada, was even more explicit when she remarked, "Our whole purpose was to integrate objects from the world of machines and industry in the world of art." Her photomontages intersperse and overlap photographs of car tires, engines, BMW logos, whole autos, cogs, gears, ball bearings, and images of past and contemporary political leaders. Contrary to the conventional interpretation of Dada as an anti-technological art movement, the Berlin group believed that technology, if properly harnessed, was essential to the development of a new political and social order.

Both Hausmann and Höch employed the collage technique, a particularly popular medium at the time, especially among the Dadaists. Collage dates back to the early teens, when Georges Braque and Pablo Picasso glued scraps of paper, cut from newspapers, magazines, and sample books, to cardboard, paper, and canvas supports. Collage, first developed by Cubists, came at a stage when Cubist art had become spatially flat, highly abstract, and difficult to read. The incorporation of actual objects into the work had several consequences: it opened up the space in front of the picture plane; it reintroduced a certain legibility into art; it allowed artists to contrast a new range of forms and textures; and it could express the fragmentary and simultaneous experiences of the modern world.

Images of automobiles derived from photographs occur in several collages and assemblages of the twenties. The degree of meaning attached to the car in these works varies greatly. In the "Merz" collages of Cologne Dadaist Kurt Schwitters, and in *Design for a Manifesto* (1920) by Hanover Dadaist Max Ernst, the auto images function as one part of many formal and contextual scraps, and the particulars are devoid of individual symbolism. In other collages, assemblages, and photomontages, such as Yuri Annenkov's *Rolls Royce* (1921), Alexander Rodchenko's *Self-Portrait*

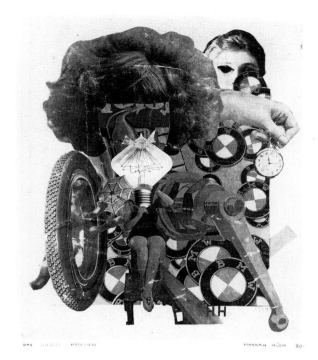

Hannan Höch. The Pretty Girl. *1920. Collage, 13¾ × 11½". Private collection, Hamburg, West Germany*

Marianne Brandt. Sport-Sport. *1928. Collage, 19¾ × 13". Collection Merrill C. Berman, New York City*

Re-
klame-
plakat

Foto-
plastik:
MO-
HOLY-
NAGY

108

László Moholy-Nagy. Pneumatik. *Lithograph reproduced in* Malerie, Fotografie, Film, *vol. 8 of Bauhausbücher, 1927. The Robert Gore Rifkind Foundation, Beverly Hills, California*

(1922), László Moholy-Nagy's *Pneumatik* (1925), Arthur Dove's *Long Island* (1925), Marianne Brandt's *Sport-Sport* (1928), and Vinicio Paladini's *Movement and Space* (1928), the automobile functions more symbolically. In *Rolls Royce,* the image of the motorcar serves as one of many indigenous British artifacts, which include English boots, lace doubling as Gothic tracery, a Mark Cross logo, and a native handbill. Alexander Rodchenko photographed cars and car parts in a brilliantly composed series of city streets and auto factories, which were shot from unusual angles. He also assembled photomontages that contained car parts, such as horns and wheels. His *Self-Portrait,* recalling Picabia's object-portraits and Hausmann's photocollage of Rodchenko's colleague Tatlin, consists of several photographs in which the artist is shown attached to a gear and straddling a tire. László Moholy-Nagy, working at the German Bauhaus, employed photocollage in his poster *Pneumatik,* a clever combination of large abstract sweeps, one arc spelling out "PNEUMATIK" as it expressively recedes into space, forming a funneling plane that is reminiscent of a racetrack.

Dove included car images in several paintings and organicized their forms so that they would harmonize with the natural world. In *Long Island,* he juxtaposed a cutout of a car with various natural elements: twigs, leaves, grass, and shells. All suggest a ride along the shore.

Marianne Brandt's collage, an anthology of locomotion from boats and bicycles to race cars and airplanes, depicts another modern symbol, the Eiffel Tower: the compendium of imagery is augmented with several illustrations of the pneumatic tire. Vinicio Paladini, a second-generation Futurist artist, carried the Futurist interest in movement into the twenties with his photocollage *Movement and Space,* which depicts a series of overlapping, spiraling motifs, including a curving racetrack, a descending staircase, and a dynamic baroque sculpture.

The inclusion of reproductions of actual automobiles in mixed mediums of the twenties was accompanied by a growing interest in the abstract, autonomous beauty of machines. Constructivism, De Stijl, Purism, and the Bauhaus in Europe, and Precisionism in America participated in an aesthetic current that promoted the inherent formal beauty of the machine, though the European movements were more utilitarian and design-oriented, abstracting aesthetic principles from the machine world to be applied to merging the creation of art and everyday objects. The automobile was generally regarded as the archetypal machine source of design principles. In *Toward a New Architecture,* Le Corbusier juxtaposed photographs of Greek temples with photographs of automobiles, comparing a 1907 car with the Temple of Hera at Paestum and a 1921 auto with the Parthenon. He compared the Parthenon, which represents the culmination of refinement in classical temples, to automobile design, which he believed was evolving toward a state of consummate development. Le Corbusier believed that architects should look to automobile design and construction to discover models upon which to base modern architectural principles. *Citrohan,* one of his early housing design programs for a prefabricated, modular system, was based on the name Citroën, the European auto manufacturer, supporting Le Corbusier's postulate that "houses must go up all of a piece, made by machine tools in a factory, assembled as Ford assembles cars, on moving conveyor belts."

Arthur Dove. Long Island. *1925. Collage on painted panel, 15 × 20¾". Museum of Fine Arts, Boston*

Le Corbusier. Two pages from Toward A New Architecture, *1928 edition. Art Library, University of California at Los Angeles*

Le Corbusier and Pierre Jeanneret. Drawings for a Voiture maximum. *1928. Fondation Le Corbusier, Paris*

The idea that mechanical objects evolve functionally toward a more ideal form had wide currency in the teens and twenties. Fernand Léger, whose hard-edged volumetric forms were much influenced by the machine, argued in "Machine Aesthetics," a 1924 article published in the avant-garde journal *L'Effort Moderne,* that "in the case of the evolution of the automobile ...the more the machine perfects its utilitarian functions, the more beautiful it becomes." Léger, who worked closely with the Purists in the early twenties, has described this evolution: "[At first] vertical lines dominated—which were not in keeping with the car's aim—it was ugly: the horse was lacking, and people said 'horseless carriage.' But when to facilitate speed, the chassis was lowered and elongated...horizontal lines balanced by curves came to dominate, and the car acquired a perfect unity, organized in keeping with its aim—it was beautiful...."

Several artists associated with machine-conscious art movements of the twenties designed or modified actual automobiles. As early as 1911 the Purist artist Amedée Ozenfant helped design the motorcar Hispano-Suiza and dubbed it the Hispano Ozenfant. In 1928, Le Corbusier proposed a brilliant forerunner to the modern-day subcompact. Aerodynamically sound and efficient, this rear-engine vehicle was never built. In the early thirties, the Bauhaus artist Walter Gropius produced several car bodies and interiors for the highly luxurious Adler Cabriolet, though his elegant designs lack the innovativeness of Le Corbusier's project. When the Bauhaus artists decided to study the artistic production of the Bugatti family, they ignored the work of two sculptors in the family and concentrated on Ettore Bugatti's renowned automobile designs.

The Purist program, like earlier Futurist ideology, endeavored to cull pandemic principles from technological developments, with the eventual utopian goal of constructing a new world, though Futurism and Purism held differing views of what technology had to offer. The Futurists concentrated on the intoxicating emotions and dynamic sensations available through use of new technology, while the Purists, hoping to restore order to

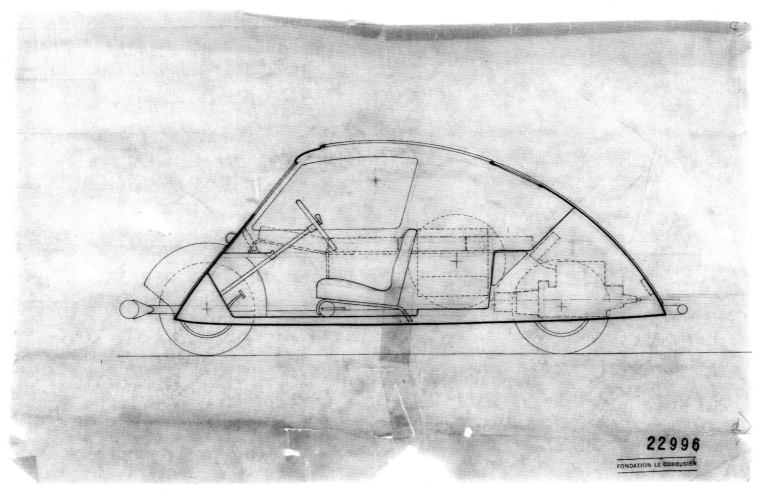

Le Corbusier and Pierre Jeanneret. Drawing for a Voiture maximum *(cross section). 1928. Fondation Le Corbusier, Paris*

a world devastated by war, resurrected the classicist devotion to proportion, harmony, and control. Believing in the possibility of attaining an ideal aesthetic mechanical state, they focused on forms of the machine and other technological objects.

Although Le Corbusier and his Purist colleague Amedée Ozenfant considered the automobile to be a paradigm of the machine aesthetic, they seldom included its image in their art, but attempted instead to structure their art and other artifacts around the principles of contemporaneous automotive design. The American counterpart to the European movement, Precisionism, was also attracted to the beauty of technological forms, and it, too, avoided using the automobile itself as subject matter in art. Art influenced by the machine aesthetic attempted to establish canons of order, geometry, precision, and efficiency, while eschewing the particular and the individual. As the Precisionist Charles Sheeler remarked: "I'm interested in a man-made world, depopulated landscapes, in that there's never people; it's my illustration of what a beautiful world it would be if there were no people in it." Since the car was a more personal and individual means of transportation, it was only occasionally used as a subject matter in Precisionist art.

One example of its appearance occurs in Charles Demuth's *I Saw the Figure 5 in Gold* (1929), one of a series of paintings he

Charles Demuth. I Saw the Figure 5 in Gold. *1929. Oil on composition board, 36 × 29¾″. The Metropolitan Museum of Art, New York City. The Alfred Stieglitz Collection*

called poster-portraits. A symbolic portrait of the poet William Carlos Williams, *I Saw the Figure 5 in Gold* is based on a Williams poem called "The Great Figure," published in the collection *Sour Grapes* in 1921. The painting represents a pictorial translation of the poet's experience of observing a speeding firetruck. Repeating gold "5s" recede into a vortex, and combine with fragmentary glimpses of street lamps, advertising signs, neon lights, and skyscrapers, to capture the staccato tempo and drama of the original Williams poem:

> Among the rain
> and lights
> I saw the figure 5
> in gold
> on a red
> firetruck
> moving
> with weight and urgency
> tense
> unheeded
> to gong clangs
> siren howls
> and wheels rumbling
> through the dark city.

Albert Gleizes. The Astor Cup Race (Flags). *1915. Oil and gouache on canvas, 39¼ × 29¼". The Solomon R. Guggenheim Museum, New York City*

As a poster-portrait, Demuth's painting intentionally alludes to contemporary advertising; the word "Bill" refers to Williams's name and to billposters, and the word "Carlo" is depicted as emblazoned in neon lights. The whole is summarized by the image of a billboard intentionally cut off by the frame so that it spells "Art Co." With its brash colors and its emphasis on crisp, emblematic forms, the work evokes the vivid hues and bold shapes of the urban environment, especially those of billboards and electronic advertising.

Demuth's poster-portrait suggests the significant role that Picabia's object-portraits played in the auto iconography of the teens and twenties. Although he did not always directly influence subsequent generations of artists, Picabia's ideas informed much art involved with the automobile as image and subject matter. His focus on the automobile as an emblem of American culture was elaborated upon by the painter Albert Gleizes in a 1915 oil *The Astor Cup Race (Flags)*, a work commemorating the race held in Brooklyn in 1915, a popular event that attracted one hundred thousand spectators. *The Astor Cup Race (Flags)*, along with paintings of the Brooklyn Bridge, Broadway, and neon advertising, was one of several typical New York scenes executed by Gleizes not long after his arrival in the United States. Dominated by sweeping arc-shapes that suggest wheels, draped flags and banners, numbers on cars, and perhaps even the oval of the racetrack, the piece radiates a buoyant spirit appropriate to Gleizes's enthrallment with modern American life.

Beginning in 1917, two years after Picabia's *291* drawings and continuing for thirty years, Alfred Stieglitz shot some five hundred negatives of Georgia O'Keeffe, recording fragments of her body, at times in conjunction with other objects. He juxtaposed O'Keeffe's hands with a car wheel and hubcap and framed her face by a car window, in two of the most cele-

Alfred Stieglitz. Hand and Wheel. *1933. Gelatin silver print, 9½ × 7½". The Cleveland Museum of Art. Gift of Cary Ross*

Ralph Steiner. Ford Car. 1929. Gelatin silver print, 7⅛ × 9⅝". © 1976 Ralph Steiner

brated photographs. The images, especially *Hand and Wheel,* reflect the prevailing aesthetic concerns among American artists and photographers in the first third of the twentieth century. Picabia's notion that a portrait need not begin with a likeness of the face must have been something of an inspiration for Stieglitz. Picabia's aesthetic scrutiny of machines, particularly car parts, was paralleled in 1917, when the photographer Paul Strand, who had been exhibiting at the gallery 291 since 1915, did a group of severely cropped photographs of machines; several included a camera, others, a motorcar's wheel. Part of a group of dramatically composed photographic images that are cut off and outsized in scale, the works carried Stieglitz's aesthetic of emphasis on a motif's inherent formal qualities to a radical extreme. This approach and vision—honing in on a portion of the automobile, radically cropping it, and carefully arranging the patterns of light and shade—produced striking abstract patterns, an approach pursued by several photographers associated with Stieglitz and Strand. Ralph Steiner's 1929 *Ford Car,* focusing on the wheel, headlight, and fenders of an automobile, is part of a sequence of shots he labeled "post-Strand." Paul Outerbridge's *Untitled* photo of the same year, in its stark representation of a portion of the luxurious Marmon motorcar's crankshaft, also reveals Strand's influence. Edward Weston, who did several photos of automobiles, including *Burned Car: Mojave Desert* (1938) and *Wrecked Car: Crescent Beach* (1939), concentrated on the front end of an automobile in *Car Lights* (1930), a suave composition counterposing darks and lights, circles and rectangles, and elegant curves with several series of repeating verticals.

In the O'Keeffe series, Stieglitz, who had earlier used a car to chronicle the progress of technology and urbanism in *Old and New New York,* was probably more interested in the automobile as an object of formal beauty than as a symbol of cultural advancement. Stieglitz disliked American commercialism and was particularly disgusted by Henry Ford, whom he considered to be the personification of American materialism and consumerism. When Sherwood Anderson compared Stieglitz's and Ford's contributions to American society, he called the photographer "the craftsman of genius" and the industrialist, manufacturer of "ugly and ill-smelling" objects. Stieglitz wrote Anderson, complimenting the writer on his perceptiveness.

Photographer Edward Steichen, a close friend and early advisor of Stieglitz, eventually turned from pictorialism to straight photography, and finally to fashion photography; he was appointed chief photographer for *Vogue* and *Vanity Fair* in the mid-twenties. His stylistic emphasis on wealth and style typified the way the auto was promoted during the "jazz age" and the "roaring twenties." Advertising frequently paired elegant women and elegant cars, as demonstrated by many of the posters of the period, such as R. E. Schreiber's work for Mercedes Daimler, Marcelle Pichon's for Renault, and others by Guy Sabran, Charles Loupot, A. E. Marty, and René Vincent.

Tamara de Lempicka's *Self-Portrait* of the twenties, though not a poster, is perhaps the consummate image representing "automobile-chic" of the period. Lempicka was a fiercely independent, liberated, and controversial Polish-born artist; trained as a Cubist and attracted to Art Nouveau and Art Deco, she traveled in high society, whose members were often the subjects of her work. Her self-portrait captured a coolness tinged

Paul Strand. Wire Wheel, New York. *c. 1920. Platinum print, 12¾ × 10¼." Collection Van Deren Coke, San Francisco*

Sonia Delaunay. Above: Design for clothes and car (Talbot). 1928. Below: Design for clothes and car (Citroën B12). 1925

with hauteur, even defiance; with leather-gloved hands holding the steering wheel of a car, swaddled in gray racing garb, Lempicka exudes a Teutonic arrogance, her steel gray-blue eyes arched with pencil-thin eyebrows, and porcelain skin contrasted with her blood-red lips. The image adorned the cover of two magazines—the exclusive feminist journal *Die Dame* and the *Galerie des Arts*, in an issue called the "Roaring Twenties," captioned "Tamara de Lempicka: Symbol of Women's Liberation, 1925."

Although emphasizing elegance and chic, many of the depictions of women and cars suggest that the automobile contributed to the liberation of women during an age of increased consciousness of women's rights. Several of the first major American sociological studies to examine the impact of new technologies on social structure—such as President Hoover's Commission of Social Trends, William F. Ogburn's many studies of the impact of the auto on society, and Robert and Helen Lynd's analyses of small-town American life in *Middletown: A Study of Modern American Culture* (1929) and *Middletown in Transition: A Study in Cultural Conflicts* (1937)—credited the car with greatly expanding the roles of women. The automobile freed women from the home, provided opportunities to increase their outside social contacts, and encouraged them to actively pursue work, leisure activities, and romance.

During this period, the automobile was assimilated into art and culture, and many artists, especially those associated with graphic design, established a close relationship with the automobile and industry. Combining the beauty and efficiency of mechanical design with their own aesthetic sensibilities, artists channeled their efforts into the production of functional objects. In an attempt to leave a more direct imprint on the everyday world, these design-conscious artists fashioned objects as ambitious as automobiles or as modest as posters. Consequently, the distinctions between high art and design became intentionally blurred. Sonia Delaunay, the French artist and designer, created customized coordinated fashions and motorcars in the mid-twenties for Talbot and Citroën. She decorated car and clothing with multicolored arrangements of rectangles or triangles based on a color principle that she had been exploring in her painting. Known as "the simultaneous contrast of colors," this theory held that certain juxtapositions of color produced dynamic optical pulsations related to the dynamic, simultaneous structure of reality. In turn, Georges Lepape, who had been a pupil in the same atelier where Picabia and Marie Laurencin had studied, designed a *Vogue* cover that was derived from Delaunay's designs. This was a period of cross-fertilization among high art, the machine world, and commercial art. Artists developed aesthetics based on machines, and they applied their aesthetic visions to the design of functional objects. Commercial artists borrowed from the bold and radical developments in modern art and photography to create more arresting commercial images.

Even though the Futurist euphoric attitude toward the automobile was tempered in the post–World War I period, artists continued to treat the automobile optimistically in their work. Eventually, the attitudes expressed by the artists and illustrators who depicted the car as a chic symbol of liberation and progress lost much substance with the economic collapse of 1929. Automobile advertisements continued to represent the car as a thrilling object of glamour and status, but many artists were unable to maintain values that ran so strongly counter to reality.

R.E. Schreiber. Mercedes Daimler. *1914. Color lithograph, 43¼ × 28½". Staatsgalerie, Stuttgart*

Tamara de Lempicka. Self-Portrait. *c. 1925. Oil on board, 35 × 26". Private collection, Basel*

R E A L I T Y   A N D
B E Y O N D
T H E   R E A L

The development of automobile iconography in the late 1920s and 1930s can be summarized by Charles Sheeler's photographs and paintings of the Ford Motor Company's River Rouge plant and by Diego Rivera's murals of *Detroit Industry*. The subject matter of these works acknowledges the importance of the car to contemporaneous society, while expanding to concentrate on industrial production and the auto factory. The automobile continued to represent social status and glamour, though as the product of advanced and revolutionary American industrial methods, it came to symbolize progress and the hegemony of American technology.

By the mid- to late twenties, fifteen million Model T's had been built, cranked out at a rate of one every ten seconds, and sold for the relatively modest price of $290 each. Yet the euphoria of the twenties, characterized by the Hoover slogan, "a chicken in every pot, two cars in every garage," soon gave way to the realities of the Great Depression. The optimism that had greeted the development of the assembly line was tempered by the realization that it contained the potential to exploit and dehumanize its labor force.

In 1927, the Ford Motor Company hired the American artist and photographer Charles Sheeler to do a series of documentary photographs of its River Rouge plant, one of the world's largest industrial structures. This mammoth architectural complex, conceived in 1915 by Henry Ford, was erected outside Detroit and expanded over many years under the direction of the architect Albert Kahn. Ford's dream of building a factory complex large enough to include all facets of automobile production, from the manufacture of steel to the casting of parts, was realized in 1927 when the company's main automated assembly line was transferred from the Highland Park plant to the Rouge. Between 1929 and 1936, the Rouge reached its peak in size and production; the company boasted that the factory "could supply all the homes in Boston with electricity, uses as much water as Detroit, Washington, and Cincinnati combined, has 110 miles of railroad tracks, 22 diesel locomotives, 81 miles of conveyer belts, and 4 bus

If the word "auto" was writ large across Middletown's [read America's] life in 1925, this was even more apparent in 1935, despite six years of depression.... Car ownership in Middletown was one of the most depression-proof elements of the city's life following 1929.... They want...their great symbol of advancement—an automobile. Car ownership stands to them for a large share of the "American Dream"; they cling to it as they cling to self-respect.

—Robert and Helen Lynd, *Middletown in Transition*, 1937

Dorothea Lange. Funeral Cortege, End of an Era in a Small Valley Town, California. *1938. Gelatin silver print, 14 × 11". The Dorothea Lange Collection, The Oakland Museum, Oakland, California. © 1983 The City of Oakland, The Oakland Museum*

Charles Sheeler. Classic Landscape. *1931. Oil on canvas, 25 × 32¼". Private collection*

lines." Constructed during what has been called the "Fordist era," the River Rouge operation symbolized Henry Ford's ascent from farm boy to billionaire, and attested to the central role played by the assembly line in propelling United States industry to a position of world primacy.

Sheeler used the automobile assembly factory to portray America's industrial productivity and wealth. He regarded the Ford series as "portraits of industry," and his photos of the plant and the later drawings and paintings derived from them—*American Landscape* (1930), *Classic Landscape* (1931), *City Interior #2* (1935)—reflect a serenity and clarity that may have been influenced by Picabia's object-portrait style. Since the photos were commissioned by the company to be used in publicity campaigns, Sheeler undoubtedly carefully selected his sites, though Henry Ford was compulsive about the factory's image and employed a maintenance staff of five thousand employees.

Sheeler's aesthetic vision was well matched with the face of the Rouge. When first confronted with the Rouge, Sheeler, echoing a Purist sensibility, remarked that "the forms...looked right because they had been designed with their eventual utility in view and in the successful fulfillment of their purpose it was inevitable that beauty should be attained." As the leading exponent of Precisionism, Sheeler searched for native artifacts and architecture possessing geometric clarity of form, upon which he imposed compositional order and structure. Formal purity and efficiency of design were to be found in many sources: in addition to factories, Sheeler's favorite subjects included machinery, modern urban architecture, particularly skyscrapers, and Shaker buildings and crafts. He much admired the photography of Paul Strand and Alfred Stieglitz, and shared their beliefs that photography was a worthy and independent artform. Sheeler understood the camera to be a mechanism that was able to transmit objective information and thereby intensify formal visual arrangements, rather than the emotional associations, of the objects represented.

In his photographs, drawings, and paintings of the Rouge, Sheeler focused on views of the plant's exterior. Since the scenes rarely contain human figures, the geometric shapes of the machines and the architecture powerfully assert themselves as the central focus. His best-known paintings from the series, *Classic Landscape* and *American Landscape,* demonstrate his passionate commitment to formal purity, precision, and efficiency. *American Landscape* and *Classic Landscape* identify the new American industrial scene with the values of the classical world: both expressed the search for beauty, truth, and rationality through the creation of a world of clarity, order, harmony, and proportion. Sheeler's works reflect the American nineteenth-century tendency to aggrandize and idealize the landscape as a symbol of America's greatness. Yet the pastoral landscape had been industrialized and the myth of the American wilderness was supplanted by the myth of boundless productive capacity. Manifest destiny was now being fulfilled in industrial terms.

In February 1928, one of Sheeler's Rouge photographs, *Criss-Crossed Conveyors* (1927), graced an issue of *Vanity Fair.* That a portrait of machinery appeared in a magazine noted for its chic snob appeal reveals a certain shift in consciousness about the automobile, especially in regard to its position in American life. By the late twenties, there were over

Charles Sheeler. Criss-Crossed Conveyors. *1927. Photograph, 10½ × 9¼". Henry Ford Museum, The Edison Institute, Dearborn, Michigan*

twenty-six million cars registered in the United States, one for nearly every five people. Eighty percent of the world's motorized vehicles were in the United States. In 1926, one could purchase a Model T, or Tin Lizzie as it was often called, for under three hundred dollars, and three quarters of all cars were bought on credit, making the purchase of a car even easier. As the Lynds wrote in *Middletown,* their analysis of a typical American town: "ownership of an automobile has now reached the point of being an essential part of normal living." As car ownership became democratized, the significance of the auto industry in American society increased. By the late twenties, employment in the auto industry approached a half-million workers, and wages reached eight hundred million dollars. Another million-and-a-half people worked at jobs dependent on car manufacture. This was the age in which "mass automobility" emerged in America, as auto historian James J. Flink would characterize it.

Great controversy exists over Henry Ford's contribution to automobile history, but history and public perception seldom agree, and clearly the public understood that Ford's role in the expansion of car ownership and the automobile industry was enormous. For many, Ford personified the American belief in technological and material progress, a belief that commonly assumed religious connotations. Capturing the mood of the twenties, Calvin Coolidge once remarked, "The man who builds a factory builds a temple; the man who works there worships there," and Ford himself proclaimed in 1922, "Machinery is the New Messiah."

Sheeler's *Criss-Crossed Conveyors* was accompanied by the caption, "By Their Works Ye Shall Know Them," and the copy continued: "The Ford automobile factories...lay claim to being the most significant public monument in America...an American altar of the God-Objective of Mass Production...America's Mecca." Sheeler later used this photo at the center of three shots called Industry, arranged like a religious triptych.

If the factory was likened to a religious structure, then Ford himself was imbued with godlike traits. In *Vanity Fair,* he was described as "the Colossus of Business, an almost divine Master-Mind." Matthew Josephson, a friend of Sheeler's and editor of the avant-garde journal *Broom,* wrote an essay on Ford in a 1923 issue that contained a major spread on Sheeler. Josephson termed Ford "not a human creature. He is a principle, or better a relentless process.... Let Ford be president. Let him *assemble* us all into his machine." Josephson's words echoed a popular sentiment; in the early twenties, "Ford for President" groups were founded and membership swelled, though Ford could not be persuaded to run for office and disappointment led to anger among some of his supporters. As Raymond Wik reported in *Henry Ford and Grass-Roots America,* one campaigner accused Ford of "chicken[ing] out, leaving us...who thought we had a leader for the great Armageddon...[for] the fight...between Christ and Satan. We now wonder if we haven't been worshipping a Tin God."

Nevertheless, the Ford myth in America was tremendous: in a survey among college students, he was selected as the third most important historical figure behind Jesus Christ and Napoleon Bonaparte. His fame also spread to Europe. In Germany, the word *Fordismus* meant "mass production"; in Russia, where in 1927 the name Henry Ford was better known than Josef Stalin, the term "Fordize" meant "Americanize."

In the twenties, the United States came to be recognized as the home of automobile manufacture and use. In a vast land where progress was often measured in terms of mobility and geographic expansion, the automobile symbolized progress and advancement. Even before the motorcar was invented, the notion of mobility as a central part of American self-consciousness had been formulated. The highway stood as a tool of manifest destiny, progress, and unity. Walt Whitman was a most ardent and eloquent spokesman, and his philosophy of the "Open Road" runs throughout the entire history of auto iconography. In fact, the ideas expressed in Whitman's poetry—that technological progress would shrink the globe, and that reality was characterized by vital, dynamic forces—inspired many of the movements attracted to the subject of the automobile and modern technology. The Italian Futurists admired Whitman, and many modernist painters of the urban scene, including Sheeler himself, were deeply moved by Whitman's verse. The centrality of the car to American life received its first expression in the twenties; it is no accident that in *Studies in Classic American Literature* of 1923, D.H. Lawrence cast Whitman's ideology in automotive terms:

> He drove an automobile with a fierce headlight, along the track of a fixed idea, through the darkness of this world. And he saw everything that way. Just as a motorist does in the night.
>
> I, seeing Walt go by in his great fierce poetic machine, think to myself: What a funny world that fellow sees!
>
> ONE DIRECTION! toots Walt in the car, whizzing along it ...
>
> ONE DIRECTION! Whoops America, and sets off also in an automobile.

As America took to the Open Road, a new form of advertising—the billboard—was designed for this swift and mobile audience. Matthew Josephson, in a 1922 *Broom* essay entitled "The Great American Billposter," explained that "the [billboard] advertisements contain the fables of her people." Throughout his essay, Josephson argued for an expansion of the definition of "art," which, in the modern world, must include what might be thought of as "popular culture." In his fascination with billboards, advertising, and roadside culture, he crystallized a sentiment that unifies the auto iconography inspired by billboards and ads, from Francis Picabia's object-portraits and Charles Demuth's poster portraits, through Walker Evans's photographs, and from Stuart Davis and Edward Hopper, to the British and American Pop artists.

Begun in 1927, the Sheeler series reflected a popular belief in the seminal role that Henry Ford, his factory, and his automobiles played in fostering an era of prosperity. The Great Depression, however, rocked the auto industry as severely as it rocked the nation, and one of the common practices of the industry—buying on credit—was held partly responsible for the economic collapse. The twenties' emphasis on the marvels of mass production was replaced by the thirties' concern for the effects of modern industry. Sheeler's belief in an ideal, unpopulated world of geometric, pure, and efficient machines was countered by representations of unemployment, strikes, migrant workers, and unfair labor practices.

Throughout the thirties, the River Rouge plant was the

Diego Rivera. Detroit Industry. *1932–33. Fresco, north wall. The Detroit Institute of Arts. Founders Society Purchase, Edsel B. Ford and gift of Edsel B. Ford*

scene of violent clashes between striking auto workers and local police, and Sheeler's vision of the plant as a beautiful arrangement of harmonious forms seems shocking in its disregard of these events. Diego Rivera's provocative murals *Detroit Industry,* commissioned by the Detroit Institute of Arts in 1931 and completed in 1933, more accurately represented the actual working conditions of the factory.

Located in the interior garden court of the Detroit Institute of Arts, the murals cover four walls. The two major frescoes are devoted to auto manufacturing: the north wall shows parts production and motor construction; the south wall, body presses and final assembly of the automobile. Both of the auto-manufacturing frescoes are flanked by smaller scenes, some of which represent such other industries as pharmaceuticals and medicine. The smaller east and west walls represent scenes of the origins of human life and technology, scenes of aviation, and other aspects of the auto industry.

The main frescoes portray a multitude of automobile-plant functions, compressed into a space that in reality could not contain so much activity. Sweeping and sinuous forms unite the mechanized men and the anthropomorphized machines into one gigantic interdependent organo-mechanism. Row upon row of workers perform identical tasks, twisting and bending in slightly different poses, which, like animation frames, document the sequential progress of the assembly line. In his Mexican murals, Rivera elucidated the magnificent cultural achievements of "Old America"; in Detroit, he portrayed the assembly line as a personification of the myth, ritual, and historical actuality of the "New America."

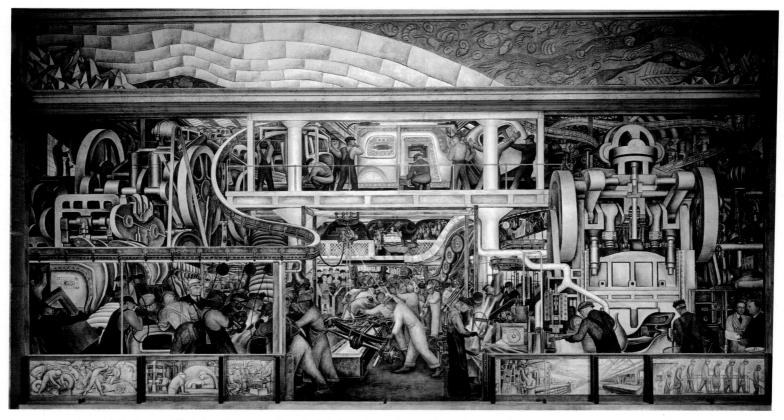

Diego Rivera. Detroit Industry. *1932–33. Fresco, south wall. The Detroit Institute of Arts. Founders Society Purchase, Edsel B. Ford and gift of Edsel B. Ford*

Earlier in the century, the unification of man and machine was represented as a heady, enriching experience, but Rivera saw it as something with both destructive and constructive potential. Rivera was fully aware of the exploitative and dehumanizing nature of Ford's assembly line at the Rouge, and he chronicled man's subjugation to the relentless demand of programmed machines and man's role as a cog in a vast, unfeeling mechanism. His condemnation of the abuses of the assembly line were common in the thirties, and his murals have important cinematic and literary parallels.

Charlie Chaplin's indictment of mass production in the movie *Modern Times* of 1936 was probably modeled after Detroit assembly-line techniques, and his sets may have been influenced by the parts production sequence of Rivera's murals. Rivera returned the favor and compliment, representing Chaplin, no less than three times, in his *Pan American Unity* frescoes (1941) in San Francisco. John Dos Passos, the American novelist who espoused left-wing sympathies in the thirties, documented worker degradation at the Rouge in his book *The Big Money,* the final part of the *USA* trilogy: "At Ford's, production was improving all the time; less waste, more spotters, strawbosses, stool-pigeons (fifteen minutes for lunch, three minutes to go to the toilet, the Taylorized speed-up everywhere, reachunder, adjustwasher, screwdown bolt, shove in cotterpin, reachunder, adjustwasher, screwdown bolt, reachunderadjustscrewdownreachunderadjust, until every ounce of life was sucked off into production and at night the workmen went home gray shaking husks)."

Although they represent the ills created by mass production techniques, Rivera's murals also express the potential benefits of indus-

Diego Rivera. Edsel B. Ford. *1932. Oil on canvas on masonite, 38½ × 49¼". The Detroit Institute of Arts. Bequest of Eleanor Clay Ford*

trial advancement. He believed that North America's rapid industrialism represented a level of achievement comparable to that of the ancient cultures of Central and South America, writing:

> I have always maintained that art in America... will be the product of a fusion between the marvelous indigenous art which derives from the immemorial depths of time in the center and south of the continent (Mexico, Central America, Bolivia, and Peru) and that of the industrial worker of the north. The dynamic productive sculptures which are the mechanical masterpieces of the factories, are active works of art, the result of the genius of the industrial country... which canalized the plastic genius of the superior and gifted individual within the broad stream of the workers for the creation of industrial mechanical art. Bridges... machinery, scientific instruments, automobiles, and airplanes are all examples... of this new collective art.

An avowed Communist, Rivera regarded assembly-line work as a prime example of collectivism; the organization of the assembly line could be seen as a model for a society in which the efficient management of tasks could reduce strenuous labor and provide basic goods and services.

Rivera recognized formal beauty in the mechanical world, an attitude paradoxically close to Sheeler's vision. Rivera argued: "In all the constructions of man's past—pyramids, Roman roads and aqueducts, cathedrals and palaces, there is nothing to equal these.... The best architects of our age are finding their aesthetic and functional inspiration in American industrial buildings, machine-design and engineering, the greatest expression of the plastic genius of this New World." Rivera respected the potential beneficial application of assembly-line methods, and admired the aesthetics of modern industry, architecture, and engineering.

Rivera thus understood the constructive and destructive potential of technology. This dichotomy is made clear in several series of paired images in the frescoes. In the parts-production murals, beneficent pharmaceuticals are contrasted with poison gas. On the west entrance wall, the left portions are filled with benign images and the right side with malignant ones: a half-face half-skull divides the two sections. On the left side men build planes, on the right they are about to fight in them; on the left a dove flies gracefully, on the right a hawk attacks its prey; an auto worker who somewhat resembles Rivera stands on the left, balanced on the right by a single portrait of close friends Henry Ford, auto magnate, and Thomas Edison, inventor.

Rivera intended to address the mythic proportions of American industrialism and its dual potentials, and depicted the body press machine to resemble Coatlicue, the Aztec symbol of good and evil, simultaneously elevating the machine to mythic levels while reiterating the positive-negative polarity of new technology. As Rivera told a friend visiting the Rouge at the time, "You were down in our country [Mexico] and you felt the grandeur of the old gods that our people carved on the pyramids and on the mountains." Then, pointing to the factory machines, he continued, "Those big figures are just the same as these."

Rivera's murals raised a storm of controversy, and objec-

tions were voiced from many quarters. The press, the city council, the clergy, museum patrons, and visitors saw certain panels as blasphemous and pornographic, and the whole as Communist. The Catholic church protested against the modern pharmaceutical mural's resemblance to a nativity scene. Rivera, like Sheeler, was attuned to the view of technology as a secular religion. Henry's son Edsel Ford, second in command at the Ford Motor Company and member of the Arts Commission that sponsored the frescoes, defended Rivera and his murals. Rivera's working relationship with Edsel Ford and William Valentiner, president of the Detroit Institute of Arts, was generally amicable and professional; in the murals, Rivera pays them tribute by representing them in the traditional guise of donors. Rivera later painted a separate oil portrait of Edsel Ford, placing his subject near a drafting table on which rest the tools of designer and engineer. Ford's head and shoulders blend harmoniously with the sketch of a car on a wall behind, and an inscription reads: "A true portrait of Mr. Edsel B. Ford, industrial engineer and president of the Arts Commission of the City of Detroit, State of Michigan, U.S. of America. I painted it. Diego Rivera, 23 November, 1932." The mind conceives and the hand executes a product of utility and beauty. Art and industry work in concert.

The criticism of technology and outcry against the plight of the worker were precipitated by the economic collapse of 1929. The optimistic roar of the twenties was replaced by the more sober tones of the thirties, as the Great Depression brought into question the entire social, political, and economic structure of American society. The Depression encouraged a reexamination of American roots, a search intended to determine the future direction of American arts and life. This investigation brought forth American Scene art; documentary photographs commissioned by the Farm Security Administration; drawings reproducing native American crafts for the Index of American Design; photos and text of Walker Evans's and James Agee's *Let Us Now Praise Famous Men;* Margaret Bourke-White and her husband Erskine Caldwell's collaboration *You Have Seen Their Faces;* and the second half of the study of the typical American town *Middletown in Transition.*

Under the general category of American Scene painting, a somewhat isolationist, nationalist form of representational art depicting American urban and rural life, two groups emerged: the Regionalists, a politically conservative circle that exalted traditional country values; and the more politically radical Social or Urban Realists, whose concentration on urban squalor marked them as heirs of the Ashcan legacy. While the political lines were not always clearly drawn, both groups exhibited an artistic conservatism reminiscent of the realist tradition of the nineteenth and early twentieth centuries.

In the exploration of American values, the automobile, previously thought of as a symbol of the American dream, came to represent betrayal of that dream. On one hand, Thomas Hart Benton, responding to the economic growth of the twenties, extolled technological progress: cars that brought settlers to mine the potential riches of a prospering new town line the streets of his 1928 oil *Boom Town.* On the other hand, Grant Wood cast automobiles as villains in *Death on the Ridge Road* (1935). The whole painting reels like a world out of control: the road snakes menacingly across

Thomas Hart Benton. Boom Town. *1928. Oil on canvas, 45 × 54". Memorial Art Gallery of the University of Rochester, New York. Marion Stratton Gould Fund*

Aaron Bohrod. Landscape Near Chicago. 1934. Oil on composition board, 24×32". Whitney Museum of American Art, New York City

John Steuart Curry. Baptism in Kansas. 1928. Oil on canvas, 40×50". Whitney Museum of American Art, New York City

Edward Hopper. Jo in Wyoming. 1946. Watercolor on paper, 13¾×20". Whitney Museum of American Art, New York City. Bequest of Josephine N. Hopper

the canvas, telephone poles and wires loom like impending grave markers. Space is distorted, conveying a derangement suggestive of an accident; the spectator is located on a winding hill, the unknown at its crest awaits him. Provoked by the death of a friend in a car crash, Wood's *Death on the Ridge Road* fuses personal tragedy with misgivings about technological progress.

Benton, generally conservative in temperament, antiurban, and wary of modernity, was nevertheless intrigued by machinery, especially cars, trains, and farm vehicles; he initially did not consider them a threat to his crackerbarrel values, although as he grew older, he became less enamored of the mechanical world. In a series of 1933 murals exhibited at the Chicago World's Fair and now exhibited at the University of Indiana Auditorium at Bloomington, Benton paid tribute to the state of Indiana, cataloguing an anthology of mechanical invention from the Haynes motorcar, one of America's first internal-combustion vehicles, to the Indianapolis Speedway.

Aaron Bohrod's *Landscape Near Chicago* (1934) depicts a struggling or abandoned auto parts business in the Skokie Valley: brokendown cars, junk, and a dilapidated shack and garage. The piece equates the deteriorating auto business and junked cars, former symbols of prosperity and mobility, with the collapse and stagnation of the economy. The scumbly surface of the painting evinces a material atrophy appropriate to these physically rotting objects.

Bohrod, who studied with John Sloan at the Art Student's League in New York and who wished to transplant Sloan's penetrating, reportorial vision to Chicago, attached no special social significance to this work. While the press looked unkindly on the raw, "hard-boiled" quality of the piece, Bohrod replied: "[This press] notice...neither deterred nor specifically encouraged additional investigation of the city's auto graveyards and other unprepossessing places. These were simply some of the unlovely subjects that interested me." Whereas such American artists as Charles Sheeler perpetuated the machine aesthetic sensibility that had been popular in the twenties, Bohrod's aesthetic philosophy drew him to the shabbier side of culture. As Bohrod continued, in response to the negative *Landscape Near Chicago* press notice: "I have always felt that intrinsic beauty in a subject is a handicap.... What can an artist really say about a beautiful sunset...a brand new shining automobile...a newly completed chunk of modern architecture?"

For the most part, American Scene images of the automobile offer ambiguous assessments of the car's role in American life. John Steuart Curry's *Baptism in Kansas* (1928) does not represent the auto as a glamorous, dynamic subject, but implies that it provides the mobility necessary to bring folks together in important community rituals, especially in rural areas where vast distances hinder the traditional establishment of community. The painting is composed of a series of concentric circles. At the center, a preacher prepares to baptize a young woman. They are encircled by a singing congregation that is enclosed by a ring of automobiles. In the far right and back of the composition one straight road suggests infinite distance, it is the artery that connects the entire community.

The routes along which the automobile traveled developed unique features that appealed to the sensibility of many American commen-

Edward Hopper. Gas. *1940. Oil on canvas, 26¼ × 40¼". The Museum of Modern Art, New York City. Mrs. Simon Guggenheim Fund*

Edward Hopper. Western Motel. *1957. Oil on canvas, 30¼ × 50". Yale University Art Gallery, New Haven, Connecticut. Bequest of Stephen Carleton Clark*

tators, from Walt Whitman to visual artists of today. Particularly in the 1960s, two distinct kinds of auto routes defined the American road: the sterile superhighway, and the cluttered store- and shopping-mall-laden strip. Pop art traveled both routes, finding standardization and boredom in one, excitement and confusion in the other, and disorientation in both. These divergent sensibilities were first explored by Stuart Davis and Edward Hopper, who investigated the visual and thematic possibilities of roadside culture from the late teens to the 1960s.

Davis discovered a pulsating and clamorous world through car windows and mirrors, where multiple sensory impressions would vie for the viewer's attention. He remarked in 1921, "I too feel the thing Whitman felt—and I too will express it in pictures—America the wonderful place we live in." Hopper sensed emptiness and alienation on the road; his devotion to themes of transience encouraged an exploration of the poetry of solitude produced through mobility. He claimed that many of his artistic ideas came to him while traveling in his car, and the watercolor *Jo in Wyoming* (1946) makes special reference to this source of inspiration. Hopper portrayed his wife in the passenger seat of their auto, sketching mountains from the roadside, establishing a dialogue between interior and exterior space, a characteristic and essential element in Hopper's work.

Gas (1940) represents a typical example of Hopper's sensibility; by placing the spectator's point of view inside looking out of a car pulling into a roadside service station, he recreates a sense of isolation and rootlessness. *Gas* sets up a disturbing contrast between the adventurous expectations of journeying, and the genuine banality of the American roadside, a paradox ironically embodied in the Mobil Gas Company's Pegasus trademark, whose promise of soaring flight is contradicted by the dullness of the actual scene. The gas station attendant's boredom and resignation is especially ironic, since he dispenses the gasoline that makes mobility and adventure possible. This almost archetypal image was composed from several road sketches that Hopper amalgamated in his studio.

Hopper perceived sterility in the roadside culture. *Western Motel* (1957) portrays an impassive figure stoically waiting to get back on the road, resigned to the fact that tomorrow's motel will be much like today's. Hopper's commentary on the American roadside has a compelling parallel in Vladimir Nabokov's nearly contemporaneous novel *Lolita,* with its descriptions of roadside lodgings and "the would-be enticements of their repetitious names—all those Sunset Motels, U-Beam Cottages, Hillcrest Courts, Pine View Courts, Mountain View Courts, Skyline Courts, Park Plaza Courts, Green Acres, Mac's Courts." In *Lolita,* fascination with the superficially romantic qualities of the roadside is transformed into dread of its inescapable banality. Nabokov's protagonist Humbert Humbert ponders, "by putting the geography of the United States into motion, I did my best for hours on end to give her [Lolita] the impression of 'going places,' of rolling on to some definite destination, to some unusual delight ... voraciously we consumed those long highways, in rapt silence we glided over their glossy black dance floors. But movement brings no progress. Arid hopelessness is all that remains."

The power of Hopper's art lies in the way he imposes a formal structure to intensify psychological essence and exert an independent pictorial force. Beginning with laconic and uncluttered subject matter, Hop-

Grant Wood. Death on the Ridge Road. *1935. Oil on masonite, 32 × 39". Williams College Museum of Art, Williamstown, Massachusetts. Gift of Cole Porter*

Edward Weston. Woodlawn Plantation. *1941. Photograph, 8 × 10".*
Center for Creative Photography, University of Arizona, Tucson.
© 1981 Arizona Board of Regents

John Gutmann. Yes, Columbus Did Discover America! San Francisco, 1938. *Gelatin silver print, 14 × 17". Fraenkel Gallery, San*
Francisco

per eliminates and refines, expunging extraneous incidentals and emphasizing the economy of structure. His oeuvre transcends the American Scene
label and identification as mere geographically and temporally rooted nostalgic propaganda.

Hopper, like Davis, used the architecture and symbols of
the American roadside to express experiences and to invent an autonomously
valid pictorial structure. The accuracy of their visions and the validity of
their expressions find a logical extension in the automobile-related art of the
sixties, which continues to investigate the emotional, perceptual, and alienated view of the American road, with its frenetic and dynamic possibilities.

The photographs done for the Farm Security Administra-
tion in the thirties represent the most poignant expressions of the American
relationship to the automobile. The government provided funds to put photographers to work, documenting the state of the countryside; to collect visual statistics; and to encourage and mobilize support for the rural poor. With
the help of the automobile, these artists crossed the country in search of thematic material.

The FSA photographers—Walker Evans, Dorothea
Lange, Russell Lee, Arthur Rothstein, and John Vachon, to mention several—usually portrayed scenes from small town life and roadside culture:
streets lined with cars, autos and trucks carrying migrant families in search
of employment, garages, gas stations, billboards, and auto graveyards.
Sinclair Lewis had described this world in his book *The Man Who Knew*
Coolidge (1928): the "plain dirt road running through a lot of unkempt farms,"
which was being transformed through the "dandy up-to-date hot dog
stand—some like log cabins and some like Chinese pagodas or Indian wig-
wams or little imitations of Mount Vernon about ten feet high...and of
course up-to-date billboards...and garages...and auto camps."

The FSA images of nomadic workers, depicted in shots by
Dorothea Lange and Russell Lee, visually capture a theme pursued by John
Steinbeck in his novel, *The Grapes of Wrath* (1939). Steinbeck's pronounce-
ment, "the highway became their home and movement their medium of
expression," epitomizes the spirit of much FSA work. In *The Grapes of*
Wrath, for which Thomas Hart Benton did illustrations in an early forties lim-

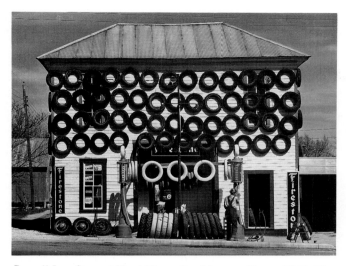

Russell Lee. Second-Hand Tires, San Marcos, Texas. *1940. Photograph, 11 × 14". Library of Congress, Washington, D.C.*

Dorothea Lange. The Road West, New Mexico. *c. 1941. Gelatin silver print, 8½ × 13½". The Dorothea Lange Collection, The Oakland Museum, Oakland, California. © 1983 The City of Oakland, The Oakland Museum*

ited edition, automobiles bring the bankers and real estate men to the farm to announce the tenant farmers' evictions: the tractors, "snub-nosed monsters, raping methodically, raping without passion," raze the shacks and rip up the land. Yet the tenant farmers' salvation is another car, a "rolling junk" that takes them to California. While it brings much hardship and heartbreak, it remains, throughout the novel, the family's only means of mobility. Steinbeck writes:

> They were not farm men anymore, but migrant men. And the thought, the planning, the long staring silence that had gone out to the fields, went now to the roads, to the distance, to the West. That man whose mind had been bound with acres lived with narrow concrete miles. And his thought and his worry were not anymore with rainfall, with wind and dust, with the thrust of the crops. Eyes watched the tires, ears listened to the clattering motors, and minds struggled with oil, with gasoline, with the thinning rubber between air and road.

Dorothea Lange. Small Independent Gas Station During Cotton Strike, Kern County, California. *1938. Gelatin silver print, 11 × 14". The Dorothea Lange Collection, The Oakland Museum, Oakland, California. © 1983 The City of Oakland, The Oakland Museum*

This folk culture, chronicled in photographs and novels, was part of the balladeer Woody Guthrie's world, remembered in such songs as "I Ain't Got No Home," "Going Down the Road," and "Talking Dust Bowl." "Back in 1927, I had a little farm, and I called that Heaven," Guthrie sang: "But the rain quit and the wind got high/ Black old dust storm filled the sky;/ I traded my farm for a Ford machine/ poured it full of this gas-i-line/ And started—rockin' and a-rollin/ Deserts and mountains—to California."

The eyes of the FSA photographers, and such others as Edward Weston, Margaret Bourke-White, and John Gutmann, were attuned to the look of rural, mobile America. Russell Lee and Walker Evans spotted a certain naive beauty in the arrangement of gas stations and garages, and Evans and Edward Weston recognized abstract power in wrecked, abandoned autos or weathered, decaying billboards. But the formal force of the images was not all that attracted these artists. Evans's *Joe's Auto Graveyard, Pennsylvania* (1936), portrays a cluster of junked cars in a spare, pristine landscape. Evans captured the dreams shattered by the Great Depression of American agricultural and industrial richness. The tombstone-cars in the auto graveyard speak of death: the death of hope, of a way of life, of a system

Walker Evans. Bucket Seat Model T, Alabama Town. *1936. Gelatin silver print, 7½ × 9½". Menil Foundation Collection, Houston*

Walker Evans. Joe's Auto Graveyard, Pennsylvania. *1936. Gelatin silver print, 8 × 10″. Menil Foundation Collection, Houston*

of values. No event since the Civil War had so rocked the foundations of American society as had the Depression. William Carlos Williams's unpublished judgment of Lincoln Kirstein's essay accompanying a Walker Evans exhibition in 1938 at the Museum of Modern Art commented on this connection: "There is a pointed reference in Mr. Kirstein's notice to the work of (Mathew) Brady during the war between the States. In Evans's pictures also we are seeing fields of battle after the withdrawal of the forces engaged. The jumbled wreckage, human and material, is not always so grim in the present case but for all the detachment of the approach the effect is often no less poignant."

The sense of detachment suffusing Evans's photographs results partially from a visual clarity and purity. But the crisp visual austerity also imbues his subjects with dignity, lends the mundane or commonplace an often riveting presence, and makes the potential social message seem less calculated or contrived. Heir to the tradition of straight photography practiced by Alfred Stieglitz and carried on by Paul Strand, Charles Sheeler, and Ralph Steiner, Evans exploited formal structure to intensify the psychological essence of a situation. He was among the first to think that an auto scrap heap could become evocative subject matter.

One particularly popular 1930s billboard of a smiling "all-American" family in a gleaming new automobile, figured in the work of at least two well-known photographers. In 1937, Dorothea Lange used it in *There is No Way Like the American Way,* as did Margaret Bourke-White in

Margaret Bourke-White. At the Time of the Louisville Flood. *1937. Gelatin silver print, 9¾ × 13¼". International Museum of Photography at George Eastman House, Rochester, New York. © 1937 Margaret Bourke-White,* Life Magazine, *Time Inc.*

At the Time of the Louisville Flood. Lange lets it stand alone; Bourke-White pairs it with a row of Ohio River flood victims waiting for support from a relief agency. Both seem to carry the same ironic message that during the Depression this depiction of an ideal American family appears unrealistic, even insulting. Bourke-White's image seems more didactic, ostensibly using the car to symbolize the bankruptcy of the American dream.

This billboard demonstrates the unwillingness of the advertising community to relinquish its pitch for economic improvement through consumption or to face the economic and social realities created by the Depression. Most automobile advertisements from this period continued to hold out the temptations of luxury, status, and glamour. As one Lincoln ad of 1934 claimed: "However much events of the past few years may have restrained the purchase of fine things, desire for them has been constant. People who, momentarily, feared that they could not afford the best are discovering now that its possession can give confidence, can build morale… from $3200." The ad is arrogant, to say the least, considering that the average yearly income in America at the time was under one thousand dollars.

Sex and chic continued to be used as thematic material in auto ads, as evidenced by the famous 1934 Fiat poster by Marcello Dudovich. The Vatican objected to this poster because of its explicit view of a woman's tightly clothed backside, the shapes of her body and apparel echoing the design of the car. In general, automotive posters of the period placed an implicit emphasis on engineering and automotive design, which was displayed with a

Marcello Dudovich. Fiat Balilla. 1934. Color lithograph, 79 × 56". Fiat Collection (Centro Storico Fiat), Turin, Italy

related boldness and efficiency of graphic layout, particularly in the ads done for Chrysler by Ashley Havinden.

The Italians, in the forefront of car design, often hired established visual artists to create their posters. Mario Sironi, who had been affiliated with the Futurist movement, did paintings of cars and trucks on city streets. In the thirties and the fifties, he produced publicity campaigns for Fiat. One of his designs from the thirties contrasts the car with the legendary she-wolf of Rome, a juxtaposition that was appropriate to the classical revival and to the emphasis on Roman heritage, popular during that time.

Giorgio de Chirico was also employed by Fiat in the fifties. Best known as a metaphysical artist in the teens and twenties, de Chirico found there was poetry and mystery in the everyday world, and was especially intrigued by the sense of anxiety and loneliness that characterized the Italian townscape. To convey these feelings he used odd, disorienting perspectives, and contrasted ostensibly unrelated objects in his compositions. By the twenties, he had developed a strong interest in classical themes, which he portrayed with loose brushstrokes and unpleasant color combinations. Working in this later style, he situated a Fiat Model 1400 within a lineage of locomotion that progressed from Pegasus and Bellerephon through an early motorcar. De Chirico's vision of the world would later appeal to the Surrealists. He exulted in the potential hidden higher states of objects, and evoked a poetry created through unlikely juxtapositions.

The Surrealists maintained conflicting views about modern technology and science. André Breton, poet and leader of the Surrealist movement, felt a certain affinity toward modern science. He believed that the Surrealists, by investigating the imagination, were like scientists exploring natural phenomena. But on the whole, the Surrealists regarded technology as dehumanizing, destructive, and evil.

The Surrealists were interested in myth, the unconscious, and repressed aspects of sexuality, and rarely used automobile imagery. When the image of a car does occur, as in René Magritte's *The Anger of the Gods* (1960), Victor Brauner's *L'Amour Propulsateur* (1940), Louis Guglielmi's *Terror in Brooklyn* (1941), or Man Ray's *Auto-Mobile* (1932), its meaning is not explicit. Magritte recast the opposition between car and horse to an ambiguous and disorienting effect: a galloping horse, caught midstride, hovers in the air above a seemingly immobile automobile. Brauner, founder and editor of the avant-garde journal *75HP*, created a primitive concoction of man, machine, and lovemaking in *L'Amour Propulsateur*, one of a group of car-related pieces that are stylistically close to Salvador Dali's art. Guglielmi, obsessed with grief and death, described his work as "the terror of three pelvic beatitudes in the test-tube of a bell. The street, a premonition of war and tragedy." Man Ray's *Auto-Mobile* assemblage was probably destroyed, but its existence was recorded in the artist's photographs. *Auto-Mobile* seems to have been created in the spirit of a Dada verbal-visual pun; a spring and ball project from a car's steering wheel that rests on a wooden frame fitted with casters. It moves only if it is pushed—thus "auto-mobile." The spring and ball dance and jerk in the spirit of the fledgling mobile, an artform pioneered by Alexander Calder in Paris in 1932. Man Ray was something of a car enthusiast, though; the auto played an important part in his films and photos, and he did several portraits of artists, including Picabia and Derain, seated behind the wheel of a motorcar.

Giorgio de Chirico. Fiat 1400. *1950. Color lithograph, 52×35". Fiat Collection (Centro Storico Fiat), Turin, Italy*

Louis Guglielmi. Terror in Brooklyn. *1941. Oil on canvas, 34×30". Whitney Museum of American Art, New York City*

Salvador Dali. Ghosts of Two Automobiles. *c. 1925. Collage and oil on posterboard, 19¾ × 15½". Teatre Museo Dali, Figueres, Spain*

Salvador Dali often approached the theme of the automobile, though the scatalogical and abtruse nature of his symbolism militates against specific interpretations of his automobile imagery. In such works as *The Automobile Fossil of Cape Creus* (1936), *Ghosts of Two Automobiles* (c. 1925), *Paranoic Critical Solitude* (1935), *Debris of an Automobile Giving Birth to a Blind Horse Biting a Telephone (1938)*, *Apparition of the City of Delft* (1935–36), and several watercolors used to illustrate the *Chants du Maldoror,* he seemed to follow a common thematic thread—locating a petrified or fossilized automobile in a grotesque landscape. In a poetically justifiable turn of events, the car and modern technology, having wreaked havoc on nature, are now victimized by it.

In *Automobile Fossil of Cape Creus,* Dali created a land that hardens everything it touches. In a poem about the painting, the artist described a "fossil-auto" as a "decayed ass" which "has the shape of an immense and very antique automobile/ of pink marble/ carved/ at the point of a rock/ and suspended over the abyss/ in the attitude/ of a victory of Samothrace." Dali's comparison of the automobile to the *Victory of Samothrace* brings to mind Marinetti's earlier pairing of the two, and reveals a changed artistic attitude toward technology. To Marinetti, the *Victory of Samothrace,* frozen in flight, symbolized the stultification of art and society caused by the anachronistic devotion to outworn values, while the car symbolized man's emancipation through technology. In Dali's nightmarish image, the car is congealed in the mountainside of a bizarre landscape, symbolizing stagnation and regression.

Dali's ambitious, ambiguous *Rainy Taxi* (1938), represents the car and mankind in decay, as both are overrun by the unrelenting forces of nature. This environmental assemblage consists of an abandoned taxi, adorned with vegetation, and rigged to unleash torrential downpours on its two mannequin-occupants—one a shark-headed driver, the other a sleazy blond passenger ensconced in a bed of lettuce and infested with live Burgundy snails. The atmosphere of perversity and abnormality perfusing Dali's apocalyptic images of cars impaled on trees, frozen into mountains, or overgrown with vegetation reflects a distortion of values in which the viewer feels more comfortable with technology's assault on nature than he does with nature's revenge on technology.

The Surrealists generally expressed their negative attitudes toward technology by ignoring it as subject matter. This attitude continued into the art of the 1940s, when the Abstract Expressionists avoided using figurative images partially because of their disgust with the nature of that society. An interest in myth, the impact of the Surrealist theory of automatism, and the emergence of existential philosophy all contributed to an artistic sensibility that, for the most part, shunned representation.

Automobile manufacture virtually ceased during these years because the industry was redirected toward war production. Certainly, art that included the automobile as subject matter was done in the 1940s, though the major artists of the period were only occasionally attracted to it. Generally, the art of the forties either reflects a sensibility related to the Depression outlook of the 1930s or foreshadows the boom in auto images that occurred in the postwar years, especially in Pop art and assemblage.

CULTURAL RECONSTRUCTION, EXPLOSION, AND REFLECTION

The image of the automobile appears often in art produced after World War II, attesting to the car's widespread impact on society, and to the visual artist's increasing involvement with popular subject matter. Initially, an aesthetic interest in popular imagery and attitudes resulted when two distinct tendencies merged: the phenomenal postwar growth of mass or popular culture, and the general disaffection in the postwar artistic community with what was regarded as the metaphysical pomposity and indulgent subjectivity of Abstract Expressionism.

The notion of popular culture developed out of and around those elements of life that are designed to be mass produced, mass marketed, and mass consumed—consumer goods, radio and television, advertising, magazines and newspapers, film, and music. It was the consequence, in part, of a refinement in mass-production techniques developed during World War II, which was then applied to the production of peacetime consumer goods. Advertising was used to sell these goods, and the postwar era witnessed the growth of increasingly sophisticated marketing techniques. Advertising was disseminated through the mass media, which swelled in the early 1950s, particularly with the commercial development of television. The prosperity of the postwar years encouraged consumption. After two decades of depression and war, the public exercised its renewed purchasing power with a vengeance. During the war years, automobile production had virtually halted, but in the early fifties, auto manufacturers responded to the market created by a widespread demand for autos. With the initiation of the Interstate Highway System and the expansion of suburban housing complexes and shopping malls, the car became a necessity for many segments of society.

Because it offered instant mobility and possible adventure, the car symbolized a *freedom*—political, social, cultural, and economic—that had been cramped and threatened by war and economic deprivation. The postwar artist began turning outward rather than inward, and recognized that the burgeoning mass culture could provide a subject

Mad road driving men ahead—the madroad, lonely, leading around the bend into the openings of space toward the horizon.

—Jack Kerouac, Introduction to Robert Frank's *The Americans,* 1959

Arman. Long Term Parking. *1975–82. 60 automobiles embedded in concrete, 65×20×20'. The Sculpture Park at Le Montcel, Jouy-en-Josas, France*

matter and a form that was antielitist, unemotional, and direct in its expression.

Pop art emerged in Great Britain in the early fifties and reached its fullest expression in the United States in the early sixties. Many earlier art movements had explored popular imagery, but Pop art was unique because it incorporated aspects of popular culture that were visually depicted in advertising, newspaper photos, magazine illustrations, and television commercials. Pop pieces were often executed using techniques and styles familiar in the commercial world of graphic design: silkscreen, airbrush, and retouched photos.

The automobile became one of the most frequently represented popular images. Artists who immersed themselves in popular culture found that the idea was best expressed in the way cars were produced, marketed, and consumed. As the pioneer product of Ford's assembly-line techniques, the car had become an ideal symbol of mass production, and the fifties ushered in a new period in automotive history. The industry perfected techniques first introduced in the late twenties by the president of General Motors, Alfred P. Sloan, Jr., who at the time shifted emphasis away from production and toward marketing. Sloan realized that Fordist concentration on production had saturated the car market. In order to sell more cars and make more money, it was necessary to improve consumption. And he was successful. Despite the hoopla surrounding Henry Ford, by the late twenties General Motor's Chevrolet had begun to outsell the basic Ford Model T.

When the Depression and the war curtailed consumer purchasing ability, Sloan's techniques were played down for several decades, only to be resumed in the postwar boom years. His techniques involved several strategies based upon the principle of obsolescence. Cars were built to last only so long, and the changes in model styles became a subtle and sophisticated maneuver to make the car owner feel that his old auto was inferior in workmanship and in design to the new model lines. Distinctions among cars were often *created*, usually by attaching a glamorous and romantic "image" to a particular vehicle. Extensive mass media advertising campaigns were used to publicize these images and to convince the consumer of their existence. Cars were produced, marketed, and sold not simply as means of transportation, but as packages of dreams, fantasies, and illusions. The Pop artists seized these imagistic aspects of the auto culture as viable artistic subject matter.

Although mass consumer culture developed most fully in America in the early fifties, the artists of Great Britain were the first to introduce the form and content of popular mediums into their art. A group of British artists and intellectuals, among them Richard Hamilton, Eduardo Paolozzi, Peter and Alison Smithson, Reyner Banham, Lawrence Alloway, John McHale, and Nigel Henderson, formed the Independent Group (IG), began meeting at the Institute of Contemporary Arts (ICA) in London, and established what art historians now call "British Pop." The major topics of discussion at these gatherings were, as Alloway recalled: "...mass-produced urban culture: movies, advertising, science fiction, Pop music, color photography, TV, automobile styling...Hollywood, Detroit, and Madison Avenue were, in terms of our interests, producing the best popular culture.... Subjects of the IG season in 1954–55 included: Banham on car styling (Detroit and sex symbolism); the Smithsons on the real dreams of ads versus architectural ideals; Richard Hamilton on consumer goods; and Frank Cordell on popular music."

Not unlike the Futurists a half-century earlier, who regarded the recent technological revolutions in transportation and communication as an inspiration for a new aesthetic, the British Pop artists, experiencing a sense of postwar lethargy, turned toward technological advances for artistic source material and subject matter. Avant-garde artists who are dissatisfied with the nature of art have often looked to "life" as a rejuvenating alternative.

Neither Italy in the early part of the century nor Britain in the early fifties were the major centers of technological ferment, and both countries sought inspiration in other societies. The United States was a source for both, and it is likely that the romantic and glamorous treatment of Pop-technological culture was, in part, the result of observing this phenomenon through the distorted lenses of geographic separation. British Pop artist Gerald Laing aptly expressed this sentiment: "...that Utopian dream of the USA which I, in common with most of my contemporaries in London believed in, ... made it inevitable that I should eventually choose to depict those gleaming, exotic images and extravagant attitudes so heavily propagandised in Europe and which, for us, implied not only an optimistic, classless society, but also that every American had his hot-rod and his surfboard."

It was no accident that aspects of British Pop bear resemblance to Italian Futurism, since one of Pop's most influential members, Reyner Banham, conducted extensive research into the activities of the Italian movement. In 1959, Banham published an English translation of the introduction to the "Founding and Manifesto of Futurism," claiming that it contained the "unconscious prophecies [that] trailer the attitudes of the Beat Generation at a range of forty years," and that it "resolves itself in an orgy of untrammeled automobilism, unlike anything else before [Jack Kerouac's] *On the Road* and concludes with a car crash that is rendered as sort of a secular mystical experience." For Banham, the Futurists were "long-lost ancestors," whose manifestoes were the "farthest familiar landmark in the fog of history, the first point in which we can recognize an image of our Machine Age attitudes....As Richard [Hamilton] and I and the rest of us came down the stairs from the Institute of Contemporary Arts those combative evenings in the early fifties, we stepped into a London that Boccioni had described clairvoyantly. We were at home in the promised land that the Futurists had been denied...."

It should come as no surprise that the automobile would reemerge as a prominent symbol in Pop art. In a direct reference to the Futurist treatment of the car, Richard Hamilton, the most famous of British Pop artists, wrote: "One wasn't just concerned with the car and the idea of speed, but [with] the way it was presented to us in the mass media...presenting a glamorous object by all the devices that glamorous advertising can add."

Like Picabia, the British Pop artists were infatuated with automobile advertising, though they concentrated on its presentation in popular, mass-circulation magazines rather than on mechanical diagrams in technical trade journals. Whereas Picabia recognized and exploited these images in terms of imagined correspondences with human personalities, the British Pop artists viewed car ads as symbols of society in general. Auto-

Eduardo Paolozzi. Untitled. *1949. Collage, 11 × 19". Collection the artist, London*

Jean Dubuffet. Touring Club. *1946. Oil on canvas, 38 × 51". Collection Richard S. Zeisler, New York City*

mobile advertisements documented the glamour and excitement of contemporary Pop-technological culture, while incisively revealing its superficial and highly materialistic values.

A page from Eduardo Paolozzi's untitled scrapbook, assembled in 1949 and officially exhibited some time later, may be the first example of the automobile in British Pop. Paolozzi juxtaposed an ad for the 1949 Raymond Loewy Studebaker with an image of an auto stylist who is at a drafting table, putting the finishing touches on a car design. This piece from Paolozzi's scrapbook, along with many others containing car ads, was assembled by collaging pictures culled from *Life Magazine,* which was something of a Bible to British Pop. These images emphasize the connections between the automobile and styling, fantasies, and glamorous images, and express Paolozzi's fascination with the products of mass culture and their underlying meanings.

Paolozzi's process of collaging media material attempts to uncover the nature of the real environment, in which one is constantly inundated by information. His extension of the collage approach into three dimensions resulted in a kind of proto-assemblage sculpture. Paolozzi combined all sorts of junk—"found objects, assorted wheels and electrical parts...various unidentified objects...Model automobiles. Reject die castings from factory tip sites"—and created from them plaster casts for bronze sculptures. Several finished bronzes, as well as related prints and drawings, portrayed human heads; echoing the work of the sixteenth-century Mannerist artist Arcimboldo, Paolozzi presented what he called "A world within a world. A landscape within a face." Just as Duchamp used automotive analogies to suggest the complexities of human behavior and internal processes, Paolozzi, in his handmade paper *Automobile Head* (1954), filled a human head with automobile parts to represent his belief in the "interplay between technology and man," and in the "multi-evocative" potential of popular imagery, which "describes the world of dreams better than any conventional art language. In 1980, he did a piece called *Paper Head* from handmade paper.

Unlike the true assemblage artists, Paolozzi does not display junk material in its original state; however, his early interest and use of detritus as part of the artistic process did anticipate this later artform. Paolozzi's work is more closely aligned with the *art brut* style of Jean Dubuffet's doodley drawings and scabrous-surfaced paintings and sculpture, or with Pablo Picasso's sculptures that were constituted from common objects. Paolozzi acknowledged the influence of both.

Beginning in the mid-forties and early fifties, Dubuffet and Picasso did works incorporating automobile imagery. The subject of the car occurs most often in the work Dubuffet produced in the mid-forties and early sixties. The forties works, such as *Touring Club* (1946), *Car Ride* (1944), and *Asphalt Gamboller* (1945), meld the crude and the playful. In *Touring Club,* four riders packed in an auto are mimicked by a hood ornament; in *Asphalt Gamboller,* an anguished woman walking her dog contrasts with a car that is bumping along in the background. Dense slabs of impasto sometimes mixed with gravel and stone, these pieces relate to Dubuffet's Macadam series, where the canvas is built up with fat layers of paint, like the asphalt on a highway. Space is nearly flat, nonvolumetric figures are awkwardly or savagely delineated, and the entire surface, thick and tactile, is congested with pictorial incident.

Haddon H. Sundblom. Drive Refreshed. *1950. Oil on canvas, 14½ × 27". The Archives: The Coca Cola Company, Atlanta, Georgia*

Eduardo Paolozzi. Paper Head. *1980. Handmade paper, 19¼ × 12¼". Collection the artist, London*

Although this series is not as whimsical and diverting as might be expected of Dubuffet, it seems less menacing than his works from the early sixties. Most of the later works are part of the Paris Circus series. In *Paris-Montparnasse* (1961), *Two Automobiles* (1961), *Rue Turlupet* (1961), *Rue Pifre* (1961), and *Major Thoroughfares* (1961), cars seem to be prisonlike cubicles on wheels, about to devour their harried occupants. In *Rue Pifre,* a flat space produced by a thick coating of pigment and elimination of modeling creates feelings of confinement, of a world from which there is no escape. A series of car images worked into the paint read like bubbles of armor protecting their generally lone occupants, whose anxious and fearful expressions add to the mood of dread and apprehension.

In Picasso's *Baboon and Young* (1951), two bronzed-over toy cars are arranged bottom to bottom to form the head of the mother baboon, whose eyes are fitted behind the car windshield, cheeks and ears growing out of fenders, and mouth and lips developed from radiators, bumpers, and the meeting-point of the two toys; a steel automobile spring defines the mother's spine and tail. The incorporation of real objects into the piece demonstrates Picasso's exploration of the potential of collage, a medium he had helped to invent nearly forty years earlier. As is often the case in Picasso's art, autobiography conditions the work: here, the toy cars had originally been given to his son, Claude.

Paolozzi's exploitation of pulp imagery and junk materials, auto ads, and auto scrap, was part of his attempt to integrate objects from popular culture into the domain of art. In the mid-fifties at the ICA, the Independent Group organized several exhibitions that were specifically designed to encourage interaction between art and the everyday world. The titles of the exhibitions, "Parallel of Life and Art" (1954), "Man, Machine and Motion" (1955), and "This is Tomorrow" (1956), revealed this intended interaction and strongly suggested the spirit of Italian Futurism. In the catalogue to "Man, Machine and Motion," Reyner Banham wrote:

> ...this exhibition is devoted to machines which extend the powers of the human body in a special way.... The relationship between man & machine is a kind of union. The two act together like a single creature. The ancient union of horse & rider, fused into a composite creature with an unruly character of its own, always potentially anarchic and fearsome, never entirely predictable, was symbolized in the myth of the centaur. The new union of man & machine possesses as positive a composite character and liberates a deeper, more fearsome human impulse.

Although helicopters, aqualung equipment, and bicycles were also included, the primary machine displayed was the automobile.

An image of a race car that Richard Hamilton had derived from a Jacques-Henri Lartigue photograph of the 1912 Grand Prix of the Automobile Club of France adorned the cover of the exhibition catalogue. Hamilton intensified the sense of speed and motion by blurring, cropping, and "negativizing" the shot, reversing its dark and light tones. Hamilton's selection of this speeding-auto scene underscores the affinity of interest between British Pop and early twentieth-century attitudes toward the automobile.

Pablo Picasso. Baboon and Young. *1951. Bronze cast 1955 (after found objects), 21 × 13¼ × 7". The Museum of Modern Art, New York City. Mrs. Simon Guggenheim Fund*

The cover for the "Man, Machine and Motion," catalogue was among the first of Hamilton's works to incorporate the automobile. The collage of 1956 titled *Just what is it that makes today's homes so different, so appealing?* is considered by some to be the pioneering work of modern Pop art. It was initially conceived to be a poster for the 1956 Independent Group exhibition "This is Tomorrow," and was to some extent part of the commercial world about which it comments. The collage contains an anthology of Pop images from comic strips and body builders to television, tape recorders, and the latest model vacuum cleaner. The presence of the automobile surfaces in the Ford Motor Company logo that emblazons a lamp shade.

Hamilton, who tended to recast the past in terms of the present, alluded to Jan Van Eyck's fifteenth-century masterpiece *The Arnolfini Wedding,* a work in the National Gallery in London. The art historian Richard Martin was the first to suggest the affinity between these works; Hamilton subsequently confirmed his dependence on the Flemish master. The visual correspondences between the two works seem obvious enough—both contain scenes in the home, with a window at the back left. Van Eyck's placement of the fashionable man and his wife-to-be is echoed in Hamilton's placement of his two nudes. The bed behind the young bride has its modern equivalent in a couch. The oversized phallic Tootsie Pop, held like half a dumbbell by the muscleman, might imply a sexual act that confers the status of Father, or "Pop," a fitting consummation to Van Eyck's betrothal scene. Since Flemish fashion makes the wife-to-be appear pregnant in our eyes (a feature often commented on and joked about), the sexual explanation of Hamilton's work seems even more inviting. With the gargantuan lollipop, Hamilton predicts later developments, in which common objects were altered in scale and size, usually monumentalized, to create Pop sculpture.

The Ford logo, attached to a lamp shade, has a counterpart in Arnolfini's candelabra: both are similarly placed, and both serve to illuminate the scene. The Arnolfini candelabra contains one lit candle, a symbol for the all-seeing eye of God, an appropriate presence at the sacred event of marriage. Does Hamilton mean that Ford, or the automobile, or the car industry are God? Fellow Briton Aldous Huxley, in this *Brave New World* of 1932, had already transformed "Our Lord" into "Our Ford," emphasizing Henry Ford's gospel "History is more or less bunk," a perfect motto for the Pop movement in which the new reigned supreme.

For Hamilton, the motorcar became a god of sorts: in the late 1950s, it was his most popular subject, and he would invariably suggest its omnipresence in the contemporary mythology of Pop culture. The car plays a central role in several of his early Pop pieces—*Hommage à Chrysler Corp.* (1957), *Hers is a Lush Situation* (1958), *Glorious Techniculture* (1961–64), and *AAH!* (1962). Though Lawrence Alloway expressed serious reservations about the merit of Hamilton's art, he did compare these works to Duchamp's *Large Glass,* as all are "enigmatic gatherings into single works of many discrete elements from esoteric sources." Hamilton, a devotee of Duchamp, aspired to create a popular culture equivalent to the *Large Glass,* which borrowed automotive nomenclature to describe its operation. Duchamp, incorporating the forces of nature into his piece through convoluted and subtle procedures, set his sights on metaphysical targets, evoked the mysteries of life, and raised questions about the nature of art.

Richard Hamilton. Just what is it that makes today's homes so different, so appealing? 1956. Collage, 10¼ × 9¾". Kunsthalle Tübingen, West Germany. Collection Dr. Georg Zundel

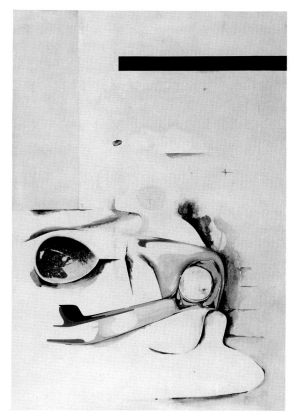

Richard Hamilton. Hommage à Chrysler Corp. 1957. Oil, metal foil, collage on panel, 48 × 32". Private collection, London

Hamilton instead dealt with popular culture as raw material, and his complex process of incorporating this material into his art poses provocative, though less metaphysical, questions about the nature of art and life. At the time Hamilton executed these works, he was exploring Duchamp's activities and working on reconstructions of the *Large Glass* and the *Green Box;* throughout this period he remained in close contact with Duchamp.

Of this early output, *Hommage à Chrysler Corp.,* a collage, is perhaps the most successful attempt at achieving a popular culture parallel to Duchamp's *Large Glass.* Hamilton, who often provides commentaries on his work, explained some of the background of *Hommage:* "Partly as a result of the Man, Machine and Motion exhibition, biased by the pop-art pre-occupation of the Independent Group at the ICA and using directly some material investigated by Reyner Banham in his auto styling research, I had been working on a group of paintings and drawings which portray the American automobile as expressed in the mag-ads."

The two main elements of the work are a car ("taken from Chrysler's Plymouth and Imperial ads, there is some General Motors material and a bit of Pontiac") and a woman ("sex symbol, as so often happens in the ads, engaged in a display of affection for the vehicle...constructed from two main elements—the Exquisite Form bra diagram and Voluptua's lips"). On the most obvious level, the juxtaposition of a sexy woman and a car, whose lines literally flow into one another, comments on the automobile as sex object and on the advertising techniques that exploit these associations. The work also depicts man's attachment to machines and the sense of intimacy he develops toward them, ideas explored throughout the history of the automobile in art.

Many subtle messages are imbedded in Hamilton's collage. In the title, by means of a typically Duchampian pun, Hamilton suggests the shift of the art scene away from France to the United States, away from traditional aesthetics toward a more blatant commercial sensibility: "homage" is now paid to a United States corporation, which, of course, has bases throughout the world. Where once the wonders of technology were expressed in art through "homages" to race car drivers and aviators, the modern corporation has usurped that position, becoming society's new technological hero.

Hamilton also made reference to other works and styles of art, alluding to Duchamp in the dotted lines encircling the front right headlight. Derived from *Nude Descending a Staircase,* these white blips, which originally signified the nude's motion, are attached to an immobile car in a "kind of International Style Showroom, represented by a token suggestion of Mondrian and Saarinen." Hamilton claimed that the figure of the woman "evoked the faint echo of the Winged Victory of Samothrace," yet he wanted to "suppress the allusion" because "Marinetti's dictum 'a racing car...is more beautiful than the Winged Victory of Samothrace' made it impossibly corny. In spite of a distaste for the notion it still exists." In the small cross shape at the middle right, Hamilton refers to a number of earlier works involved with problems of kinetics, including *Carapace* (1954), which punned on the car's speed of motion and its potential to be a protective shell, and the Trainsition series (1954), which attempted to recreate the visual perceptions of a landscape and speeding car seen from a speeding car and a speeding train.

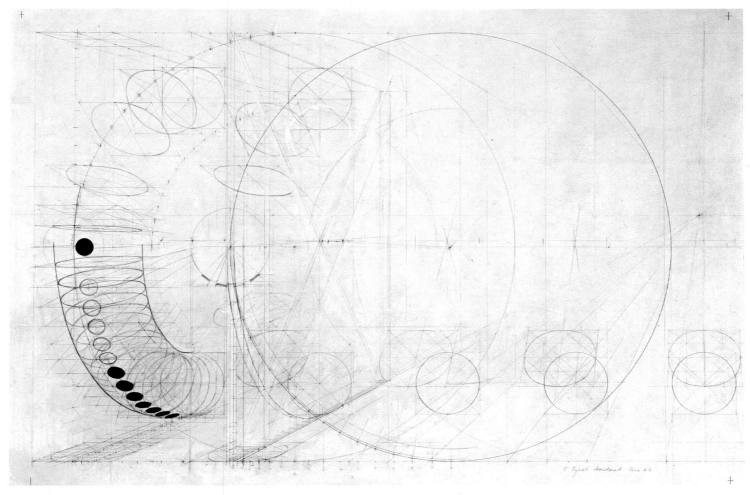

Richard Hamilton. Five Tyres Abandoned. *1963. Colored pencil and ink on paper, 19 × 28¼". Kunsthalle Tübingen, West Germany. Collection Dr. Georg Zundel*

Hommage à Chrysler Corp. is by no means a simple or straightforward work; many of Hamilton's visual devices recall Picabia's use of car parts as extended symbols. What appears to be a car's front left headlight is actually a "jet-intake," a device found on American cars in the fifties. The spirals of Voluptua's bra were taken from an ad that described its unique "floating action," which Hamilton described as "a suspension problem"; and the overall resemblance of the auto to a "Bug-eyed monster," connotes the automobile's highly organic quality. Faithful in technique to its advertising origins, the original collage contains a number of commercial art devices: "plastitone and mechanical tints," and an area of aluminum foil simulating the area of chrome on the car. Hamilton's art contains a rare combination of wit and sobriety, involution and obviousness, banality and sophistication, in a provocative visual arrangement of flowing, eliding forms, and of discrete, almost diagrammatic ciphers.

Of Hamilton's early Pop works, three others explore the automobile as primary subject matter, uniting a stream of complex associations that combine high and commercial art. Sex and the automobile remain major themes, cleverly expressed in *AAH!*, where a delicate finger approaches a gearshift in a gesture evocative of sexual anticipation, and of the life-imbuing "creation of Adam" gesture on the Sistine ceiling. In *Glorious Techniculture*, the form of a rifle doubles as a rear or side window of a car. The title, a play on the cinema term "glorious technicolor," implies a vibrant world of media influences, where images and fantasies of adventure, violence, and glamour become so strong that culture begins to resemble a Hollywood extravaganza. In *Hers is a Lush Situation*, the car-woman association is taken out of the showroom and into "the writhing sea of jostling metal" of the street. The cross-fertilization between life, art, and media-hype insinuated in *Glorious Techniculture* is finally realized in the title of *Hers is a Lush Situation*, which was actually derived from an *Industrial Design* review of the 1957 Buick: "The driver sits at the dead calm center of all this motion. Hers is a lush situation."

In another series of works involved with the automobile, Hamilton focused on a single part of the car, the tire. *Five Tyres Abandoned* (1963) consists of computer-derived perspective constructions of tire treads, and was based on an article detailing the evolution of automobile tires that curiously resemble the sieves in Duchamp's *Large Glass*. The tire was a common element found in Dada collage, and frequently appeared in other Pop pieces. An item from the popular and technological worlds, distinguished by a geometric, symmetric shape and a repetitive abstract tread design, the tire could be used to synthesize the distinction between pure formalism and popular imagery.

Other British Pop artists pursued themes related to the automobile, particularly in the 1960s. Peter Blake, in *Beach Boys Car* (1964) paired the Beach Boys with one of their favorite subjects, automobiles. Gerald Laing, who perceived the world of auto racing as a modern-day successor to medieval and Renaissance heraldry, did bold, flat, vivid paintings of speedsters. He later produced abstract, sculptural, shaped canvases, inspired, as he put it, by that "elaborate piece of sculpture on wheels," the race car.

Not everyone agreed with Laing's sentiment. In the midst of the Pop art revolution in Britain, sculptor Alberto Giacometti offered an opposing judgment in an essay "The Automobile Demystified," initially published in *Paris Review* in 1958. Giacometti wrote:

> You asked me what relationship there may be between a car and a sculpture or even, to what degree a "beautiful" chassis might be a sculpture. I immediately went to the Automobile Fair.... Throughout my visit, I never once thought of sculpture. Well, yes, there *was* one time: on the front of a car there was something like a tiny Winged Victory....The car is... functioning with its eyes, its mouth, its heart, its innards, eating and drinking, running until it breaks down, a strange imitation of living beings. But the automobile, like any other mechanical object, has nothing to do with sculpture.

In the early sixties, British Pop artist Allen Jones did a series of paintings and drawings portraying buses: *6th Bus/Palette Bus* (1962), *Special Bus* (1962), and *Transports of Delight* (1963). They are spatially flat and the paint was loosely applied. The composition divides into horizontal registers housing multicolored wheels at the bottom, the body of the bus at the center, and passengers—scribbled, crude forms like Dubuffet's—often engaged in erotic activities at the top. Jones's use of vehicles and erotica is paralleled in Peter Phillips's abrasive collaged images of automobiles, sex, and violence in the Custom series. This tougher, sleazier side of the Pop world finds an intriguing literary analogue in Anthony Burgess's exploration of depravity and savagery in the novel *A Clockwork Orange*. Written in 1962, this purportedly futuristic novel took as its subject the subculture of Britain's Mods and Rockers, and contains passages similar in theme and tone to the introduction of the "Founding and Manifesto of Futurism."

> *Founding and Manifesto of Futurism*
> I stretched myself on my machine like a corpse on its bier, but revived at once under the steering wheel, a guillotine threatening my stomach.
>
> And we sped on, flattening watchdogs on doorsteps, curling them up under our flying tyres like collars under the flat-iron.

> *A Clockwork Orange*
> ...and I turned on the ignition and started her up and she grumbled away real horrowshow, a nice warm vibraty feeling grumbling all through your guttiwuts.
>
> We fillied round what was called the backtown for a bit, scaring old vecks and cheenas, that were crossing the roads, and zigzagging after cats and that.

British Pop became the first major art movement since Futurism to treat automobile imagery with such frequency and fervor, and it laid the foundations for a renewed interest in it by artists of the sixties, seventies, and eighties. British Pop's fascination with consumer-technological culture differed from Futurism's unquestioning belief in the promise of a technological nirvana. Recognizing the humor and, to some degree, the absurdity of this new culture, the British Pop artists, influenced by Dubuffet, Picasso, Picabia, and Duchamp, injected wit and irony into their depictions of the automobile.

When Pop art emerged in America, the romantic haze of the separating ocean dissipated, and American dispassion replaced British

Larry Rivers. The Accident. *1957. Oil on canvas, 84 × 90". Joseph E. Seagram & Sons, Inc., New York City*

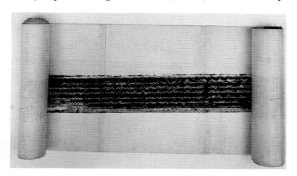

Robert Rauschenberg. Automobile Tire Print. *1951. Monoprint on paper (mounted on canvas), 22'1½" × 16½". Collection the artist, New York City*

fascination as an attitude toward consumer society. American artists, participating more directly in the experiences of mass culture, perceived a sense of dehumanization that lay beyond "those gleaming exotic images and extravagant attitudes" that so mesmerized the British. American Pop's discovery of images from popular culture, and simultaneous reaction against the excessive subjectivity of Abstract Expressionist art (less a factor in Great Britain), resulted in an art that was ostensibly cool, objective, and detached. This attitude of neutrality, enhanced by Pop's stylistic adoption of commercial techniques, proved to be a necessary prerequisite for examining popular culture with a devastating, critical eye. Although many Pop artists have denied the symbolic significance of their imagery, their themes are saturated with associative meanings that demand interpretation. Nearly all the major Pop artists had something critical to say about the car's role in society, and many of the negative attitudes expressed toward the automobile in the art of the sixties and beyond were initiated in American Pop art.

The artists sometimes considered to be forerunners of Pop—Larry Rivers and Robert Rauschenberg—depicted auto imagery and helped to shape the American Pop mentality. By applying the Abstract Expressionist "energetic brushstroke" to the representation of common objects, these artists attempted to expose the myth of the "existential gesture." One might say that they extracted the "meta" from Abstract Expressionism's metaphysic, leaving only the physical aspects of the work of art. Larry Rivers's *Buick Painting with p* (1960) creates the image of an automobile out of slabs of lush brushstrokes: a car painted in an Abstract Expressionist style.

This procedure may have neutralized the angst of the Abstract Expressionist autograph by affixing it to everyday motifs, but it also embodied a violence appropriate to certain automobile subjects. In Rivers's *The Accident* (1957), linear and painterly pictorial incident is scattered across the canvas, exploiting an Abstract Expressionist field effect to convey the sense of disorientation characteristic of an accident.

Robert Rauschenberg, infatuated with the perceptual and psychological mosaic of modern life, incorporated car images into his collages, combines, photographs, and silkscreens. His most explicit use of automobile symbolism appeared in his *Dante's Inferno* suite of the early sixties. In the transfer drawings, each sheet represents a canto, and contemporary objects and figures replace Dante's characters: for example, Virgil is played by Adlai Stevenson, Dante by John Kennedy, and demons are represented by automobiles.

In his 1951 monoprint *Automobile Tire Print,* Rauschenberg placed sheets of paper on Fulton Street in Manhattan, and enlisted his friend, the avant-garde composer John Cage, to drive his Model A Ford through a pool of ink and then onto the paper. Chance became a determinant in the production of the piece, although this strange method ironically imparted a rigorous visual regularity. In a sense, Rauschenberg was returning to the machine-world objects that often inspired Bauhaus principles of design. The black and white repetitive arrangement verges on a Zen "boredom" that Cage no doubt appreciated; it sardonically mimics the "all-over" quality of Abstract Expressionist painting. The extreme horizontality of the monoprint asserts the importance of the overall shape of the piece.

Rauschenberg's ambivalence about Willem de Kooning's art led him to produce another work using unusual Dadaist procedures. Rauschenberg erased a de Kooning drawing, then signed, and exhibited the vestigial remains as his own. De Kooning is sometimes credited with pointing the way toward the use of media images because he chose Marilyn Monroe and fifties pin-ups as subject matter, and because he included actual advertisement cutouts such as the "Camel T-Zone" mouth for his 1950 collage *Woman*.

In the late 1950s, the Swiss-born photographer Robert Frank published an important suite of photographs, *Les Américains* (The Americans), the outcome of the first Guggenheim Fellowship awarded to a European. As Picabia, Duchamp, and Gleizes had done some forty years earlier, Frank, who came to the United States in 1947, opened American eyes to an aspect of its visual and psychological character that natives had yet to recognize. Frank's photographs occupy a critical position in the history of photography. In one respect, they are a continuation and variation of the FSA tradition, except that Frank did not approach America with a prescribed reformism.

It has been suggested that the format and structure of *The Americans* was derived from Walker Evans's earlier volume of photos called *American Photographs* (1938). The correspondence between the two suites is compelling, though Evans focused primarily on rural America, and Frank's range appears more comprehensive. Frank's oblique and idiosyncratically constructed photographic images broke most rules of the tradition of unmanipulated photography, which Evans had helped to perpetuate. From the standpoint of the fifties, Frank's intentionally grainy, blurred, and unfocused imagery struck many as casual, random, and careless in composition. These apparent haphazard, gritty, and eccentric qualities led to a hostile reception by contemporary critics, who branded this vision "warped," "bitter," "prejudiced," and "joyless." While some of the critical response to *The Americans* concentrated on Frank's subject matter—what Evans called "pictures of people, of roadside landscapes and urban cauldrons and of semi-living, semi-satanic children,"—the strongest reactions were directed against his style, which seemed to drain his subjects of dignity.

While Evans and Frank frequently approached comparable motifs to create brilliant documents of American life, Evans's clarity, focus, careful arrangement of forms, and scrupulous sense of tone created a sense of stolidity and order, hope and rationality. The feeling of complicity between Evans and his subjects, perhaps somewhat paradoxically enforced by his use of a view camera, reveals a mutual respect and pride. To the contrary, Frank's photos read like exposés: the figures seem neither posed nor composed; they often glare with hostility and suspicion: dwellers of a seemingly chaotic, disordered pictorial universe that functioned as a metaphor for an actual world that was spinning apart. But by no means was Frank's work produced accidentally; rather, through his coherent, convincing, and intelligent vision, he was able to convey a sense of recklessness and improvisation and to capture the spirit of the "blues."

Frank viewed this universe in a beat-up used car. In an introduction to *The Americans*, Jack Kerouac wrote of "the humor, the sadness, the EVERYTHING-ness and American-ness of these pictures!":

Robert Frank. Assembly Line—Detroit. *1955–58. Gelatin silver print, 8½×12¾". International Museum of Photography at George Eastman House, Rochester, New York*

Robert Frank. U.S. 91 Leaving Blackfoot, Idaho. *1955–58. Gelatin silver print, 11×16¾". International Museum of Photography at George Eastman House, Rochester, New York*

Robert Frank. Motorama—Los Angeles. *1955–58. Gelatin silver print, 9¼ × 13¾". International Museum of Photography at George Eastman House, Rochester, New York*

Harry Callahan. Chicago. *1943. Gelatin silver print, 11 × 14". Collection Peter MacGill, New York City. © 1976 Harry Callahan*

Car shrouded in fancy expensive designed tarpolin (I knew a truck driver pronounced it "tarpolian") to keep soots of no-soot Malibu from falling on new simonize job as owner who is a two-dollar-an-hour carpenter snoozes in house with wife and TV, all under palm trees for nothing ... In Idaho three crosses where the cars crashed, where that long thin cowboy just barely made it to Madison Square Garden as he was about a mile down the road then—*"I told you to wait in the car,"* say people in America so Robert sneaks around and photographs little kids waiting in the car, whether three little boys in a motorama limousine, ompious & opiful, or poor little kids can't keep their eyes open on Route 90 Texas at 4 A.M. as dad goes to the bushes and stretches—The gasoline monsters stand in the New Mexico flats under big sign says SAVE....

Frank's vision, though applied to many different motifs, retains a distinctly urban flavor, a kind of multifocused, heterogeneous tenor. It is an urban outlook typified in the photographs of Louis Faurer, whose work sometimes suggests compositional instability, and a grainy and shadowy quality reminiscent of the *film noir* cinema of the forties. Faurer's photos capture the teeming restlessness of the postwar American city, with its low-slung cars prowling the night. Friends in the forties at the *Harper's Bazaar* studio, Faurer and Frank were unquestionably kindred spirits.

The photographs of Faurer, Helen Levitt, and to a lesser extent, Harry Callahan, serve as an antidote to the rural, middle-American projections fostered by the FSA. Levitt, who studied with Walker Evans and collaborated with James Agee to produce the film *In the Street,* casts a sympathetic and compassionate eye on the cityscape and its residents, treating the urban milieu as a form of living theater.

Noted for his eloquent photos of nature, from which he extracted linear, graphic patterns, Harry Callahan did city photographs that have been traditionally characterized as cold, alienated, and depersonalized. *Chicago* (1943) was shot just before he began working for the General Motors photographic lab. The clever exposure creates ghostly patterns of movement that also appear to expunge any figure of emotion.

Two contemporary photographers—Garry Winogrand and Lee Friedlander—have done works, beginning in the late 1950s and continuing to the present, inspired by Frank's approach to overlooked, odd, yet characteristic American motifs. Winogrand, like Frank, exploits the spatial potential of a wide-angle lens, adeptly traps fleeting sensations and gestures in shots that are often congested with pictorial incident. In Winogrand's photograph *Los Angeles* (1964), he treats the open car as a moving balcony, where the public and private spheres meet and overlap. The convertible barely creates a frame or enclosure around its figures, and thus promotes telling juxtapositions with the objects around it. The occupants of this "exposed" type of car inhabit a space where privacy is sacrificed for the sake of display or narcissism.

Friedlander explores the visual potential of unusual juxtapositions. He finds oddity in the landscape, often through placing seemingly intrusive vertical elements at the compositional center, where they operate as potent, independent pictorial forces, to create visual tension between a banal landscape and the formal photographic properties. In *Butte, Montana,*

Garry Winogrand. Los Angeles. *1964. Gelatin silver print, 14 × 17". Collection the artist, Los Angeles*

Lee Friedlander. Butte, Montana. *1970. Gelatin silver print, 11 × 14". Fraenkel Gallery, San Francisco*

Andy Warhol. Five Deaths Twice. *1963. Silkscreen on canvas, 50×30". Private collection, Ghent, Belgium*

Friedlander tinkers with the autobiographical implications of Lee Avenue, which is affixed precisely to the compositional element that exerts the most powerful formal pressure. Friedlander also likes reflections and mirrors: the car's side-view mirror, figuring in some self-portraits, creates a spatial disjunction, and at times reveals the photographer, camera in hand, as a multiple reminder of the artist's presence in the work. In the photographs of Winogrand and Friedlander, the car and road are a testimony to Robert Frank's vision and influence; after the publication of *The Americans*, traveling in the United States became something of a photographic rite of passage.

Jim Dine. The Car Crash. *1960. Happening. Reuben Gallery, New York City*

Much has been made of the neutral stance of many Pop artists, although it seems odd that they often selected similar subjects fraught with meaning about which they supposedly had little interest. The work of Andy Warhol, perhaps the most notorious of the American Pop artists, offers an ideal example of how Pop's detachment actually expressed the essential nature of mass culture. Warhol himself has characterized his own imagery as "a statement of the harsh, impersonal products and brash materialistic objects on which America is built today." His slogan, "I think everybody should be a machine," and his name for his studio and its activities, The Factory, suggest extreme examples of modern mechanomorphism. Warhol's Car Crash series, part of the *Black and White Disaster* group, hardly glamorizes the auto culture, seeming rather to comment on the atavistic nature of technological advancement, and on the anesthetizing effects of American mass-produced life. As Warhol phrased it: "When you see a gruesome picture over and over, it really doesn't have any effect." Warhol has also stated that one of his aims was "to see it as a black and white design...just like a dress fabric." This sensation of numbness and ennui recurs in Jean-Luc Godard's film *Weekend*, in which car wrecks become symbolic of the paradox of progress. Through repetition and stylization of violent acts, Godard created a humorous situation that becomes a horrible one. After scores of crashes, the idea of another crash becomes ludicrous, but the viewer, catching himself laughing at these grisly events, feels shameful and confused about his response. Both Warhol and Godard have pointed up the savage assault of mass culture on the mind and the body, and the reduction of "advanced" civilization into a mental and physical wasteland. As Allen Ginsberg suggests in his poem "The Car Crash," death and destruction by auto have become a central, mad fact of modern life.

The American Pop artist James Rosenquist depicted another kind of "car crash" in *Ultra-Violet Car Touch* (1966). The piece consists of two large motorized oil-on-canvas panels; one contains the image of the shining, protruding front end of an automobile, the other a slightly battered car's rear end, and the two rhythmically and relentlessly "bump" one another in a metaphor for the sexual act. The metaphor is hardly original: Mario de Leone's 1914 Futurist poem "Fornicazione di Automobili" (Fornication of Automobiles) compared a collision to a primitive rite of love. Similar expressions can be found in Jim Dine's famous happening of 1960, *Car Crash*, in which people who represent crashing cars performed an erotic "dance of death," and in J. G. Ballard's scatalogical novel *Crash*, which intertwines unrelenting graphic descriptions of car accidents and their victims with a vast array of sexual fantasies.

Rosenquist's work demonstrates Pop's exploitation of the emotional and psychological effects of the automobile and mass culture, and

James Rosenquist. I Love You With My Ford. *1961. Oil on canvas, 6' 10¾" × 7' 9½". Moderna Museet, Stockholm*

Tom Wesselmann. Landscape #5. *1965. Oil, acrylic, collage on canvas, 84" × 12' 1½" × 18". Collection the artist, New York City*

also comments on the perceptual impact of "highway culture": billboards, strip architecture and clutter, and superhighway sterility. Trained as a billboard painter, Rosenquist's paintings often represent food, sex, and cars (e.g. *I Love You With My Ford* [1962], *Silver Skies* [1962], *President Elect* [1960–61], *Lanai* [1964], and *Smoked Glass* [1962]). They reflect, through leaps in scale and fragmentation of images, the disorientation and confusion of the modern environment. As the Beat writer Neil Cassady pattered in his hip travelogue, *The First Third:* "Billboards, billboards, drink this, eat that, use all manner of things. Everyone, the best, the cheapest, the purest and most satisfying...."

The title of Rosenquist's popular image icon *I Love You with My Ford* suggests that one loves with the help of a car because it provides a physical setting for sex, it inflates the ego, and impresses and excites the opposite sex. The visual components of the painting reinforce the car-sex theme. The image of the lovers, who resemble stars on a movie screen and overscaled billboard imagery, suggests the drive-in theater as a dual trysting spot for lovers on screen and in a car's back seat.

Tom Wesselmann, Robert Indiana, Allan D'Arcangelo, and Ed Ruscha have also made extensive use of billboards, road signs, and the highway as formal and thematic artistic sources. Wesselmann, best known for his slick images of nude women, did a series of landscapes begun in 1964, consisting of large Volkswagen images placed in a landscape, several accompanied by tape recordings of the starting and shifting of a Volkswagen's motor and gears. In *Landscape #5* (1965), Wesselmann used an actual cutout from a billboard of a Volkswagen. The car, just under life-size and in profile, stands directly on the floor. A foot-and-a-half behind it, a large oil painting of a simplified landscape serves as a background. Billboard and oil painting delightfully confound the Pop boundaries between art and the commercial world.

In a world where "signs were more profuse than trees," Robert Indiana adopted the hard, precise style of billboards and road signs as the formal basis for an art that could reflect the new landscape. Indiana also captured the essence of information transfer through an investigation of roadside signs. His paintings are visually arresting and associative, just as highway markers must be bold and symbolic to attract attention and extend information. At a time when the literal shape of the painting's supports was treated as an important formal element of the work, Indiana exploited actual sign contours: the railroad crossing X, the diamond-shaped warning sign, and the rectangular information sign. Indiana borrowed colors from stoplights, gas stations, and warning signs, and derived letters and numerals from highway markers. His works of art address many topics: corrupted American values, racial discrimination, other works of art, and autobiographical concerns. Indiana's own commentaries provide excellent explanations of the design and meaning of his paintings. The following abbreviated example describes *USA 666* (1964–66):

> [its shape]... the unmistakable black and yellow high visibility ... X-shaped railway crossing danger sign that punctuated the Indiana roads of my youth where instant death befell the occupants of stalled cars, school buses in foggy weather or of autos racing into serious miscalculations before the onrushing always irresistible locomotive.

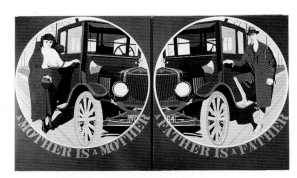

Robert Indiana. Mother and Father. *1963–67. Oil on canvas, two panels, each 72 × 60". Collection the artist, Vinalhaven, Maine*

But USA 66 actually comes from multiple sources:...the Phillips 66 sign of the gasoline company [my father] worked for—the one sign that loomed largest in my life casting its shadow across the very route that [he] took daily to and from his work and standing high in a blue sky, red and green...the company colors...(Which three colors make up half of the 'Sixth Dream' series)....It also conjurs up Route #66, the highway west for Kerouac and other Americans for whom 'Go West' is a common imperative,...it is 'Use 666'...on small metal plates affixed to farmers' fence...alternating with the even more ubiquitous Burma-Shave advertisements that brought elementary poetry as well to the farms and byways....the EAT signs that signalled the roadside diners that were usually originally converted railway cars...when the motorbus ruined and put that system out of business in the thirties. In similar cheap cafes my mother supported herself and son by offering 'home-cooked' meals for 25¢ when father disappeared behind the big 66 sign in a westerly direction out Route #66.

Indiana translates memories and feelings into emblems and ciphers that trigger these sometimes humorous, sometimes tragic original associations. In nearly all his "autoportraits," as he calls these paintings, Indiana uses a pictorial language appropriate to this new roadside environment. "...the automobile...created a need for a new scale and method of communication," architect and theorist Robert Venturi posited. "...the way the motel and the supermarket communicate their message with signs has a fantastic vitality...relevant to the man going 60 m.p.h. in an auto....Symbols ...can evoke the instant association crucial for today's vast spaces, fast speeds, complex programs, and perhaps, jaded senses which respond only to bold stimuli."

The diptych *Mother and Father* (1963–67) depicts Indiana's parents posed in separate panels, flanking the family car, "the keystone of their dreams—the chugging chariot carrying them on to greener pastures and redder passion," as the artist related it. Mother and Father do not interact except through the car, as Indiana alluded: "He (father) wooed her (mother) on wheels (LOVE) and she was crazy for it. That was until she became fat and middle-aged when he ditched her and went shopping for a new model— built-in obsolescence Yankee-Style: new wives, new cars, new art." Indiana credits Arshile Gorky's *The Artist and His Mother* as his inspiration for the work, but A. E. Marty's illustration *Garage* exists as a more compelling source. Its round shape, derived from signs, was also a popular format for Renaissance nativity paintings. Since *Mother and Father* contains a Model T with a license plate "IND 27, " and the artist was born in 1928, the license plate may refer to the date and place of his conception.

Allan D'Arcangelo recognized an affinity between the physical appearance of the modern highway and modern abstract art. His paintings incorporate the clean surfaces and spare forms of the geometric interstate and of minimalist art. *Holy Family* (1963) refers to the experiences of the contemporary family unit, a modern-day Mary, Joseph, and Jesus, who speed across the desolate American Interstate Highway System, where rest stops are Burger Kings and Great Western Motel Lodges. D'Arcangelo often compared old and modern ways of travel; in *Rising Moon* (1963), ancient navigational guides—the moon, stars, and constellations—are replaced by new guideposts: gas stations, service areas, exits, and route signs. In many works, D'Arcangelo includes an image of a car's rear-view mirror to heighten the suggestion that what approaches is identical to what has passed, a device evoking a chilling feeling that "with the passage of time, nothing has happened," as the artist himself assessed it.

Los Angeles artists Vija Celmins and Ed Ruscha have done work that addresses experiences related to perceptions of the modern freeway. Celmins's *Freeway* (1966), a meticulously painted oil on canvas, is done in a range of colors that simulates the photograph from which the image is derived. Celmins did several works in the mid-sixties dealing with auto imagery; here she places the viewer behind the dashboard of a car on a freeway, the place, as Harvey Mudd describes in his ode to *L. A. The Plain of Smokes*, where "shark-colored air/. . . eats the lung/ negotiating/ the monotonous circles/ van nuys/ to southgate/ boyle heights/ to watts/ LAX/ to the beach at venice." The subtle range of tones and careful treatment of perspective create an almost contemplative mood; car windshield again serves as framer, mediator, and demonstrator, a calm "eye" within a perceptual and emotional storm.

Some of Ed Ruscha's art deals with experiences of "highway hypnosis" and superhighway standardization. His antiseptic, laconic *Cheesemold Standard with Olive* (1969) concentrates on the clean, bold lines and forms of a gas station. Sign and roof line form a single hard edge that bisects the composition and exerts a directional pull that produces the sense of endless distance characteristic of the modern highway and its attendant services. Ruscha chose to represent a "Standard" station rather than Gulf or Shell because it could be any station, anywhere, anytime. Ruscha's photo-essays *Twenty-Six Gas Stations* and *Thirty-four Parking Lots*, reflect on the sameness of these architectural types related to the automobile.

In George Segal's *The Gas Station* (1963), the artist frames his characteristic roughhewn, white-plaster figures in a rigid, architectonic, three dimensional environment, creating a haunting dialogue between personal figures based on his local gas station attendants and the sameness of service station architecture. The real objects in the tableau—oilcans, tires, coke machines—contrast with the almost apparitional sculptural representations.

Segal's environments, analyzed by one artist as "walk-in" Hoppers, suggest comparisons with Vladimir Nabokov's novel *Lolita*. Nabokov's account of a gas station closely parallels the visual sense of Segal's environment, with "its stationery trivialities. . . that green garbage can, those very black, very white-walled tires for sale, those bright cans of motor oil, that red icebox with assorted drinks, the four, five, seven discarded bottles within the incompleted crossword puzzle of their wooden cells." Elizabeth Bishop, in her poem "Filling Station," created another version of a gas station that nevertheless echoes Segal's imagery: ". . . Somebody/ arranges the rows of cans/ so that they softly say/ ESSO-----so-----so-----so/ to highstrung automobiles."

Segal's works are called "environments" because they occupy space that approximates the space and scale relationships existing in

Vija Celmins. Freeway. *1966. Oil on canvas, 17½ × 26½". Collection Harold Cook, New York City*

George Segal. The Gas Station. *1963. Plaster and mixed media environment, 8'6" × 24' × 4'8". The National Gallery of Canada, Ottawa*

Allan D'Arcangelo. Highway US 1—Panel 3. *1963. Acrylic on canvas, 69½ × 81″. Collection Sydney and Frances Lewis*

Edward Ruscha. Cheesemold Standard with Olive. *1969. Eight-color screenprint, 26 × 40". Collection Danna Ruscha, Los Angeles*

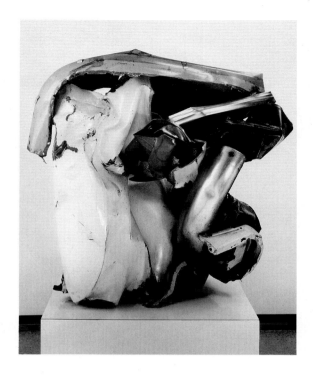

the real world, a space in which spectators are often free to enter. Environments grew out of several art traditions. They are ambitious extensions of the collage aesthetic of attaching everyday objects to an artwork, and of utilizing the space in front of the painting's support. They combine elements of painting and sculpture. Environments have roots in twentieth-century performance art, such as Futurist "evenings" and Dada cabarets, in which the sets and activities of a stage are designed to be visually aesthetic experiences rather than merely dramatic ones. They are related to contemporary assemblages, in which artists combine everyday objects to form sculptures, and to happenings, in which artists create transient scenarios of time, space, and movement that exist, briefly, as works of visual art.

The vast proliferation of mass-produced material objects has resulted in a huge amount of junk—one of the byproducts of an advanced industrial society. The automobile industry's principle of obsolescence has contributed enormously to the scrap heap. Several sculptors, Richard Stankiewicz, Jason Seley, John Chamberlain, César, and George Herms have raided the junkyard for raw material, rendering the dross of car cadavers into the aesthetic gold of sculpture, establishing the technique known as "Assemblage," in a process Marshall McLuhan labeled the "phoenix syndrome."

John Chamberlain, one of the first artists to use car scrap as sculpture material, has recalled: "I was looking around for another kind of material because I ran out of material. . . . I went out to Larry Rivers's place and he had some old car parts out there—a '29 Ford, and it was a different proposition. . . . It occurred to me that there were all of these junkyards around and it was fantastic—just free material—free material at that time was essential. And here it was, free steel that was already painted." Chamberlain welds together auto scrap, creating beautiful relational sculpture. Crumpled, squeezed, and dented chunks of lustrous-hued metal, streaked with rust and pitted chrome, buckle and warp into deep folds and protrusions like the drapery on Gothic and Baroque sculptures. Begun in the 1950s, Chamberlain's energetic pieces, in which shards of vibrantly colored metal abut with tremendous force, develop in three dimensions the gestural and dynamic potential of the Abstract Expressionist works of Willem de Kooning and Franz Kline.

But gesture does not come directly from the artist's hand; it is wedded with industrial process. Chamberlain takes industrial products that have undergone mechanical and natural wear, tear, and abuse, and employs industrial techniques to assemble sculpture; his works are involved with issues of process, both mechanical and natural.

César, the French sculptor associated with the new realism movement, a French parallel to Pop art, crushes cars in an industrial compactor and consecrates them as sculpture. In these Compressions, as they are known, César eradicates the glamorous and dynamic associations of the vehicle's once baroque fins, fenders, and bumpers, creating a monolithic static hulk that sardonically foreshadows the emergence of Minimalist sculpture, while it functions as a kind of reverse monument to the motorcar. Several ironic parallels to César's sculpture can be found in everyday life. A British newspaper reported the story of a woman who so loved her 1932 Austin that she could not bear the thought of anyone else owning it. She had it crushed into a column of metal, first to be an ornament in her garden, then to act as the headstone for her grave. As implied in a clever contemporary

Volkswagen advertisement, the company, in its emphasis on quality control, created scores of César sculptures every day. *The Washington Post* once carried the story of a man who had his 1975 twelve thousand dollar Lincoln Continental "smashed to a small cube as a demonstration of why people should buy smaller cars instead of 'gas guzzlers.'"

These assemblage artists, salvaging and recycling spent and useless materials, transform environmental chaos into artistic order. Each assemblage becomes a kind of archeological statement attesting to the profligacy of society. Like Pop art, assemblage borrows techniques from the industrial and commercial worlds in the making of a work. But the Pop acceptance of and emphasis on the lack of uniqueness of mass culture differs from the assemblage-art conversion of the mass-produced object into a unique work of art. Assemblage artists perpetuate the original collage tradition, extending it to include the products and processes of the industrial world.

Other contemporary artists, American and European, and primarily painters rather than sculptors (Lowell Nesbitt, Joseph Hirsch, Jean-Olivier Hucleaux, Erro, Robert Longo [who makes reliefs], and John Salt) use the auto graveyard or abandoned cars as visual or imagistic raw material, developing motifs that the photographer Walker Evans was among the first to explore. Lowell Nesbitt's series New York in Ruins, part of his Athens in Ruins/Rome in Ruins/New York in Ruins series, contrasts the decay of great ancient civilizations with that of contemporary society. Whereas artists earlier in the century compared cars with classical and ancient civilizations to suggest the greatness of the automobile, more contemporary artists use the analogy to suggest the demise of modern civilization. Robert Longo's 1982–83 lacquer on aluminum relief with cast bronze bonding *Love Police: Engines in Us (The Doors)* juxtaposes a bronze-colored stack of junked cars with a candy-apple red depiction of the upper torso, arms, and head of two figures. Longo goes in for the appearance of a big statement, one loaded with potential meaning, which is often thwarted by a sense of ambiguity. The tangle of wrecked cars was made to resemble a grand bronze relief, and initially reads as a monument to the death or destruction of a civilization. But the figures above, a powerful, stoic, neoclassical male, and a female whose laughter borders on anguish, confound this interpretation. The work seems to be about how clichéd gestures or techniques are borrowed to make monumental statements. Longo's piece explores the modern appropriation of formulas used during the Classical, Renaissance, and Baroque periods, and reused during the neoclassical period. As Pop artists consciously borrowed aesthetic techniques and strategies from the commercial world, Longo takes them from art historical sources. The concept of appropriation becomes one of the major points of this kind of art.

John Salt, a photo-realist painter, executed soft-focused, hazy, airbrushed paintings of auto interiors, generally located in the auto scrap heap. To Salt, car interiors are "the place where people leave their mark." Like haunting memories filtering through the layers of the past, Salt's paintings center on their present reformulations, remain romantic and nostalgic, evoking a sense of the history of a car's owners and passengers.

In the late 1960s and early 1970s, artists loosely grouped together as the photo-realists began painting works of art directly from photographs. They were inspired by the Pop art technique of working from ob-

Every now and then a VW runs into a little trouble at the factory.

Volkswagen advertisement. Every now and then a VW runs into a little trouble at the factory. *1966.*

Opposite, above: John Chamberlain. Ravyredd. *1962. Welded and painted steel, 34 × 31 × 58". Collection Robert Halff, Los Angeles*

Opposite, below: César. Compression. *1980. Compressed automobiles, 60 × 21 × 20". Collection Pontus Hulten, Los Angeles*

Robert Longo. Love Police: Engines in Us (The Doors). *1982–83. Lacquer on cast aluminum bonding, 264 × 90 × 24". Collection Sidney Kahn, New York City*

jects represented in the media, and by the sense of detachment resulting from such a procedure. They surmised that starting with a reproduction of a scene or object and establishing an actual physical distance from the original source tended to prevent emotional involvement with the subject matter and to encourage exploration of formal matters. Since the photographs translated the three-dimensional world into two dimensions, the photo-realists could emphasize the abutment of colors and shapes on the canvas surface, the crispness and high resolution of color photos, and the ambiguity or tension between the illusion of depth and the arrangement of forms on the surface. Photo-realism was part of a widespread sixties sensibility of coolness, detachment, and objectivity, characterized by hard-edged, tightly brushed, antiexpressionist forms, and psychologically and emotionally neutral subject matter.

By using photographs as their primary sources, the photo-realists question the widespread but inaccurate interpretation of photographs as documents of reality. Photographs are no closer to reality than any other artform; monocular lenses of varying focal lengths do not correspond to the way the eye sees. The camera focuses, slices, scans, and crops the visual world; human visual perception operates differently. If the camera were an objective, impersonal recorder of visual data, photographers would not have individual, distinctive, and recognizable styles. In making paintings that look like photographs, although the paintings are customarily very large, the photo-realists add another layer of produced, manipulated illusion between the spectator and the image that is mistakenly interpreted to be a record of reality.

A cataloguing of photo-realist painting reveals a striking unanimity of subject matter, taken from the world of the urban store front, suburban housing complex, shopping center, and parking lot. Because the automobile helped to create these environments, the car became a frequent photo-realist subject. Its inherent qualities of shape, texture, surface, color, light, and reflections offered a number of formal challenges. Such works as Don Eddy's *Bumper Section* (1972), Tom Blackwell's *34 Ford Tudor Sedan* (1971), Richard Estes's *Automobile Reflections* (1969), Ralph Goings's *Sherwin-Williams Camper* (1975), Ron Kleeman's *Mongoose* (1972), John Salt's *Demolished Arrested Auto* (1970), Robert Bechtle's *'68 Oldsmobile* (1969), and Christopher Cross's *Turbo Carrera* (1982) explore the interplay between image clarity and fuzziness in photographs, the coloristic brilliance of photographic reproductions of lustrous paint jobs, and the subtle intricacy of reflected lights complicated by windows, mirrors, and chrome, sometimes amplified by reflections from nearby store fronts. Frequently, the image is tightly cropped, recalling the compositions of earlier automobile photographs by Paul Strand and Ralph Steiner. Don Eddy's Bumper Section, a series of more than twenty paintings, focuses primarily on sections of the car's front bumper and headlights. Eddy emphasizes the abstract potential of the shapes and patterns of grills and lights, the spatial confusions of gleaming chrome and glass surfaces, and the depth-producing reflections of their surroundings.

Such formally dazzling painting may offer commentary on the role of the automobile in society. Despite these selective and seductive portrayals of the automobile and its environments, many photo-realists stress the impersonal, redundant, and potentially threatening aspects of this

John Salt. Vehicle in a Shopping Area. *1970. Oil on canvas, 37×52". Collection Harvey Schulman, New York City*

Richard Estes. Paris Street Scene. *1972. Oil on canvas, 40×60". Collection Sydney and Frances Lewis*

Robert Bechtle. '61 Pontiac. *1968–69. Oil on canvas, 59¾×84¼". The Whitney Museum of American Art, New York City*

Don Eddy. Private Parking X. *1971. Acrylic on canvas, 66×95". Collection Monroe Meyerson, New York City*

Ralph Goings. Helen's Drive-In. *1971. Oil on canvas, 35×47". O.K. Harris, New York City*

new environment. Richard Estes's paintings reveal the pictorial richness of the contemporary urban landscape, with its textures and colors and its interaction of light, shadow, and reflections. He often removes people from his paintings of the urban scene, concentrating on the spectacle of the modern world. Estes has remarked, "Making a picture out of something is a way of putting oneself in control of it, like the cavemen and their pictures of wild animals. Did the capture of the animal's form make his threat any less acute? Maybe a picture of your environment is a way of coping with it?" Estes invokes the artistic process to cope with a threatening environment.

Robert Bechtle has been called the "poet of the parking lot," and the hauntingly evocative imagery in his paintings expresses a sense of ambiguity tinged with futility. He commented: "...I am certainly aware of the social implications of the subjects. I can identify with my subject matter in a sense—I like it and I hate it. ... It deals with a very middle-class lifestyle which I tried to get away from when I was younger. But eventually I had to admit to myself that that was who I was and, like it or not, I had to deal with it." Like Estes's work, Bechtle's art suggests the impersonality of the new environment. He describes this approach as "try[ing] for a kind of neutrality or transparency of style that minimizes the artfulness that might prevent the viewer from responding directly to the subject matter." His paintings contain a number of elements, including people, yet his works invariably take their names from the cars in the pictures. Three paintings by Bechtle—one a view out the window of his home at his car parked on the street, another a reflection of the window in a mirror in his home, and a third, Bechtle and his family posed in front of the car—are all entitled *'61 Pontiac* because each contains an image of that model of car.

Bechtle seems to imply that experience is defined in terms of the automobile—the family poses in front of it, one looks out the window of his home at it. Bechtle, like other photo-realists, admits to a middle-class lifestyle and to producing art in a workmanlike, nine-to-five way. Neither bohemian nor romantic, Bechtle has a car, house, and family equally as conservative and middle-class in appearance. No wonder other photo-realist paintings, those of gleaming engines, race cars, and motorcycles, by Tom Blackwell, David Parish, and Christopher Cross, have been interpreted as "macho" images. Cars reflect their owners.

There is a duality in photo-realism, where the car is both source for a display of technical virtuosity and symbol of the contemporary environment. This duality can be demonstrated by considering *Private Parking X* (1971) by Don Eddy, an artist who opposes the classification of his art under the photo-realist rubric. Eddy disavows the significance of the subject matter of his art. In *Private Parking X*, he concentrates on the tension between the gridded patterning of the chain link fence that is nearly bonded to the picture plane, and the signs attached to it. There is an oscillation between depth and compression of the foreshortened image of a Volkswagen, a perplexity amplified by the illusion of space created by the car lot lines and negated by the dark shadows.

Formalism is only half the story in *Private Parking X*. Eddy's process of composing his painting, by selecting elements from several different photos, created curious juxtapositions. The painting depicts the way America travels—by car and by credit. Cars and credit can be thought of as providing instant gratification and freedom: the exhilaration and im-

Robert Adams. Cars on Longmont Street. *1974. Gelatin silver print, 6 × 7½". Fraenkel Gallery, San Francisco*

Lewis Baltz. Mustang Bridge Exit, Interstate 80, Nevada. *1977. Gelatin silver print, 8 × 10". Grapestake Gallery, San Francisco*

mediate mobility of a car ride; the enjoyment of goods before the pain of payment. But freedom and gratification are tempered by the actual expense of owning and operating a car, and the interest paid through credit purchase, a "false" sense of "free" money. Blue Chip Stamps offer the promise of "free gifts," which in actuality are paid for by the consumer well in advance of their redemption.

During a time when automobile advertisements perched Chevrolets on top of inaccessible mountains or spouted Byron's poetry as the incarnation of the spirit of the Camaro, the photo-realists painted the car, as in Bechtle's *'60 Chevies* or in Ralph Goings's *Helen's Drive-In* (1971) in its more natural habitat: in the shopping center, the "strip" or the ersatz rural housing complex. In their use of photographs, the kind "that tends to just be—You sense that what came before was exactly the same as what is [now] and that what comes next is going to be exactly the same," Robert Bechtle explained. The photo-realists reflect the world of banality and standardization that the Pop artists explored. As Lewis Mumford lamented: "In using the car to flee from the metropolis, the motorist finds that he has merely transferred congestion to the highway and thereby doubled it. When he reaches his destination...he finds that the countryside he has sought has disappeared: 'beyond him, thanks to the motorway, lies only another suburb, just as dull as his own.'" Or as Gertrude Stein pithily put it: "When you get there, there isn't any there there." Standardization is thus transformed into oppression or entrapment.

It is tempting to link the work of certain contemporary photographers, such as that of Robert Adams, Steven Shore, Lewis Baltz, Langdon Clay, and William Eggleston, to photo-realism. These photographers focus on images of automobiles parked on streets, near suburban housing complexes, in shopping malls, fast-food restaurants, and roadside lots, often establishing an illusion of physical distance between spectator and scene, pulling back their lenses to contrast the man-made environment with violated nature. The technical facility displayed by many photo-realists is beside the point to photographers: it is thought to be too easy, too much of a photographic cliché to emphasize complicating, disorienting reflections in tight, cropped shots. While bewildering effects might be ideal in displaying a painter's skill, they are often thought of as disreputable tricks for photographers.

Because these photographs often show landscapes altered by new construction, they have been labeled "The New Topographics." Robert Adams's photographs treat the development of tract houses, shopping centers, and drive-in theaters placed within a larger landscape setting. His photos operate within the venerable tradition of American landscape photography, begun in the nineteenth century by Mathew Brady, Timothy O'Sullivan, Carleton Watkins, Eadweard Muybridge, and William Henry Jackson, who traveled to western and southern frontiers, sometimes as members of geological expeditions. They recorded the virgin American landscape, and along the way encountered a fresh land now settled and built upon. Adams's contemporary shots of the new landscape may be interpreted as chronicling the intrusion of man-made constructions on the natural terrain, although there is a sense of uneasy détente between artifice and nature. Light and shadow help to enforce this integration and unity, promoting a pleasing visual tempo.

Stephen Shore. 20th Street and Spruce Street, Philadelphia 6/21/74. *1974. Ektacolor photograph, 11 × 14". Light Gallery, New York City*

William Eggleston. Memphis. *1971. Dye transfer photograph, 16×20". Middendorf Gallery, Washington, D.C.*

Langdon Clay. Stucco Valiant. *1977. Ektacolor photograph, 8¾ × 13". © 1983, Langdon Clay*

William Eggleston. Sumner, Mississippi, Cassidy Bayou in Background. *1971. Dye transfer photograph, 14×17". Middendorf Gallery, Washington, D.C.*

Lewis Baltz also distances and frames architecture within nature, producing laconic formal configurations. In some of his images, formal sterility conveys a sense of emotional sterility; in others, the isolated house or bar dwarfed by the surrounding landscape becomes a place of refuge, an enclosure for human interaction, no matter how lonely or puny it may seem.

Stephen Shore and Langdon Clay seem closest to the photo-realists. Both work in color, and both draw their lenses near to architecture and sparsely inhabited streets; cars, roadways, and construction fill more of the frame. Shore emphasizes space, measuring and weighing intervals between objects, and using linear silhouettes to materialize pockets of light. In its characteristic exploitation of empty space, Shore's work resembles Bechtle's painting, although Bechtle uses physical emptiness as an analogy for emotional emptiness, and Shore uses it to produce compositional rhythms.

Langdon Clay's photos are unabashed portraits of automobiles, though his works bear some resemblance to Estes's art. He shoots mostly "used" cars, eerie in the evening light, rusted, decaying, repainted, or repaired. These photos, begun in the mid-seventies, record a time when high car prices encouraged owners to keep and repair older automobiles.

Apparent contradictions activate William Eggleston's color photographs of the South. An air of detachment circulates around private and personal images. Although the photographs feel like snapshots, they are carefully organized compositions. Eggleston brings his wide-angle lens close to his subjects, causing space to distort and fan out from a core image that establishes the predominant color chord of the photo. Against this major chord, Eggleston plays a jarring syncopation of tones.

These photographers are united by their scrutiny of a car-dominated and car-altered environment. Like Robert Frank and Walker Evans, they traveled by car to record the new environment, and they continue the tradition of exploration of the American landscape that was established by photographers and painters of the nineteenth century. This landscape is no longer one of magnificent mountains, wondrous waterfalls, or awe-inspiring canyons, but a world transformed by the automobile, a land of shopping centers, tract housing, and the modern road.

Beginning in the sixties, Edward Kienholz and Claes Oldenburg provided some of the most important contemporary "auto-art," works that have roots in the tradition of Pop and assemblage that express interests in mass culture and the media. Each artist has developed a unique, trenchant repertory of auto-related imagery, and each has developed a form of auto iconography that summarizes themes addressed in the work of many contemporary artists.

Kienholz's *Back Seat Dodge '38* (1964) may be the most famous work of art involving the automobile. First exhibited in 1966 in Los Angeles, the piece was considered scandalous, and a crusade headed by County Supervisor (and candidate for governor of California) Warren Dorn branded the work as obscene and pornographic, uttering the catchy phrase, "My wife knows art, I know pornography." Dorn, unable to close the show, at least got the car door closed, to be open only during specific tours restricted to those eighteen years and older.

Edward Kienholz. Back Seat Dodge '38. *1964. Mixed media environment, 66″ × 18′4″ × 12′. Los Angeles County Museum of Art*

Mel Ramos. Kar Kween. *1964. Oil on canvas, 60 × 48″. Hirshhorn Museum and Sculpture Garden, Smithsonian Institution, Washington, D.C.*

Kenneth Price. Don't Think About Her When You're Trying To Drive. *1981. Graphite, colored pencil, watercolor on paper, 22 × 18″. Collection Bob and Laura Lee Woods, Los Angeles*

This environmental work is close in structure to Salvador Dali's *Rainy Taxi*, which was done the same year as the make of Kienholz's Dodge. Kienholz's truncated car, with its front seat removed, becomes a "bedroom-on-wheels." The sexually-engaged figures, a beer-drenched chicken-wire male and a plaster female, fuse in a single, faceless, conjugal head that contains a photograph of a salacious scene, suggesting the fantasy-reality interface of sexual activity. The license plate itself is significant: "C692, Everywhere, U.S.A."

By lining the interior windows of the car with mirrors, Kienholz short-circuited any pleasurable voyeurism, confronting the spectator with his own image as he views the scene. *Back Seat Dodge '38*, temporally located in the mid-forties and exhibited in Los Angeles in the mid-sixties, exposed the morality (or immorality) of an older generation that was currently occupied with criticizing the new sexual mores of the sixties generation.

Kienholz's work has a fascinating literary parallel in a novel by Harry Crews, entitled *Car*, in which enterprising junk dealers convert their "scrap" heap into a "scrap" book. They rechristen their auto graveyard "Car: Your History on Parade," and charge admission for entrance into a yard filled with nostalgic piles of twisted metal and broken glass. Their promotional pitch announces: "SEE THE CAR IT HAPPENED IN— THE EVENT THAT CHANGED YOUR LIFE. And they came: to relive the love affair, the accident, that first car, that last car, the time the tire went flat, the time he ran out of gas, the time he *said* he ran out of gas, the place where Junior was conceived, (You had your foot braced against the dashlight, and the other foot against the door handle, honey. Remember?)."

Automobile-related themes recur in Kienholz's oeuvre, in *Son of John Doe, After the Ball is Over* (1964), *Mayor Sam Edsel* (1965), *The American Trip* (1966), *Sawdy* (1971), *The Art Show* (1977), *Volksempfängers: The Ladder* (1977), and *5 Car Stud* (1972). This last tableau makes a harrowing commentary on the taboo subject of interracial love, and the social, psychological castration of the black man in American society.

Civil rights is the subject of James Roche's *The Bicentennial Welfare Cadillac* (1976). Roche, who employs a variety of mediums to produce works that frequently comment on American values, used an actual automobile to address issues concerning American minorities. Roche treated the car "like a large canvas," to which he attached many objects— horns, mirrors, flags, and aerials. Roche has questioned both the ability of bureaucracy to deal effectively with disadvantaged minorities, and its desire to make everyone equal.

Social rites and the relationship of the automobile and sex have surfaced throughout art and literature since the invention of the automobile. Early in the century, American songwriters composed such suggestive tunes as *In Our Little Love Mobile, Fifteen Kisses on a Gallon of Gas*, and *Tumble in a Rumble Seat*.

Many contemporary artists, including Mel Ramos, Roy Lichtenstein, Ken Price, and Luis Jimenez, have considered the subject. Ramos, in his painting *Kar Kween* (1964), resurrects the image of the spark plug to symbolize a virile man, which is fondled by one of his characteristically glossy nudes. Exploiting the ever-popular K of the "Kar Kulture," what Tom Wolfe talks about in *The Kandy Kolored Tangerine-Flake Streamline*

James Roche. The Bicentennial Welfare Cadillac. *1976. Modified and decorated 1950, 4-door, Cadillac sedan, 65" × 87" × 20' 7". Morgan Gallery, Shawnee Mission, Kansas*

153

Roy Lichtenstein. In the Car. *1963. Magna on canvas, 68 × 80". Scottish National Gallery of Modern Art, Edinburgh*

Baby, Ramos toyed with the sexual overtones of the spark plug brand name: AC. Roy Lichtenstein's *In the Car* (1963) melds a preoccupation with imagery appropriated from other two-dimensional mediums, in this instance, *True Romance*-type comic strips, with saccharin emotional formulas. Stylistically, he reveals a more general concern with the concept of framing: the piece itself serves as a frame, the comic strip box as a border, and the stylized streaks suggest a car window and windshield as another enclosure.

Ken Price, a California artist, helped develop what is sometimes called the "Los Angeles" look. Price's ceramics have pearlescent surfaces produced by lacquered glazes derived from the world of car customizing. In Price's drawings, a favored theme has been sex and death. *Don't Think About Her When You're Trying to Drive* (1981) was made in the illustrational style Price used for the drawings accompanying Harvey Mudd's elegy to Los Angeles, *The Plain of Smokes*. "You can't daydream/ in the fast lane," writes Mudd, as the driver of the automobile in Price's drawing seems to have done while fantasizing about or perhaps catching a glimpse of sex in the trailer down the road.

The idea of the car as sexual surrogate emerges in a number of contemporary works of art. In his poem "XIX," e.e. cummings describes the painstaking, delicate, and bittersweet technique of breaking in a new car as an analogy for making love to a virgin. The halting, at times almost fumbling, cadences of cummings's iconoclastic meter are supreme evocations of the tender, comical starts, halts, doubts, and reassurances of sexual initiation.

> she being Brand
> —new...
> i was back in neutral tried and
> again slo-wly;bare.ly nudg.   ing (my
> lev-er Right-
> oh and her gears being in
> A1 shape passed
> from low through
> second-in-to-high like
> greasedlightning) just as we turned the corner of Divinity
> avenue i touched the accelerator and give
> her the juice,good
> (it
> was the first ride[...]

Chicano artist Luis Jimenez is known for satirical sculptures that comment on the car as ego inflator and sexual surrogate. The lurid colors and lustrous surface of the fiberglass and epoxy *The American Dream* (1968) refer to Mexican religious sculpture and to actual automobiles. A car ravishes a voluptuous nude female, breasts rhyme visually with hubcaps and headlights, hair with fenders, belly and buttocks with hood and trunk.

Claes Oldenburg's often awkward and amusing aesthetic parodies of everyday objects are attempts to exert symbolic control over the environment. "The world frightened me," Oldenburg once said. "It would be great to control the world by creating all the objects in it...I imitate these objects because I want people to get accustomed to recognizing the power of objects, a didactic aim."

The automobile has been one of the many targets of Oldenburg's artistic acts: "Of the doubles man has made of himself, the car is the most ever-present, competitive and dangerous. Also the one which most naively represents man." Cars have figured in a number of Oldenburg's projects; they first appeared as part of his *Street* environment from 1960; parts from them were sold in his *Store* of 1961; they were the main actors of his most important happening, *Autobodys* of 1963; they provided the source for numerous drawings and sculptures in his *Chrysler Airflow* series of 1965–66.

The *Street* project of 1960 introduced a number of Oldenburg's ideas about the automobile and the environment. Oldenburg equated the street with "life" (as the Futurists had done) and regarded it as the arena of revolutionary gestures and activities (one "takes to the street"). By re-creating the "Street" within the context of the gallery, Oldenburg attempted to bring life and revolution closer to art. Because of the scale and character of contemporary urban architecture and the automobile's increasing dominance of the street, he felt that the street, home of the people, was becoming inhuman and impersonal. Changing its character, shrinking it to a human scale, reducing objects from three to two dimensions, and domesticating it within the confines of gallery walls, Oldenburg symbolically transformed the street into a less threatening part of the world. Oldenburg believed that the automobile contributed to the violent character of the street, so he made it less physically menacing by constructing it from cardboard, a flimsy and vulnerable material.

The dynamics of the street and the violent associations of the automobile functioned as dominant themes in Oldenburg's happening *Autobodys,* which was performed in Los Angeles in 1963. Automobiles played the major roles (tryouts were held to determine the best cars for the part), and the stage was a parking lot illuminated by car headlights, because Oldenburg believed the automobile was an appropriate expression of the character of Los Angeles. Even the spectators watched from cars, and the event became a kind of "drive-in happening." The happening emphasized Los Angeles's dependence on the car and the sterility of its freeway culture.

In 1965, Oldenburg began a series of works based directly on the car, selecting the 1938 Chrysler Airflow as the icon of the automobile age. The Airflow's characteristic streamlined features were softened and its dynamic essence converted to a limp and impotent state. Harking back to Picabia's use of isolated car parts for his machinist art, Oldenburg dissected the car into components and created soft Airflow engines, radiators, and tires. The Airflow was democratized and became a cardboard cutout cover for the February 1966 issue of *Art News.*

Oldenburg's original artistic strategy to tame the environment was amplified in his proposals for public monuments. He transmutes and normally enlarges such common objects as lipsticks, umbrellas, electric plugs, and baseball bats, and locates them in the environment. Oldenburg wishes, not without irony, to honor the common objects that exert a subtle but tremendous influence on our lives.

Monumentalized car parts are the subject matter of *Pro-*

Claes Oldenburg. Airflow—"First Sketch," with figure of Carl Breer. *1965. Ink on paper, 21¾ × 28". Collection Richard and Wendy Hokin, Darien, Connecticut*

Claes Oldenburg. Soft Airflow—Scale 2 (model). *1966. Canvas filled with kapok, impressed with patterns in sprayed enamel, 24¾ × 42¼ × 13″. Collection William J. Hokin, Chicago*

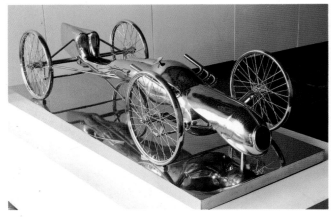

Ernest Trova. Study/Falling Man. *1966. Silicon bronze, 21 × 78½ × 31″. The Whitney Museum of American Art, New York City. Gift of Howard and Jean Lipman*

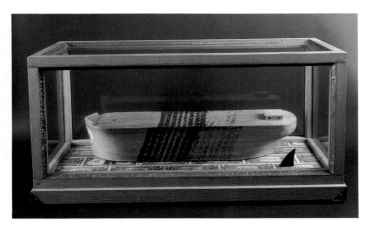

H. C. Westermann. Death Ship Run Over by a '66 Lincoln Continental. *1966. Pine, plate glass, ink, currency, 15½ × 32 × 11″. Collection Edwin Janss, Thousand Oaks, California*

posed Colossal Monument to Replace the Nelson Column in Trafalgar Square: Gearshift in Motion (1966), *Rear View Mirror in Place of Nelson's Column* (1966), and *Proposed Colossal Monument for Grant Park, Chicago: Windshield Wiper* (1967). In *Trafalgar,* the artist pays homage to the traffic that dominates the square, and in *Windshield Wiper,* he refers to Chicago's inclement weather, while expressing a personal desire to make people view an entire environment as if seen through a car windshield. The most brilliant of Oldenburg's auto-related proposals, *Proposed Monument for the Intersection of Canal and Broadway, NYC: Block of Concrete, Inscribed with the Names of War Heros* (1965), to be strategically placed at this vital New York intersection, would stymie traffic and paralyze the city. According to government reports, blockage of this intersection would eventually wreak havoc on the entire world. A fitting monument to the victims of war, *Concrete Block* sardonically points out society's all-encompassing dependence on the automobile, while it mocks the history of public monuments, which so often have obstructed the flow of traffic. Oldenburg has developed a variety of partly humorous, partly grim strategies and gestures to retaliate against the environment and the automobile: "the deepest and most natural subject I've ever had."

Claes Oldenburg. Proposed Colossal Monument to Replace the Nelson Column in Trafalgar Square: Gearshift in Motion. *1966. Crayon, watercolor, magazine clippings, 15¾ × 22¾". Private collection, New York City*

Reflections of the automobile's dominance over mankind, and artistic acts of revenge, appear in several immediately contemporary works of art and literature. Ernest Trova's chilling, science-fiction sculpture, *Study/Falling Man* (1966), extrapolates theories of evolution: man's body changes according to the use and disuse of certain parts. Trova, an American sculptor originally from the Midwest, portrayed man's dependence on the motorcar as arms and legs become wheels and axles, across which is stretched a gleaming, streamlined, sexless body, whose navel is a fuel tank (man's new umbilical cord). Francesc Torres uses the automobile as an apocalyptic symbol. His *Field of Action* (1982) consists of an actual jeep spattered with paint and fitted with TV monitors as wheels. The monitors beam images of aggression: an assembly line producing weapons; the bombing of Dresden; atomic bombs exploding; the Kennedy assassination; race car crashes and fires, and many more. Torres's charcoal drawing *Snap and/or In the Spirit of the French Commune* (1982) compares the destruction of the Vendôme Column, with the image of a Cadillac split in two. In this equation, the car becomes a symbol of modern America, and Torres's aesthetic attack on it becomes a revolutionary gesture.

In Chicago artist H. C. Westermann's beautifully crafted sculpture *Death Ship Run Over by a '66 Lincoln Continental* (1966), the artist claimed to have actually run over his pine model ship with an inked up tire—"an interesting technique," he called it, and an act reminiscent of Rauschenberg's *Automobile Tire Print*. Westermann placed the results on a sea of dollar bills punctured by a shark's fin, all of which he encased in a glass box. Microcosm and metaphor for America's rapacious materialism, Westermann's assemblage uses the car as its emblem.

The German artist Wolf Vostell has engaged in more radical attempts at controlling the environment through symbolic artistic gestures. Through happenings, Vostell has pointed up man's struggle with a hostile environment. Vostell, who modernized Marinetti's dictum of the "beauty of a speeding auto" with the statement, "When I see a speeding car,

Francesc Torres. Snap and/or In the Spirit of the French Commune. *1982. Charcoal on paper, 59 × 196¼". Herbert F. Johnson Museum of Art, Cornell University, Ithaca, New York*

Wolf Vostell. 9-Nein-de-coll/ages. *1963. Happening, Wuppertal, West Germany*

I also see an accident going by," adopted the car as his actor and the street as his arena. Some five years before Oldenburg's *Autobodys,* Vostell proposed that "The Theatre is in the Street," and instructed participants to watch and wait for car accidents. When one occurred, they were to reassemble the wreckage as sculpture on the site of the accident. Performed in 1958, Vostell's "The Theatre is in the Street" was a highly prescient event; it contained the seeds of happenings, assemblage, and the theme of the car crash as symbols of mass culture's production of mass tragedy. Although the event did not go according to plan, Vostell had wanted to impress upon people, through preservation and accumulation of individual accidents, the sheer volume of car accidents. The accumulating wrecks would eventually halt all traffic, and Vostell envisioned preventing further automobile death and destruction.

Like Oldenburg, Vostell believed that machines and buildings had usurped the street from the people. One wonders whether happenings, an extremely active form of artistic expression in the early sixties, might have encouraged political dissidents to take to the streets, something that had rarely happened since the unionization protests of the 1930s. Cars, often as symbols of violence, figure in at least eleven other sculptures, environments, and happenings by Vostell. Often he retaliates against the environment by subjecting the car to violent physical attacks. In a piece now on permanent display at the University of Chicago, he encased a Cadillac in concrete, an act of revenge against an object that has caused so much of the rest of nature to be paved over.

Perhaps Christo's wrapping of cars and highways can be evaluated in a related way: wraps function either as symbolic shrouds or to obstruct mobility and utility. His *Closed Highway Project for 5000 miles, 6 Lines—East West Across the USA* (1969) was obviously a fantasy proposal, and therefore not based on a specific roadway. Conceived before Christo had begun proposing monumental schemes that he intended to have realized, the project predicts these later works in which his involvement with many levels of government and bureaucracy would parallel the way a highway actually gets built.

As one might expect, artists eventually got around to the actual destruction of cars. Sartre wrote: "recognition that it is impossible to possess an object invokes...a violent urge to destroy it." Vostell, in his happening *9-Nein-de-coll/ages* (1963), had a car demolished by two onrushing trains, and in 1962 the French artist Arman exploded a bomb in an MG, christening the shattered remains a work of art called *White Orchid* (1963).

Arman's most famous car works, his Renault Accumulations series, are assemblages made from identical car parts. Intrigued by mass production, Arman was invited by a French magazine to decorate a car and painted 819 tiny Renaults that "line up and overlap on the body of my 'Parisienne' [and] symbolize the theme of accumulation. They bear witness to our age, in which everything is quantity. Today man no longer makes objects; he secretes them.... I didn't want to transform my car into a museum piece; it remains a 'Parisienne' ready for everyday use." In the true spirit of mass production and obsolescence, Arman used paint that would deteriorate within ten years.

Arman recently completed *Long Term Parking* (1975–82), an accumulation of sixty automobiles embedded in a concrete block that

Christo. Closed Highway Project for 5000 Miles, 6 Lines—East West Highway Across the USA. *1969. Photostat, pencil, charcoal, plexiglass collage, 28 × 22". Collection the artist, New York City*

Wolf Vostell. Silent Traffic. *1969. Car in concrete. Installation, Cologne*

Arman. White Orchid. *1963. Exploded MG sports car, 6' × 6¾" × 16'8¾". Private collection, West Germany*

is approximately sixty-five feet high and twenty feet square at the base. Arman calls it "a visual accumulation [of] the most typical object of the twentieth century. We are being invaded by cars. As a witness of this civilization dealing with accumulations, I wanted urgently to build this large statement."

Ultimately, the automobile works of Arman, Vostell, and Oldenburg form part of an aspect of contemporary art that includes *Ghost Parking Lot* (1978) by the architectural design group SITE, and the activities of Ant Farm, such as *Cadillac Ranch* (1974) and *Media Burn* (1975). In *Ghost Parking Lot,* SITE paved over twenty abandoned autos in a parking lot, to create a public sculpture that they felt "included certain subconscious connections between shopping center rituals and the mythology of the American automobile," a "fetish" undergoing "complete burial." Ant Farm's *Cadillac Ranch* consists of a row of ten Cadillacs, front ends buried, rear ends rising at a sixty degree angle from the ground on "Toad Hall" in Amarillo, Texas. In Ant Farm's 1975 event *Media Burn,* a 1959 Cadillac, dubbed "The Phantom Dream Car," plowed through a bank of forty-two burning tel-

Ant Farm (Chip Lord, Doug Michels, Curtis Schreier). Media Burn. *1975. Happening. Cow Palace, San Francisco*

Ant Farm (Chip Lord, Hudson Marquez, Doug Michels). Cadillac Ranch. *1974. Used Cadillacs. Amarillo, Texas*

Jim Wines/SITE. Ghost Parking Lot. *1978. Used automobiles, bloc bond, asphalt. Hamden Plaza Shopping Center, Hamden, Connecticut*

evision sets. As its organizers summarized it: "It is the myth that the automobile created and the myth destroyed, in the same car."

Recalling Futurist and Dada anarchic strategies and their ideas of "creation through destruction," and "masterpieces of aggression," such acts seem to transport us beyond the conventional boundaries of art. But in a world where the air we breathe can be lethal, venturing into the street can be considered an act of courage or even of folly, where nuclear war remains a constant threat and violence permeates our lives, such bleak and extreme artistic acts should hardly appear extraordinary or inappropriate.

The projects by SITE and Ant Farm, although associated with some of the more extreme contemporary gestures toward the car, are not without humor and irony. Negative artistic gestures often produce positive aesthetic results: both *Ghost Parking Lot* and *Cadillac Ranch* are works of public sculpture that visually enliven their surroundings. It was inevitable that as the automobile was assimilated into American life, there would be a cross-fertilization between automobile iconography and the fine arts. High art adorned the highway, and artists customized cars, did paintings and sculptures borrowing techniques from customizing, constructed sculptural evocations of cars, and built automobiles.

There are many examples of "highway art," from Stephen Antonakis's designs for a billboard poster advertising museums, Corita's camouflages of Boston gas towers, to exhibitions of sculptures along roads in Nebraska and Vermont. Many artists have rented billboards to use as exhibition space for original works. In 1967, *The New Yorker* ran a cartoon showing a middle-aged couple driving along the open road, admiring painted billboard reproductions of Botticelli's *Primavera,* Picasso's *Girl Before a Mirror,* and Van Gogh's *Starry Night.* The caption read: "Now, this is highway beautification." Comic fantasizing became reality two years later, when the New Jersey Highway Commission graced its turnpike with a billboard reproduction of Thomas Gainsborough's *Blue Boy.*

Since Pop artists borrowed so heavily from the media, it seemed natural that artists would eventually be hired by car companies to design advertising campaigns. In 1972, Datsun employed Salvador Dali and Robert Rauschenberg and several other artists. Dali put an image of a 610 Wagon on one of his characteristic melting watches, which was growing out of a hairy tree and suspended below a huge spider. The watch numbers spelled out "610," the model of the car, and the name of the work. Rauschenberg's *Engineer's Landscape* consisted of collaged photo images of a 510 Datsun and its parts, as a way of suggesting its fine engineering. Agam, Cruz-Diez, Arman, Vasarely, and Sonia Delaunay decorated cars for the French magazine *Connaissance des Arts.* Delaunay painted her car with brilliant contrasting colors similar to the decoration of her "Simultaneous Auto" of the twenties. Agam and Vasarely painted optically pulsating patterns like those of their more traditional works. Andy Warhol, Frank Stella, Roy Lichtenstein, and Alexander Calder "modified" BMW entries at Le Mans: Lichtenstein used his Ben-Day dots to suggest windswept forms, and Calder dotted the car with playful, colorful organic shapes, creating a true "mobile."

Several artists from the sixties, seventies, and eighties expressed a genuine fascination with the forms, shapes, and colors of the automobile. In the seventies, artist Richard Pettibone, known for his meticulous miniaturizations of famous works of art, juxtaposed painted versions of great masterpieces with racing cars. In *Ingres, Grande Odalisque, 1814; and Clay Reggazoni's Ferrari after Winning the U.S. Grand Prix at Long Beach, California, 1976,* Pettibone reveals the affinity between the sleek, suave lines and icy hauteur of the Ingres nude with the aerodynamics and streamlining of a modern race car.

Los Angeles artist Billy Al Bengston executed paintings exploiting the glossy, metallic paints and the smooth surface of the car customizing culture. Considered to be part of the "Los Angeles look" because of their lacquered acrylic surfaces, Bengston's works have a variety of subjects: one theme features motorcycle parts hovering like icons in the middle of the canvas.

Frank Stella, one of the most accomplished contemporary artists, has generally been thought of as a brilliant abstractionist, a formal composer whose works make little reference to observed phenomena even though the titles of his pieces often suggest strong associations to specific

Salvatore Scarpitta. Ardun-Cyclone. *1964–65. Racing car components, 8'6" × 64", backstop, 9 × 15'. Leo Castelli Gallery, New York City*

Don Potts. The Master Chassis. *1966–70. Assemblage, 27½ × 75½ × 27½". Collection the artist and Fuller Goldeen Gallery, San Francisco*

Tony Cragg. Highway. *1979. Toy cars and trucks. Installation, Lisson Gallery, London*

Chris Burden. B-Car. *1975. Assemblage, 31" × 8'10". Ronald Feldman Fine Arts, Inc., New York City*

Frank Stella. Polar Co-ordinates for Ronnie Peterson III. *1980. Lithograph and serigraph, 38½ × 38″. © 1980 Frank Stella*

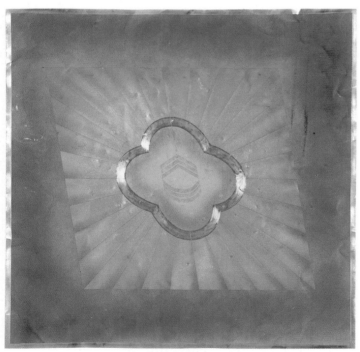

Billy Al Bengston. Holy Smoke. *1966. Polyester resin on aluminum, 48 × 48″. Collection Laura Lee Stearns, Los Angeles*

places or objects. It now appears as if some of his art has more than an oblique attachment to an observed source. As early as 1960, in *Marquis de Portago,* a piece named after a race car driver killed in a crash, Stella used metallic paint and notched the canvas to suggest the fenders of a racing car. In the early eighties, he did two series based on the world of auto racing. *Polar Co-ordinates for Ronnie Peterson III,* a memorial to another ill-fated auto racer, consists of a group of lithographs and screenprints on which boldly colored, four-part protractor curves are centered in a multihued mesh of lines echoing the central configuration. The controlled energy of the Polar Co-ordinates explodes in his Circuit series, a group of graphics and reliefs inspired by racetracks and rallies. The french curve replaces the protractor as the basic module, twisted and pulled into vertiginous arabesques suggestive of the arcs and hairpin curves of actual tracks and roads. The coruscated, exuberant reliefs, made from such materials as aluminum and fiberglass also recall John Chamberlain's relief assemblages composed of polychromed crumpled auto bodies.

Sculptors Robert Bourdon, Dennis Clive, and Tony Cragg deal with fragments or miniaturizations of automobiles. Bourdon fashions sculptural reliefs that simulate portions of cars; he paints delicate carvings of wood in sumptuous kandy-flake colors, providing three-dimensional parallels to cropped photographic images of segments of automobiles. Clive is a ceramist best known for his comical clay trucks; in *Palm Deluxe* (1983), he parks a clay version of a cream and aqua early fifties car on a coal-black street, at the curb of a white sidewalk from which sprouts a lone palm tree. Clive manipulates color, form, and scale; his colors seem bleached and baked by the sun, suggestive of the firing of glazes in the kiln; the car seems shrunken but slightly bloated, and the tree soars with amusing dignity. *Palm Deluxe* is a humorous microcosm: car, tree, sidewalk, and street, though isolated from a larger context, provide just enough information to conjure up a total environment, replete with a sense of geography and climate.

In 1979, British artist Tony Cragg arranged a series of toy cars and trucks on a gallery floor, converting the space into a miniature *Highway,* as the piece was called. Like assemblage sculptors, Cragg often uses junk and everyday objects, but rather than connecting fragments of rubble into a solid sculptural ensemble, Cragg scatters the objects on floor or wall, sometimes randomly, sometimes to form recognizable patterns. Fragments, though constituting a visual whole, remain fragments. In *Highway,* Cragg builds a mini-environment: the observer feels like an archeologist or an alien, scrutinizing a foreign world. *Highway,* however, is the observer's own world in microcosm.

Anton van Dahlen reduces cars to Mondrianesque horizontals and verticals in an attempt to demythologize the car. By isolating the automobile and distilling it into primary formal components, van Dahlen hoped that any extra-plastic elements of the car, such as associations with sex, power, and destructiveness, would be expunged. His works, which include drawings, reliefs, and both small and life-size sculpture, range from static, blocky systemic arrangements to more energetic and dynamic constructions. As he continued to analyze the car's form, van Dahlen discovered that it grew more complex in both arrangement and association. His Auto-

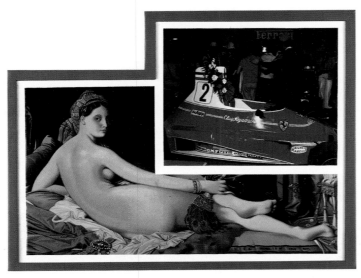

Richard Pettibone. Ingres, Grande Odalisque, 1814; and Clay Reggazoni's Ferrari after Winning the U.S. Grand Prix at Long Beach, California, 1976. *1976. Oil on canvas, 8 × 10¼". Collection the artist, Charlotteville, New York*

Dennis Clive. Palm Deluxe. *1983. Ceramic, 32 × 16 × 16". Collection the artist, Santa Rosa, California*

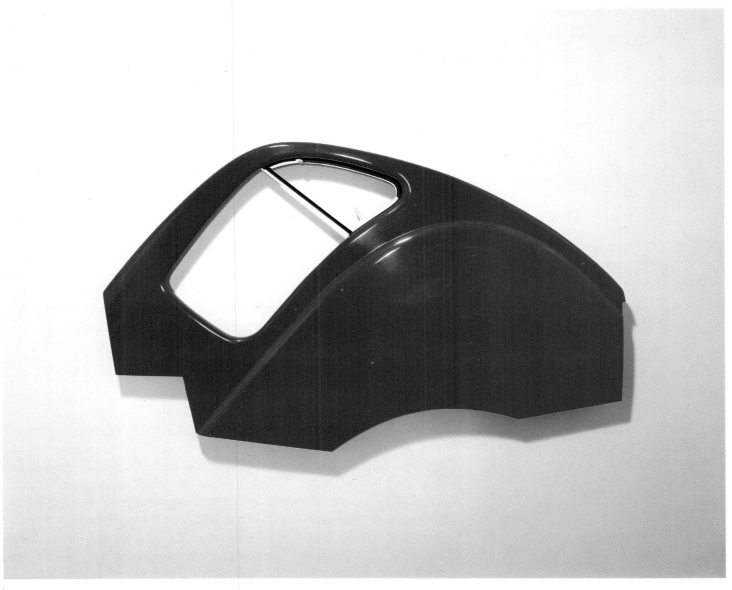

Robert Bourdon. Balzac. *1983. Painted mahogany, 70¼ × 42¾ × 2¼". Museum of Art, Carnegie Institute, Pittsburgh*

David Salle. Untitled. *1975. Mixed media on paper,*
48 × 96". Collection Larry Gagosian Gallery, Los
Angeles

spirit box (1974), for instance, in its resemblance to ziggurats or stepped pyramids, is imbued with a sense of ominous mystery. Eventually, after residing
in the United States, he began drawings and paintings in which the car's ominous aspects became more explicit.

Salvatore Scarpitta, who accepts the influence of Futur-
ism, and claims to have organized the first official dirt-track drag race in the
United States, places rebuilt, handcrafted, nonfunctional race cars with
panels of speedway announcements, totems to the world of the automobile.
Scarpitta's sculptural recreations of cars function as aesthetic objects that,
for him, carry emotional associations. Nonfunctional and illusionistic, they
remain squarely within the realm of art.

In the 1970s, several contemporary artists began building
actual automobiles. These artist-inventors, especially Don Potts and Chris
Burden, resurrected the notion of artist-engineer. In his sculptures, Don
Potts has tried to build the quintessential race car. Potts installed a huge engine into a steel armature: all wheels and motor, *The Master Chassis* (1966–
70) became a sculptural evocation of powerful horsepower. *The Stainless
Steel Body* is comprised of a stainless steel subframe attached to four bicycle
wheels supporting eighteen stainless steel scooped and gently curved aerodynamically adjustable panels. Although efficient and graceful in design, not
all of his cars are operable, and none has a seat for a driver or passenger. The
artist reintroduced the machine aesthetic dilemma: there is often little pro-
vision for humans in a world of idealized, mechanical forms.

Perhaps the most extraordinary contemporary sculptural
parallel to the automobile is *B-Car*, an operable auto designed by the west
coast conceptual and performance artist Chris Burden. In 1975, Burden
started work on the *B-Car*, which was projected to be a four-wheeled functional vehicle, capable of one hundred miles per hour speeds, and of getting
one hundred miles to the gallon. Reminiscent of the tinkering auto inventors,
Burden toiled, by trial and error, eventually completing his piece, driving it
on the streets of Paris, and exhibiting it in Europe in 1975.

Why build a car? As Burden explained it: "One of my most
cherished fantasies has always been to manufacture a car of my own—to add
the name of Burden to the list of Ford, Honda, Bugatti, Citroën, etc." This
attitude fits well with the career of an artist whose efforts have been directed
toward self-aggrandizement, and toward testing his own physical and emotional limits. Burden once purchased television air time to do a performance
in which he announced a short list of the world's greatest artists, including
Leonardo, Michelangelo and Picasso. He uttered his own name at the end of
the list.

Burden has also placed himself in grave danger as an art-
ist, risking injury and death by immolation, drowning, shooting, electrocu-
tion, and starvation. The car played a role in some of these events: in one
instance, Burden had himself crucified to the back of a Volkswagen Beetle;
in another, he was enclosed in a sack placed on a busy Los Angeles thorough-
fare. Through these extreme acts, Burden seems concerned with converting
art into an act of possible heroism and with undergoing, on an almost primitive level, a physical trial. His construction of a car is an attempt to achieve
notoriety and to reexperience the invention of one of the basic and most influential artifacts of contemporary civilization. Burden's efforts are related to

Victor Brauner. Amour propulsateur. *1945. Wax and collage on board, 14½ × 17". Private collection, Paris*

Carlos Almaraz. Beach Crash. 1982. Oil on canvas, 54 × 72". Collection the artist, Los Ange

Leonardo's visions for self-propelled vehicles in that he attempts to recapture the union between art and technology that existed in an earlier era.

Burden's art poses a paradox. On the one hand, it seems to indict the car's potential for destruction; on the other, it attempts to redefine it. His extreme measures, particularly the dangerous ones, are in the mold of other aggressive aesthetic acts involving the car, such as Vostell's various car happenings, Arman's bombing of an auto, and the Ant Farm and SITE auto burials.

Possibly the most aggressive publicized gesture was Dustin Shuler's *Death of an Era,* a 1980 performance in which a 1959 Cadillac, the car make so often the victim of these artistic assaults, was impaled on a mammoth twenty-foot-long nail. Like Dracula pierced in the heart by a wooden stake, the Cadillac is penetrated by a stainless steel spike, signaling, as its title declares, *The Death of an Era.* Enacted in the evening under a full moon, the event recalls an earlier ritual played out by Norman Mailer and friends, and described in his book *Of a Fire on the Moon.* During the summer of 1969, when America landed a man on the moon, Mailer and his friends ushered in a new age and buried an automobile. A portion of one end of the car remained above ground. Assemblage sculptor John Kearney, known for his portrayals of endangered species of animals made out of car bumpers, turned the tip of his auto into the image of an insect.

Mailer's last rites may be somewhat premature, however, as the future history of the automobile may cite the 1970s and 1980s as a time when the automobile's role in society underwent careful scrutiny. Oil shortages, inflation, low productivity, safety and pollution regulations, labor problems, retooling, recalls, and increased competition have combined to create great uncertainty about the future of the automobile.

A recent work of art addressing the car as subject matter reflects a related ambiguity. In an untitled work of 1975, David Salle employed his traditional formula of two sets of images, here placed side by side. Although the words, image, and billboardlike format point to the automobile as the theme of the work, its meaning is ambiguous.

Mark Tansey's *Action Painting* (1981) is a verbal-visual pun. The title refers to the term frequently used to describe the active physical procedures used by the Abstract Expressionists. But the approach is reversed: the subject of an exploding automobile provides the action while the artist calmly and detachedly registers it. These works seem to be concerned with techniques and ideas of art than with the impact of the automobile on society.

Carlos Almaraz's *Beach Crash* (1982) unites the recent style of "New Expressionism" and the concern with the craft of painting, and applies it to a motif appropriate to the violent expressionist brushstroke, the car crash, and to the subject of an important modern myth, the automobile.

Despite uncertainty within the auto industry, the car remains a resilient artifact, a survivor of energy crises, ecology movements, safety crusaders, government regulation, economic instability, and industrial mismanagement. No substantive alternative to automobile transport has yet been realized. As long as the car is with us, providing emotional experiences, taking lives, changing the environment, and altering perception, art will comment on and be influenced by this most inspirational of modern inventions.

THE CAR AS STAR

Of all the personalities that have lit up the silver screen, none has been more multifaceted and long-lived than the automobile. From comedy to tragedy, from "B" quickies to wide-screen epics, the car has not only been a staple part of motion picture iconography, but on occasion has also actually usurped leading roles from the actors. It is not surprising that such a unique partnership should have been formed between the film and automotive industries. Both are essentially twentieth-century developments; both were born of technological innovations and are concerned with and dependent upon motion; both rely on a mass consumer market; both, because they are geared for general as well as specialized audiences, continue to swing back and forth between predictable mediocrity and surprising excellence.

The pioneers of cinema found in the automobile a tool that could aid them in realizing the young medium's potential for capturing and altering motion. With its ability to transport quickly and reliably cumbersome film equipment and large production crews considerable distances, the auto helped to eliminate the restrictions of the early studios and canned theater, opening up a new, spontaneous, and complex world of subjects and sensory options out in the city street. Once on location, directors like D. W. Griffith took advantage of the automobile's mobility and smooth ride for traveling shots of trains, horses, and other moving objects, an innovation that broke down the static edge of the film frame and created a sense of continuous space. Whereas motion had been confined to the objects within the image, it was now transferred to the spectator, thrusting him into the action and making him a participant in the drama. As a result of the auto, film no longer only recorded preexisting activities; the audience could now escape into stories devised specifically for the virtues of the motion picture medium. With the

Opposite: The Absent-Minded Professor. *1961. Extraordinary features with standard equipment.*
Above: Jean Harlow and her 1932 Packard. Glamour amid the Depression

viewer's suspension of disbelief complete, the cinema was free to begin experimenting and developing a new language of storytelling.

Beyond these technical considerations, the early filmmakers realized that the car itself could serve as a lively subject to satisfy the audience's appetite for motion. More controllable than a train and less temperamental than a horse, the automobile was the perfect choice for scenes requiring dynamic movement and a rapid tempo, while the driver and passengers added the necessary human ingredient. The convertible was the ideal car for most sequences; not only could the filmmaker charge up a scene with a moving image, he could also keep his actors and actresses in clear view, whether they were fighting, conversing, or making love.

The silent film comedians were the first to take full advantage of this newfound freedom, performing daredevil stunts as their cars careened out of control down crowded Los Angeles streets, always just missing—or almost always—the gauntlet of pedestrians and vehicles in their path. Through the magic of the movie camera, the Keystone Kops, Harold Lloyd, and Buster Keaton became extensions of the automobile, taking on incredible machinelike power and precision: subjected to the most grueling punishment, they just kept on running. Other comedians were not so lucky. For the less physical Laurel and Hardy, the car was usually a continual source of annoyance and frustration. They so wanted to fit into the new mechanized age, but could never shake their nineteenth-century babes-in-the-woods simplicity.

1. *Dr. Jack. 1922. Harold Lloyd in a car with two roles: as prop and vehicle for traveling shots.* 2. *Scarface. 1932. The cowboy and his horse, the gangster and his auto.* 3. *Two Tars. 1928. Laurel and Hardy experiencing the frustrations of a modern convenience.* 4. The Grapes of Wrath. *1940. The auto as salvation*

Though we have laughed at the pleasurable slapstick terrors of incompetent drivers, from W. C. Fields to *It's a Mad, Mad, Mad, Mad World* (1963) and *What's Up, Doc?* (1972), the out-of-control auto has not always been used in such a lighthearted manner. Some of the most thrilling and nerve-racking film sequences have been achieved with weaving automobiles, their brake cables cut, flinging the hero down steep slopes to almost certain doom. One of the most memorable variations on this theme came in Alfred Hitchcock's *North by Northwest* (1959), in which the villains force liquor down Cary Grant's throat and send him and his car on their merry way down a twisting mountain road. On other occasions, the automobile has not only gone out of control but has actually gone berserk. Steven Spielberg's made-for-television movie *Duel* (1971) pits a feeble Dennis Weaver against an ominous dark

truck; because the driver is never seen, the truck takes on an evil presence all its own. Taking this sinister approach a step further, the star of the 1977 movie *The Car* was a possessed black machine that mowed down a good portion of a small town's population before being dynamited by the local police. The thriller is perhaps at its best when it makes such use of the auto, an object so familiar that when it turns against us, the emotional shock is that much more effective.

In the 1930s, gangster films helped promote the car from the status of a clever prop and technical device to a symbol of mythic proportion for both physical and social mobility. The Western genre's shoot-outs and holdups were transferred to the twentieth century, and the horse was replaced by the luxury sedan. The automobile had not only become a violent weapon, leaving behind the painless antics of the silent era for

the realities of the Depression, but a luxurious end in itself, a possession that represented success and the fulfillment of the American dream. The public lived its fantasies through real life figures as well, and was particularly enamored of the glitter and glamour of movie stars parading around in their Duesenbergs, Packards, and leopard-skin-lined Rolls Royces. If these dreams were not enough, many films, such as John Ford's *Grapes of Wrath* (1940), showed the ordinary man turning to the highway as a more practical means of escaping his economic predicament. At the end of *Modern Times* (1936), Charlie Chaplin and Paulette Goddard shrug off defeat, smile, and begin a journey on foot down a symbolic highway that surely led to a brighter future on the horizon.

There has always been something magnetic about movement in any medium, but the cinema could capitalize on motion unlike any previous artform. The race and chase were natural results of a medium attempting to exploit what it did best. Before 1910, the French filmmakers Ferdinand Zecca and Emile Cohl had discovered that their trick films would be much more appealing if they featured the rapid movement of a footrace or a bicycle chase. From Howard Hawks's early look at motor racing in *The Crowd Roars* (1932), to *Grand Prix* (1966), the race and chase continued to be popular motifs in movies, but it was not until the late 1960s and early 1970s, with the tour de force car chases of *Bonnie and Clyde, Bullitt,* and *The French Connection,* that the race and chase became almost obligatory components of any action film. Subsequent films like *Smokey and the Bandit* (1977), *Cannonball Run* (1980), and the television series *The Dukes of Hazzard* have attempted to top one another with ever more elaborate stunts and intricately choreographed maneuvers. "The chase," said Alfred

1. Grand Prix. 1966. The ultimate motion in the motion picture. 2. On the Waterfront. 1954. The compressive power of the automobile interior. 3. Traffic. 1971. Individuals and their individual vehicles. 4. Bullitt. 1968. The chase—choreographing chaos. 5. Taxi Driver. 1976. Film noir paranoia—in the front and backseat. 6. Weekend. 1968. The self-destructive bourgeois and its toy

Hitchcock, "seems to me the final expression of the motion picture medium." Certainly no other film motif has been capable of creating such purely visceral effects in the viewer.

The claustrophobic confines of the automobile interior have provided an ideal setting for verbal exchanges, giving us some of the greatest scenes in cinema history. The expressionistic patterns of light and shadow and the implied movement from grainy back-projections and flashing theatrical lighting are frequently associated or juxtaposed with the dialogue, intensifying the dramatic conflict. The famous encounters between Marlon Brando and Rod Steiger in *On the Waterfront* (1954) and Charlton Heston and Orson Welles in *Touch of Evil* (1958) are effective not only because of the acting and writing but because of the intrusion of a disorienting chiaroscuro in the extremely cramped and inescapable set-

ting of a moving auto. In *Wild Strawberries* (1957), Ingmar Bergman utilizes the confines of the auto to force two characters traveling together to confront the present and the past and reevaluate their deteriorating relationship. Carrying on the comedic tradition in a more subtle tone, Jacques Tati builds whole sequences around his sputtering mini-car in *Mr. Hulot's Holiday* (1953) and an entire film around the personalities of automobiles and their owners in *Traffic* (1971). On the other hand, many directors sensed in the automobile a destructive autonomy that kept people isolated and broke down traditional forms of communication. Thus a forbidding sense of alienation and destruction accompanies the appearance of the auto in such *film noir* classics as Howard Hawks's *Big Sleep* (1946), Henri-Georges Clouzot's *The Wages of Fear* (1953), and Martin Scorsese's *Taxi Driver* (1976). French

New Wave director Jean-Luc Godard argues in *Weekend* (1968) that the bourgeoisie believes that cars are means of escape from the turbulent, materialistic society they have created; of course, no such liberation is possible, as the irrationalities of their world—the automobile included—travel along with them, eventually making them victims of their delusion.

By 1970, however, the auto had once again reclaimed its position as a positive representation of manhood, sexuality, and emancipation, particularly for the counterculture and the working class—a development due in no small part to the advertising campaigns of the automobile industry. The car and the road began to function as settings for individual scenes, and as backdrops for entire stories in road films like Dennis Hopper's *Easy Rider* (1969), Monte Hellman's *Two-Lane Blacktop* (1971), Steven Spielberg's

Corvette Summer. *1978. Free spirits and competitors on the American highway*

Sugarland Express (1974), Wim Wenders's *Kings of the Road* (1976), Matthew Robbins's *Corvette Summer* (1978), and Sam Peckinpah's *Convoy* (1978).

In the late 1950s and early 1960s, television shows like *Route 66, Car 54 Where Are You?,* and *Highway Patrol* brought the same characters into our homes each week, and with them the same automobiles. Fictional characters came to be associated with their autos, and the cars occasionally became as famous as their owners. Who can recall Batman and Robin without conjuring up a picture of the outlandish Batmobile, or imagine James Bond without his fully equipped Aston Martin? The automobile had begun to function as a trademark for these individuals and for various segments of the population as well. In 1964, avant-garde filmmaker Kenneth Anger explored the compulsive world of the

custom car builder in KKK *(Kustom Kar Kommandos),* while such theatrical films as Nicholas Ray's *Rebel Without a Cause* (1955) and George Lucas's *American Graffiti* (1973) revealed just how important and complex the hot rod and its accompanying rituals were for America's youth.

In reality, a dream car may possess little more than a few gadgets and a supercharged engine, but a filmmaker's imagination need not be limited by such restrictions; the cinema abounds with automobiles possessing fantastic and supernatural powers. In *Orphée* (1950), Jean Cocteau gave us a car with a radio capable of picking up cryptic messages from Hades, while the *Twilight Zone* episode "You Drive" presented an auto that brought its owner, a man who had committed a hit-and-run accident, to justice. In *Chitty Chitty Bang Bang* (1968) and

Walt Disney's *Absent-Minded Professor* (1961), the automobiles were quite capable of flying, sailing, and helping their owners out of most predicaments. By the time these films were made, the American family had practically adopted their cars into the household, relying on them for countless errands and outings. It is not surprising that Walt Disney's *Love Bug* (1969) and television's *My Mother the Car* were not only endowed with special powers but also with human thought and emotion.

Though some visions of automobiles in the future remain earthbound, as in Stanley Kubrick's *Clockwork Orange* (1971) and *The Road Warrior* (1982), most seem to be hybrids, transporting their passengers through the air like a plane. Such filmmakers as George Lucas and Ridley Scott have kept the airborne ability of these machines to a minimum, desiring to preserve the character of the automobile. Thus the vehicle that Mark Hamill drives in *Star Wars* (1977) hovers just above the desert, and though Harrison Ford's flying contraption of *Blade Runner* (1982) is capable of reaching considerable altitudes, it is used as the only means of getting from one part of Los Angeles to another, just like the car of today.

The car is an exceptionally photogenic and filmic object, and can be used to transform a mundane scene into a memorable one. It can appear as a frightening machine or a charming character, a comedic prop or a vicious weapon. It is more than an aesthetic object, more than an anthropomorphized mechanism—the auto is an icon with an inherent rhythm and energy that it transmits to its surroundings. From the cinema's earliest days, filmmakers have innately understood the automobile's potential for creating a series of potent images; no doubt it is a partnership that will continue as long as there are movies and cars.

—KERRY BROUGHER

Convoy. *1978. The macho road*
American Graffiti. *1973. Socializing via the car*

A 1960 *Chevrolet Corvette* with "extended wave-curl flames"

It is a warm summer Saturday afternoon in San Diego in 1959. Workers at the Convair Division of the General Dynamics Corporation aircraft assembly plant on Pacific Coast Highway are on the weekend shift, feverishly installing electrical cables in the gleaming aluminum structure of a nearly finished Convair 880 jetliner, preparing for its first test flight several weeks off. But they are distracted by an odd sight visible through the floor-to-ceiling glass windows that make up the building's east wall. An irregular procession of sleek and immaculately painted cars is making repeated slow passes along the street. Each car contains a young male driver—sometimes alone, sometimes with a buddy or a girlfriend riding shotgun—and all are gazing intently toward the aircraft and the workers with only an occasional glance down the road. Over and over again, first in one direction, then in the other, the same cars creep by. Sometimes the passenger ducks down in the seat, disappearing from sight, to let the driver get a better view.

What is going on here? Why are these drivers and passengers looking into the assembly building so intently? Do we have here a gratifying expression of interest in the industry that keeps southern California's economy moving? Is it an example of youth's fascination with the miracle of flight? Not at all. These children of the machine age are not looking *in* the windows; they are looking *at* the windows, and what they see is the reflection of themselves and, more important, of their cars.

These are not just any cars. Car owners from all over San Diego County have driven to Pacific Coast Highway, to the block-long glass walls of the Convair assembly buildings, to gaze lovingly and critically at re-

GO OR SHOW

flections of the cars they have customized. Check out that '55 Chevy Two-Ten sedan. The front has been lowered, headlights and taillights frenched, hood shaved, grille replaced, interior redone in tuck-and-roll Naugahyde, and the exterior painted with forty hand-rubbed coats of black lacquer. Look at this '51 Merc with the chopped top, '52 rear fenders, and '54 taillights. To the rodders and customizers of San Diego County, the Convair factory is nothing but a series of block-long mirrors.

It is 1940, just past 10:30 on a cold winter night three hundred miles north of San Diego in the dusty central California valley town of Fresno. A single overhead 100-watt light bulb illuminates the interior of a wood-sided double garage standing under several oak trees behind a small white bungalow. A grease-covered young man, twenty-two years old and dressed in coveralls, leans over the engine of a car, wrench in hand, bolting down one of a pair of new cylinder heads he picked up earlier that day for his 1932 Ford roadster. Outside the garage, rusting away in a heap, are a couple of sets of fenders, a pair of bumpers, a pair of running boards, and a hood—items for which he has no more use.

What is this man doing? This time the answer is easy. He is working on his hot rod.

Twenty years and three hundred miles apart, the drivers cruising on Pacific Coast Highway in San Diego and the man torquing down the cylinder head in Fresno are part of the same phenomenon: the art of taking the passenger car, that epitome of mass production and uniformity, and making it one's own by modifying it or customizing it. Hot rodding is one way to do it and customizing another.

IN PURSUIT
OF SPEED

Hot rods and street racing go together, and the classic form of street racing is the drag race—a side-by-side, straight-line, standing-start acceleration contest. The heyday of street drag racing occurred just after the end of World War II, in the mid- to late forties, but the phenomenon began a lot earlier, back to a time when teenagers were first able to drive their own—or their parents'—cars. The first drags were spontaneous, as they often still are today. Tony Nancy, Los Angeles drag racer and custom upholsterer extraordinaire, remembers it like this in Tom Madigan's 1974 biography, *The Loner: The Story of a Drag Racer.* "Somewhere on a forgotten, lonely road, two cars stopped. The drivers looked one at another. A new phrase was struck: 'Do you wanta drag?'... There were no set distances; sometimes a half-mile, sometimes less. It really didn't matter. It was competition. Drag racing was easy too: just pull up to a stop sign or slow down to a crawl and then let 'er rip."

There was nothing necessarily special about the cars used in these speed contests, nor is there about the cars used in drag racing today. Popular history is full of unfortunate examples of the graduating senior borrowing the family Buick sedan on prom night and breaking a rocker arm or blowing up the engine while engaged in precisely the activity he had solemnly promised not to engage in. But certain cars have always been better suited to the sport than others, from the point of view of both performance and image—light cars, inexpensive cars, coupés or roadsters, as opposed to sedans, and V-8s instead of fours and sixes. From the very beginning, an inclination to work on the engine and the body to extract a little more power and subtract a little more weight has dwelt in every dragster's heart.

In the late thirties and early forties, light cars with hot engines became widely available, and this inclination began to be fully expressed. Groups of racers meeting in the parking lot of a drive-in restaurant might plan a rendezvous on some little-used section of a straight, flat road. When they arrived, they would close it off, mark off a quarter or half mile, and race. George Barris, who reached the top of the custom car world in the

Tom and Bill Spalding's pre-World War II modified roadster

Danny Sakai's modified Ford V-8 roadster

Opposite: The Xydias-Batchelor So-Cal Special at Bonneville, Utah salt flats in 1950

Dean Batchelor's classic '32 Ford roadster streaking across El Mirage dry lake on a 125 mile-per-hour run in 1948

mid-fifties, recalls groups of kids numbering in the hundreds gathering at the Piccadilly drive-in in Culver City and setting up races on Sepulveda Boulevard. With the road blocked off, the two cars whose drivers had been goaded by the crowd into racing each other would start toward the finish line about a mile and a half away. Marking this line would be the headlights of the last pair of a long row of cars facing each other across the road. According to Barris, the two drivers had to be very confident in their machines, since they raced for pink slips, and the loser lost not only the race but his car.

Needless to say, the response of parents and police to this activity was less than enthusiastic, so it was inevitable that some kind of organization would appear, and that some drag racers, especially as they grew older, would be driven toward legitimacy and respectability. In southern California, in 1937, the Southern California Timing Association was formed, and under its aegis, street racers ran high-speed races, pushing their machines to top speed in official, timed events on the dry lake beds in the Mojave Desert northeast of Los Angeles. The timing events naturally encouraged side activities, and drag races were eventually organized. Hot rodders from all over southern California would converge on places like Muroc and El Mirage to "run what you brung."

What they brought were vehicles that departed to greater and lesser degrees from the coupés and roadsters to be found in the local car dealer's showroom. Some were built from scratch; many were entirely stock. Tom and Bill Spalding's Riley overhead valve V-8 would have been found on the flats (as the dry lakes were called) in 1941. The vehicle shows all the elegance of a battered pickup truck, but the Roots blower projecting through the hood demonstrates the seriousness of the builders' quest for speed. (A blower, or supercharger, is a device that uses mechanical energy supplied by the engine to force the fuel-air mixture into the engine, instead of relying on natural atmospheric pressure. It can double an engine's output.)

Danny Sakai's sleek and aggressive V-8-modified shows much more finesse, and in 1941 it reached a top speed of 128 miles per hour. Modifications to the Ford flathead engine included new cylinder heads, manifold, and ignition. The body was handmade, fabricated from scratch, and it has a La Salle grille.

Vehicles closer to stock, typically modified Ford roadsters, stripped of fenders, running boards, and windshields, were more common. Unlike the specials, these cars could usually be driven on the road as well as the flats.

The hot rodders had only squatters' rights to the flats, and after the war, they were forced to share them with the Air Force, which was moving in with experimental jets and rocket planes. Chuck Yeager broke the sound barrier in the Bell X-1 over Muroc in October 1947. Drag racers and experimental aircraft pilots loved the dry lakes for the same reasons: they were smooth, they were flat, they were big, and they were out of the way.

While the jets and rocket planes were taking over the air, an observer at the flats could have been forgiven for thinking that they were taking over the ground as well—in the small, slippery forms of the "lakesters" and "belly tankers." Inside, these racers were like traditional hot rods, with flathead Ford or, a little later, overhead-valve Cadillac or Oldsmobile power plants. Outside, they were something else entirely—little aluminum bullets, barely large enough for the the rear-mounted engine and driver. The bodies were made from surplus "drop tanks," expendable fuel tanks suspended from the wings or bellies of aircraft to extend range, which were discarded by the military after the war. Alex Xydias's Ford V-8-60-powered open-wheeler was created by building a simple frame and mounting the engine at the rear. It was covered by a war surplus drop tank from a Lockheed P-38, which originally held 315 gallons of aviation gas. Little of the original shape was changed, except for the addition of the cockpit opening and the head fairing. It reached 132 miles per hour at El Mirage in 1948.

Later, Lake Muroc would become Edwards Air Force Base, Skyrockets and X-15s would fly to the edge of space, and—much later—the Space Shuttle would return to earth there. By 1950, entirely new and more sophisticated lakesters were built from scratch, and the California lake beds began to show wear, so the center of racing action was shifted to the Great Salt Lake flats of Bonneville, Utah. There, monstrous, sleek cars would eventually push beyond three hundred, four hundred, five hundred, and even six hundred miles per hour, sometimes in vehicles that were little more than jet aircraft with fancy wheels and no wings.

The Xydias-Batchelor So-Cal Special was an early example of these special-bodied lakesters. Its shape was very similar to the classic teardrop of Xydias's belly tanker because it was the same car, in a new body. Xydias and Batchelor removed the body, narrowed the track, and had a streamlined body built on the chassis by Valley Custom Shop in Burbank. In 1949 and 1950, it was the fastest car in America, with a top speed of 210 miles per hour with a 208 two-way average.

Organization was not limited to the flats, but crept in closer to home. In the late forties, the era of the quarter-mile drag strip began, with organizers sometimes taking advantage of military airstrips that had been quickly built for the war and abandoned after it. In southern California, quarter-mile strips were opened on an airstrip at Santa Ana, and at Pomona and Fontana, using specially built facilities, but the drag strip was by no means an exclusive Californian phenomenon.

Quarter-mile strips appeared throughout the country, and, in 1951, the National Hot Rod Association was organized under the leadership of Wally Parks. For several years, it sponsored the drag racing Safety Safari, a portable drag strip caravan that traveled around the country promoting the sport. It emphasized safety regulations and organized cars into different classes according to body type, weight, fuel type, and engine size. National championships, especially the NHRA's Winternationals, attracted lots of money and big crowds.

As the sport became a big-time enterprise, the cars did too, and often attracted major commercial sponsors. The hot rod roadster was eclipsed by more sophisticated dragsters built from scratch exclusively for racing at the strip. In the early fifties, the simple and well-loved Ford flatheads were displaced by the newer overhead-valve V-8s from Oldsmobile, Cadillac, Chrysler, and eventually Chevrolet. (The terms "flathead" and "overhead valve" refer to different ways of arranging the components that allow the fuel-air mixture into the combustion chamber, and the exhaust mixture out. The flathead arrangement is older and less efficient, but simple and effective.)

Alex Xydias's "belly-tanker" powered by a Ford V-8-60 at El Mirage in 1948

Bill Faris's '32 Ford roadster before a run at El Mirage

Jerry Stroner's channeled '32 Ford Model B roadster (Deuce) at El Mirage

By 1957, drag racing reached the point where *Life* magazine felt it warranted a cover story. *Life* reported that there were 130 drag strips in 40 states, 2.5 million drag race spectators, 100,000 hot rods, and 15,000 car clubs, whose ranks were swelling at the rate of 1,500 new members per month. The record speed over the quarter mile in 1957 was 166.97 miles per hour, with good dragsters routinely attaining speeds of over 100 miles per hour. The legal, controlled sport of drag racing was gaining respectability, to the relief of those who believed it would reduce illegal street racing, and to the dismay of those who believed it would only encourage it. The Southern California Timing Association and the National Hot Rod Association worked hard to promote an image of responsibility and safety, encouraging car clubs to participate in civic projects, and to avoid illegal street racing. Meanwhile, of course, a couple of hot rods would be sitting at the stoplight, engines idling, waiting for the light to change. These street rods were the heart and soul of the rodding phenomenon.

In the beginning, a hot rod was just a passenger car whose drive train—the engine, transmission, differential, wheels, and tires—had been modified for increased acceleration and speed. Usually, these modified cars could be driven on the streets, although, under close scrutiny by the local traffic patrolman, certain technical discrepancies (such as missing front brakes for the sake of reduced weight) were sometimes uncovered and citations issued. For most rodders, the challenge was to get a car that was quick and street-legal. Any intersection with two lanes and a traffic light could then serve as the point of departure for two rodders who wanted to blur the line between street transportation and street racing.

A hot rod could, in principle, be put together out of a car of almost any model and year. The favorite cars of the early hot rodders, and later of the early customizers, were Fords, particularly 1928 to 1935 Ford roadsters. During the late thirties, these Fords fulfilled the primary hot rod

A hybrid roadster made from a narrowed Chevrolet body, with doors filled in, sitting on a Ford V-8 running gear. Front tires are from a motorcycle

Bert Letner's modified roadster was based on a 1925 Model T body, had a custom front end, Ford V-8 engine and running gear; at El Mirage in 1948

requirements of availability and cheapness better than any other car, and the cars themselves were light and simple. With a little work, virtually anyone could make them go fast, and many did. Bill Faris's '32 roadster, from the Glendale Sidewinder's club, ran in a stock body class against roadsters with comparable engines.

In addition to changes in the engine and drive train, other essential modifications consisted of the removal of extraneous body pieces. But hot rodders would often go much further with the body than simply taking things off. Jerry Stroner's '32 Ford roadster (Deuce), for instance, shows the effect of channeling, a profile-lowering technique. Other channeled machines from about the same time—a Chevy-bodied, Ford-powered roadster with split-V windshield, and Bert Letner's modified '25 Model T—were sleek examples of the art of custom fabrication.

The engine was the heart of the machine. In 1932, Ford introduced a new flathead V-8, which remained in production for the next twenty years, not to be replaced until 1954, when Ford offered a new, overhead-valve V-8. It was unusual for an inexpensive car like a Ford to have a V-8, but this engine was simple, easy to work on, and easy to modify for increased power (to produce speed) and increased torque (to produce acceleration). It was even possible to buy an overhead valve conversion kit. The Ardun heads (named after the engineer Zora Arkus-Duntov, who would later direct the Corvette program at General Motors) were extremely important to the engine's long and successful career. The flathead, even as an overhead, inspired a sense of loyalty among hot rodders that survives today.

For reasons like these, early hot rodding came to be closely identified with Ford. Once this had begun to happen, the innate conservatism of hot rodders—who would carefully adhere to an unwritten code of what was proper in the process of expressing their individuality — took over and helped to solidify Ford's status as *the* hot rodder's vehicle.

The quintessential hot rod was—and still is—the 1932 Ford Model B, affectionately known as the Deuce. Although Model B sedans, coupés, and pickups all had their places, the most popular style was the roadster. (A sedan is a closed automobile with two or four doors, and front and rear seats. A coupé is a two-door sedan that has been shortened by eliminating some or all of the backseat area. A roadster is an open car with a single seat.)

One of the most famous Ford roadsters, and one of the most famous hot rods of all time, is Tom McMullen's 1932 Ford highboy, which was built in the late fifties. The car is significant because of its intrinsic excellence, because everything about it was done right, and because it embodies the essence of the classic Ford hot rod. All nonessential components—that is, all parts not contributing to speed or accelerative power—were removed, including the running boards, fenders, bumpers, ornaments, and handles. The car was raked: the rear raised and the front lowered. Aggressive-looking tires and cast magnesium wheels replaced the originals. The front suspension trailing arm was drilled for lightness and chromed. The car was painted a deep black to show off the quality of the bodywork, and simple pinstripes were added to define the major body lines. Flames lick out from behind the radiator and the extensively louvered hood. In other hot rods, the engine covers and other body panels might also be removed, sometimes to be replaced by custom-built lightweight components.

There was more behind these modifications than simple weight reduction and the improvement of aerodynamics. The actual weight of a chrome ornament is negligible, and the removal of certain items, such as fenders, can actually degrade aerodynamic performance (understanding of automotive aerodynamics was limited before the 1960s). What is really behind these changes is the cultivation of an image: the image of the single-minded, no-nonsense pursuit of speed.

The more radical techniques employed by hot rodders (and customizers) promoted this image even more powerfully. Chopping, for instance, lowers the roof by shortening the window posts; and channeling lowers the car body on its frame rails. Changes like this can improve performance by lowering the car's center of gravity and reducing its wind resistance, but at best the effects are minimal. The true reason for these changes is aesthetic effect. Especially in the case of chopping, the effect produced is mean-eyed and sinister—just the ticket to set a rodder's heart on fire.

Rodders also made any number of modifications to the mechanical components of their cars, often beginning by blue-printing the engine: taking it apart, cleaning, polishing, and balancing its parts, and lovingly reassembling it precisely according to specifications. Carburetors, intake and exhaust manifolds, cylinder heads, pistons, camshafts, valves, flywheels—any or all of these could be changed to increase the stock engine's power and torque. The hot rodder could replace the engine completely, with a later version of the original (in which case the work would be relatively easy) or with an entirely different engine from a different make. The hot rodder could and probably would make changes to the electrical, exhaust, suspension, fuel, cooling, steering, brake, and drive train systems. High-performance wheels and tires would certainly be added. In general, the hot rodder's art was the art of nuts and bolts: if a part could be unscrewed, it was, to be cleaned, polished, balanced, chromed, replaced, or thrown away.

As with any such phenomenon, the art developed and evolved. During the forties, the modifications to hot rods used for dry lake racing became so extreme that many cars were no longer street-legal; the lakesters and belly tankers lost all resemblance to the classic roadster.

Where did the hot rodders come from? Why did they develop in the thirties the way they did, and why did they flourish in the late forties and fifties? The phenomenon was clearly inevitable, in view of the development of the automobile during the twenties and thirties as a significant factor in American life—in view, that is, of the developing American love affair with the car. The automobile became essential as a mode of transportation, but more than that, it became an extension of the owner's personality.

There were other factors at work, too. Teen culture, that hotbed of energy, with its own music, dancing, movies, clothing, and slang, was burgeoning during the thirties and forties. The car provided the perfect outlet for adolescent urges, both sexual and aggressive. It provided a means for expressing rebellion. A chance to show off. An arena for competition. A way to attract a girl and a place to have her once you got her. ("Nice car, nice girl.") An opportunity to be away from parents and to be together with one's friends. A sense of belonging to a special group with its own rites, rituals, cult objects, heroes, codes, proprieties, and language. Working on a car was the perfect pastime for the typical teenager who had lots of time, little money, and a fetish about appearance.

Hot rodding went beyond teen culture, however. In the earliest days of the automobile, professional auto racing tended to be a rich man's pastime—who else could even afford to own a motor-driven vehicle? As it became possible in the twenties and thirties for almost anybody to own a car, it became possible for almost anybody to modify that car, and, as the number of automobiles increased, so did the number of mechanics, professional and amateur. Engineering and mechanical knowledge about cars and engines became as much a part of the general culture as knowledge about hunting, fishing, sewing, or cooking, to be passed over the fence from one backyard to another.

The war was important too. Countless young men streamed through car-crazy and car-knowledgeable southern California on route to the Pacific; many came back with superb training in aircraft maintenance, and they proceeded to apply those high standards to their cars. In southern California, perpetually good weather, proximity to the dry lakes, and the finest roads in the United States encouraged an explosion of hot rodding and customizing.

It would be a mistake, however, to focus entirely on external factors. When it comes down to it, the right way to look at hot rodding and customizing is from the point of view of the object itself. The car sits there just begging to be changed and improved. Drop the suspension a little here; raise it there. Bolt on a new pair of heads; polish the intake ports. Remove the fenders; paint it all the deepest possible black. Chrome the valve covers and the radius rods. With each modification, the object takes on a new form and becomes a new expression of the possibilities latent in its original form.

CUSTOMS:
WILD OR MILD

In the early forties, the hot rod phenomenon gave birth to something a little different—the street machine. Street machines, which flourished only after World War II, combined the rodder's traditional interest in speed and performance with a new interest in late- and current-model cars. The new interest developed partly because the supply of vintage roadster parts and bodies was steadily dwindling, and partly because Detroit, especially Ford, was beginning to make new cars that appealed strongly to the rodder's passion for speed and image.

A good street machine was "clean and mean": its modified engine and drive train followed the lead of the hot rodder, but its body followed the lead of the customizer, who was also beginning to blossom about the same time. The classic early street machine was the '40 Ford or '40 Mercury with a flathead V-8 loaded with every possible high-performance bolt-on. The boundary between street machines and customs has always been hard to define, and many street machines can be considered customs. Essentially, the street machine is designed to go fast; the custom is designed to look good. In the loose parlance of the car crowd, almost anything can be called a street machine, even a "sleeper," with its totally stock body, as long as it is street-legal and fast. In the fifties, the ubiquitous car clubs contained them by the thousands.

Built "low and slow" was the byword of the car nuts at opposite ends of the spectrum, from the hot rodders to the street rodders. To be sure, they all had the same roots; they were all fixated on the motor vehicle as a means for self-expression. But the classic customizer was different because in his purest form he was *only* interested in self-expression, disavowing the hot rodder's and street rodder's interest in speed and engineering for speed. The classic custom car is the lead sled, a car too loaded down with the materials of the customizer's art for racing, but just right for showing and cruising.

Like the street rodder, the customizer distinguished himself from the classic hot rodder by his interest in a wide variety of late-model

Opposite: Chevrolet Bel Air convertible with pinstriping

Two '36 Ford five-window coupés, one mild and one wild, customized in the late thirties and early forties

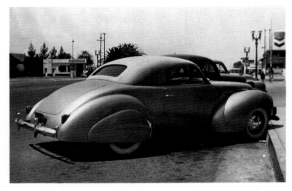

The Coachcraft shop in Hollywood customized James Wong Howe's '40 Ford coupé

Jimmie Summers customized this '40 Mercury convertible club coupé

and new cars. The car that most helped to create the split between hot rods on one hand, and customs and street rods on the other, was the '36 Ford. For several years, it was really only this car—in its original form and in later versions under the Ford and Mercury names—that aroused the interest of the vast majority of customizers. Early Chevys and Plymouths were too staid, too dowdy, simply not good-looking enough. As with the hot rod phenomenon, customizing was essentially a business of Fords and Mercurys through the end of the forties.

The two '36 Ford coupés pictured here beautifully represent the beginnings of the custom era. One is fairly close to stock, with a subtly chopped top, narrowed grille, solid hood sides, no running boards, and a meticulous maroon and silver paint job. The other car, customized by Howard Fall about 1940, is more radical. It too has a chopped top and its running boards have been removed, but the body has been channeled, the fenders raised, and an entirely new front end created, using sheet metal from a '37 Ford.

A '40 Ford coupé, owned by the Warner Brothers cinematographer James Wong Howe, and the '40 Mercury convertible pictured are perhaps even more beautiful. The body of the Ford was sectioned, a new canvas-covered top fabricated, a custom grille and small Packard taillights added. The Mercury body is stock, but it was channeled, its fenders were raised, running boards removed, and its original, very pretty grille replaced by a new, equally pretty grille modeled to resemble a '39 Buick's. The fenders were raised to allow for wheel clearance, otherwise a problem with cars lowered too far. It is an exceptionally smooth and clean car.

The incredible channeled '38 Ford convertible four-door sedan incorporated raised front fenders and a sectioned '40 Ford hood that was matched to the '40 front fenders. The radio antenna was "tunneled" (recessed), and the door handles were removed. Valley Custom added the popular Carson/Hauser convertible top, and the owner's mother hand-tooled the leather seats.

To be sure, not every early street machine or custom was a Ford or Mercury. Neil Emory's mildly customized '37 Dodge convertible coupé shows how subtle changes could improve a Chrysler product. It has a chopped windshield, a custom-made Carson convertible top, and Studebaker teardrop taillights that match the rear fender contours.

After World War II, the interest in late-model cars continued to grow, and with increasing prosperity the trend of customizing new showroom cars began. The appearance of cars from General Motors improved—even Chevrolets were becoming longer, lower, and wider, with swept-back windshields, sloping roof lines, and fenders that faded away in a sweeping line back along the doors, sometimes clear to the rear fender. These fadeaways were often defined by a strip of chrome; as design conventions changed and the separate fender disappeared entirely, the fadeaway strip often remained.

Gene Winfield's chopped '46 Ford convertible with '46 Olds grille and a Carson-style padded roof is a good example of a hot street machine. Built in 1949 and rebuilt in 1950, the car was powered by a loaded flathead, and has dual cowl spotlights—standard equipment on any street rod or custom.

As time went on, Detroit styling evolved from the heavy-fendered, bulbous look of the late forties and early fifties, to the lighter, airier, more stylized look of the mid-fifties. Window posts were thinner, there was lots of glass, wraparound windshields, and "hardtop convertibles"—that is, coupés and sedans with no central pillars and no window frames in the doors. Fenders and running boards were out; tailfins, fancy chrome strips, and modern two-tone color combinations such as turquoise and white were in. Headlights and taillights became integral parts of the car's overall styling, instead of standard components bolted on at the factory.

Customizers developed their own repertory of tricks. Customs, especially those of the late forties and early fifties, were often called "lead sleds" because the body was filled in and smoothed with lead filler in order to create uninterrupted lines and surfaces. Almost from the beginning, there were two kinds of customs: the mild and the wild. A mild custom would avoid the more radical kinds of modifications and concentrate on a multitude of smaller modification details: rounded edges, filled seams, frenched headlights and taillights, tunneled antennas, and pinstriping. (Frenching involves removing the chrome trim ring and recessing a light into the body without leaving a visible seam. A wild custom, like Howard Fall's modified '36 Ford coupé, would have radical modifications that involved major changes in bodywork: chopping, channeling, sectioning, radiusing the wheel wells, and fabricating entirely new components such as grilles or even fenders. (While chopping lowers the roof and channeling lowers the whole body over the chassis, sectioning entails the surgical removal of a horizontal band of sheet metal along the vehicle's perimeter, through fenders, doors, and other panels. To radius means to change the contours of the wheel cutout in a fender to make it conform to the circular shape of the wheel.) Some customizers seemed to enjoy using radical techniques to produce subtle changes in shape and proportion that only true *aficionados* could recognize.

The classic era of customs spanned the period from the early fifties to the early sixties. The fifties—the Fabulous Fifties, as they were sometimes called—showed rapid growth in the popularity of hot rodding and customizing. By the early part of the decade, what had been largely a regional southern Californian phenomenon had gone nationwide.

During this period, customizing retained many of the elements from the prewar era, while adding several new developments that contributed to sleeker overall appearances. The basic aesthetic was loud, fast, and colorful, and reflected an increasing concern for beauty—attention to proportion, surface, and the combination of components from various vehicles into an aesthetically unified product. Cars were often styled with a specific concept or theme in mind, and were given names like pieces of sculpture: "Miss Elegance," "Ala Kart," "Le Perle," "Predicta," "Fabula," and (perhaps carrying the bogus Latin theme a little far) "Forcasta."

The fetishistic attention to detail intensified. Customizers used paint to give their cars a personal, individual touch, to mask imperfections in bodywork by distracting the eye, and to accent the best features. The use of pearlescence, metalflake, and wide experimentation with paints led Joe Bailon to the invention of Candy Apple Red. George Barris, with whom Bailon and many other metal shapers and painters worked, developed a whole line of "Kandy Kolors"—blues, greens, oranges, purples, even

Valley Custom built this '38 Ford convertible sedan, which has a body channeled over the frame, a Carsen/Hauser custom top, and a hand-tooled leather interior

Neil Emory customized this '37 Dodge convertible coupé

Gene Winfield built this '46 Ford convertible for Al Serpa in 1949 and rebuilt it in 1950

George Barris and his customized '29 Ford pick-up "Ala Kart"

Bob McNulty's yellow pearl and black '57 Corvette with a Ferrari grille

George Barris painted Toby Hallike's '56 Buick in Kandy Cherry Burgundy, with reversed-tip airbrushed scallops, and pinstriping by Von Dutch

whites. These deep finishes were achieved by applying a base coat, usually with powdered fish scales, crushed simulated pearls, or metalflake, followed by as many as forty to fifty coats of lightly tinted, translucent lacquers that created the illusion of looking into the color through a lustrous surface. A wide array of conventional colors also became popular; purple was very important. These finishes were often completed with flames, pinstripes, or scallops. The whole enterprise became so sophisticated and specialized that even pinstripers became famous. Von Dutch and Tommy the Greek were specialists among pinstripers: Von Dutch was the abstractionist; Tommy the Greek the masterful straight liner.

Customizers found their inspiration anywhere; they could equally admire the classic elegant styling of Italian sports cars, and the futuristic styling of the dream cars that General Motors in particular sent around the country in its traveling car shows called "Motorama." A lovely Ferrari-grilled '57 Corvette by Bob McNulty, painted by George Barris in yellow pearl and black with white pinstriping, showed the subtlety with which customizers could handle the European influence. If the customizers saw something they liked, they would use it—a particular way to employ a body crease, a slight inward cant of the fender, a new grille texture.

Mild custom modifications developed in great variety during the fifties. Frenching and filling gained in popularity. Grilles were exchanged, or they were modified by removing horizontal or vertical bars, or by painting them flat black. Sharp edges were rounded off. In a technique known as shaving, chrome parts like hood ornaments, emblems, and door handles would be removed, and the bumps, ridges, or holes where they had been attached would be filled and smoothed. Decking was the same technique applied to the trunk lid. Door and trunk handles were replaced by electric solenoids activated by buttons and switches hidden under fenders, hence the phenomenon of the cool young man casually strolling up to his car and kicking the rocker panel to open the door.

Wheel cover fads abounded, from Olds Fiesta covers to small Ford hubcaps mounted on wheels painted in colors contrasting with the car's to plain spun aluminum discs. Redoing interiors was big. Upholstery had to be tuck-and-roll, pleated or piped, preferably Naugahyde, which was considered by customizers to be a substantial advance over leather. Dual sunken antennas were used at times, as were louvered hoods and scoops. Scoops on hot rods were often functional, allowing extra air into the engine or to the brakes, but scoops on lead sleds were just decorative.

The early fifties cars pictured here illustrate a vast array of techniques. The 1949–51 Ford coupés were very popular cars for customizing, not only because of their fundamentally clean lines, but because their straight sides made them easy to section. Ron Dunn's '50 Ford coupé, customized by Neil Emory and Clayton Jenson of Valley Custom, can be compared with a stock version of the car. With its frenched headlights, squared-off rear fenders and taillights, simplified grille, and radiused wheel wells, not to mention its radically altered yet balanced proportions, the car was described by *Hot Rod Magazine* as "a major attraction" on the 1952 custom car show circuit. Another '50 Ford coupé, owned by Jere Ehrich and customized by Joe Bailon, incorporated elements popular in the late fifties: two-tone side trim, here from a De Soto, and tail fins, these modeled after a '57 Ford Fairlane.

Tuck-and-roll upholstery on a Barns brothers' "Kandy Green" '58 Chevrolet Impala convertible

The Studebaker Starlight coupé was an unusual model for customizers to work on. Valley Custom built this mild job, adding a custom grille and rounded wheel cutouts

Neil Emory and Clayton Jensen customized Ron Dunn's '50 Ford coupé, which has been sectioned to lower the silhouette of the car without reducing ground clearance. It is pictured next to a stock model of the '50 Ford coupé

Left: Joe Bailon's '50 "Pacific Blue" Mercury club coupé. Right: The Barris yard in Lynwood, California, in 1957. Jerry Seaton's '55 Bel Air coupé (center) was painted in White Pearl with Kandy Cherry Red scallops

Left: The Barris brothers customized this channeled '58 Chevrolet Impala and painted it Kandy Green with an outline pinstripe. Right: The Barris brothers painted this chopped and channeled '56 Chevrolet sedan in purples, blues, burgundies, and rusts. It has side trim from a Dodge and a rear window from a '50 Mercury

Gene Winfield built the '56 Mercury "Jade Idol" in 1959 for LeRoy Kemmerer. It was found and rebuilt by Jerry Rehm, in 1980, and is now on display at Harrah's Automobile Collection in Reno, Nevada

The Barris brothers' chopped and channeled '50 Chevy hardtop showed what could be done with the sleek postwar offerings from General Motors. The car was shaved and decked, and its rear fenders were extended to enclose the imposing Continental spare tire kit. Valley Custom's '50 Olds 88 Holiday started with the same General Motors body and removed a four-inch section, a difficult and exacting job that produced excellent results. The body was dechromed, handles removed, air scoop added to squared-off rear fenders, and headlights and grille shell frenched. Painted in a color called "Orchid Flame," the car was named "The Polynesian," and was one of the most famous California customs in the 1950s.

Of all the early fifties cars, the '49 to '51 Mercurys were most coveted by the customizers. In its own way, the Merc was as important to the car culture as was the '32 Ford roadster. The classic modification to the Merc involved chopping the top and channeling the body, as in Joe Bailon's "Pacific Blue" '50 Merc club coupé, which had multitubular bumpers, frenched headlights, De Soto grille, extended taillights, Olds Fiesta hubcaps, white pinstriping, and special upholstery with one-inch horizontal pleats and chrome embellishments. Gene Winfield's '50 Merc with two-tone paint job is a classic. It was built in 1951 as a mild custom, then chopped in October 1953. Powered by a loaded flathead, this street machine was clocked on the dry lakes at 101.96 miles per hour. With its '51 Merc rear fenders holding '54 Merc taillights, the car is the embodiment of the fifties customizer's dreams: low-slung, sleek, and sinister.

Although General Motors had its moments, Fords and Mercurys held the day in the custom world until 1955. The styling of both the '55 and the '57 Chevy is a classic Detroit example of simplicity, lightness, and balance. Chevrolet's introduction of the advanced lightweight "small block" V-8 in 1955 and the introduction of a larger, fuel-injected version in 1957 did a lot to change the make's image of staidness and dowdiness. (Fuel injection is a more sophisticated and precise alternative to conventional carburetion. In the '57 Chevy, the device was extremely complicated and expensive, and very few were actually produced and sold, but the image-building impact was great.)

The '55 Chevy became an extremely desirable automobile, and was popular with the customizers. Three mild and one fairly wild Chevrolets from the era are pictured: a '55 Bel Air coupé by George and Sam Barris; a chopped, iridescent purple, blue, burgundy, and rust two-door '56 sedan; a channeled and extended-fin '57 Bel Air convertible with '59 Cadillac Eldorado taillights, and a Kandy Green '58 Impala. The Barris pearl white '55 Chevy with Kandy Cherry scallops outlined in yellow had "coordinated design" elements: double side moldings following the dip in the door line, and matching exterior and interior colors. Both the metallic "Sky Blue" '57 and the Kandy Green '58 Impala used the technique of "outline pinstriping": applying a continuous heavy stripe to bring out the body's major design elements. Speaking about cars like the '55 Chevy in the December 1955 issue, the editors of *Car Craft* noted that Detroit styling had become "so clean in pure design that only minimum modifications are deemed necessary to make the cars true customs."

The Corvette became the classic street machine, though it had appeared in 1953 as a rather tame little two-seater with a gutless six-

This '57 Chevrolet Bel Air convertible has frenched rear fenders and extended tail fins, and was painted in Sky Blue Metallic with pinstriping by Dean Jeffries at the Barris brothers' shop

 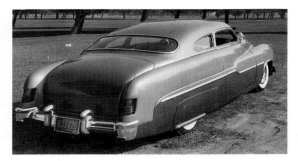

Left: Joe Bailon customized Jere Ehrich's '50 Ford coupé, adding a custom grille, side trim, and high tail fins that were popular in the mid to late fifties. Right: Gene Winfield built his '50 Mercury as a mild custom in 1951, and chopped the top in 1953

Left: George Barris's chopped and channeled '50 Chevy hardtop has extended rear fenders and a "Continental" spare. Right: Sam Barris mildly customized his wife's '55 Ford convertible, adding a custom grille and non-Ford trim that accented the two-tone paint

The "Polynesian," a '50 Oldsmobile 88 Holiday, with sectioning in progress (top) at Valley Custom in Burbank, and then shown after completion (bottom)

cylinder engine and two-speed automatic transmission. By 1958, it had blossomed into the most fearsome thing on the road. With its light V-8 and strong four-speed, even a 'Vette straight off the showroom floor was considered a fine street machine. The orange-red George Barris '60 'Vette with lime and black flames, and red, yellow, and black pinstriping was basically unmodified except for the paint job.

These fifties cars represented mild or, at most, moderately wild customizing. "Jade Idol," created by Gene Winfield for the custom car show circuit in 1959, is an unusually fine example of wild customizing taken to the extreme. Its '56 Mercury body was sectioned four inches, its rear fenders taken from a '59 Chrysler, and an entirely new canted vertical headlight assembly fabricated. It has swiveling seats, tuck-and-roll upholstery, and a television in the middle of the dashboard.

"Jade Idol" exemplifies the interest in styling futuristic, even surrealistic vehicles, which flourished in the late fifties and early sixties. Other preeminent practitioners of this art were Ed "Big Daddy" Roth, Darryl Starbird, and George Barris, all of whom had cars in custom shows throughout the country. Roth started out as a pinstriper; Starbird, famous for a series of cars with crisp lines and bubble tops, began as a draftsman for the Boeing Aircraft Company. These cars were the customizers' versions of the "Detroit idea," and were created primarily for the custom car show circuit, which played an important part in spreading the hot rod and custom phenomena across the country.

During this period, car customizing evolved from a backyard enterprise into an increasingly commercial business. Some of the most talented and committed customizers opened shops where they were able to support their own car habits by customizing other people's vehicles. It was the era of specialization in engineering, bodywork, painting, or interiors. For an entrepreneurial type, there were any number of ways to cash in on the hot rod and custom craze: one could open up a shop, promote shows, manufacture parts, or get into publishing or racing.

The automobile industry was booming. The country was optimistic about Detroit's increasingly flamboyant and futuristic styling. Aircraft design was expressed in such features as fins and wraparound windshields. Even advertising proclaimed the future; in 1957, the sensationally restyled and befinned Chrysler Corporation line was announced under the slogan, "Suddenly it's 1960."

Fierce competition among Ford, General Motors, and Chrysler led to frequent and drastic restyling. In an unprecedented step, the whole line of 1958 GM cars, which had undergone radical restyling from 1957, was replaced by cars with entirely new bodies for 1959.

All this activity provided fertile ground for the imaginations of hot rodders and customizers around the country. For some, cars were a hobby; for many others, they became an all-consuming passion. Projects could take years to complete, and many, of course, never were.

An incredible proliferation of hot rod and custom car magazines began during the fifties. Across the country, backyard customizers, and potential backyard customizers, were reading such magazines as *Hot Rod, Car Craft, Rod & Custom, Popular Hot Rodding, Street Rodder,* or the other publications that came and went over the years to find inspiration and

learn techniques. Much of what was shown in the magazines could be done with little skill and less money: just bolt one grille off and bolt another on.

The postwar baby boom had produced, by the mid-fifties, a disproportionately large number of teenagers in the population. Accustomed to economic prosperity and the social strength of their numbers, they sought their sense of individual and group identity in untraditional ways. Car clubs sprang up on every high school campus around the country. Members drove whatever street machine or pseudo street machine they could afford, usually an older car, mildly customized, often painted in flat gray primer. Such names as "The Drifters" and "The Dominators" were emblazoned on jackets, shirts, overalls, and on plaques floating in rear windows amid seas of tuck-and-roll. Drive-in restaurants were meeting places, drive-in movie theaters were for experiments in backseat sex, and main streets were for cruising.

As they grew older, graduated from high school, and found regular jobs, these young males would often put their extra time and money into better, more ambitious customizing projects. As they grew older, especially if they had gone off to college and entered a profession, these individuals tended to graduate into sports cars—Corvettes, naturally, but also Porsches, Alfa Romeos, Ferraris, and Lamborghinis.

Hollywood got into the act. On screen, from James Dean's 1955 classic *Rebel Without a Cause* to Mamie Van Doren's less memorable 1958 film *High School Confidential*, custom cars began to be an integral part of the picture. Off screen, virtually every star from Jayne Mansfield to Liberace was parading around town in a George Barris original.

As America entered the sixties, the custom car and hot rod phenomena seemed to get lost, as strong reactions developed against typical Detroit products and Detroit conventions. Cars had become steadily bigger, more luxurious, and more stylized since the end of the war. Design had become more sophisticated. Custom cars had in fact helped create this trend. Then came the Volkswagen, which was small, spartan, styleless, and successful. After the VW came Detroit's compact reactions to it: the Corvair and a host of little Pontiacs, Oldsmobiles, and Buicks from General Motors; the Falcon and Comet from Ford; and the Valiant and Lancer from Chrysler.

Then came vans—first VWs, then the domestic products. Motorcycles, especially the small ones from Japan, started becoming popular. Then came mid-sized cars, and the hopped-up mid-sized cars sometimes called "pony cars." Later still came the invasion of Toyotas, Datsuns, and Hondas.

In short, the whole automotive environment became more complicated, competitive, and international, while the hot rod and custom phenomena became highly commercialized, lost freshness and direction, as well as a large portion of their clientele, especially the affluent and classier parts. Some drifted off into the counter-culture; some into vans; some into motorcycles; and many preserved their automotive identities by indulging in fast, expensive sports cars. For some who had been mesmerized by the custom craze, or who would have been in earlier years, such cars as the original Corvette Sting Ray of 1963 was perfect just as it was from the factory. It was the cleanest, crispest thing to come out of Detroit in forty years. With a car like that sitting on the showroom floor, who needed a hot rod or a custom? In the prescient words of the December 1955 *Car Craft* story: "If the new cars get much nicer, there won't be anything left for us to customize."

Opposite: Detail of Kandy flaking

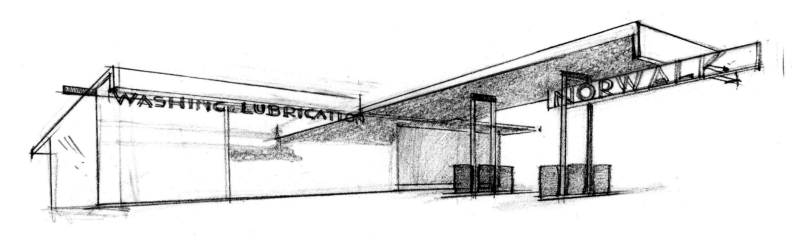

Richard Neutra. Norwalk Service Station, Bakersfield, California. 1947. Pencil sketch on paper.
Richard J. Neutra Archive, University Research Library, U.C.L.A.

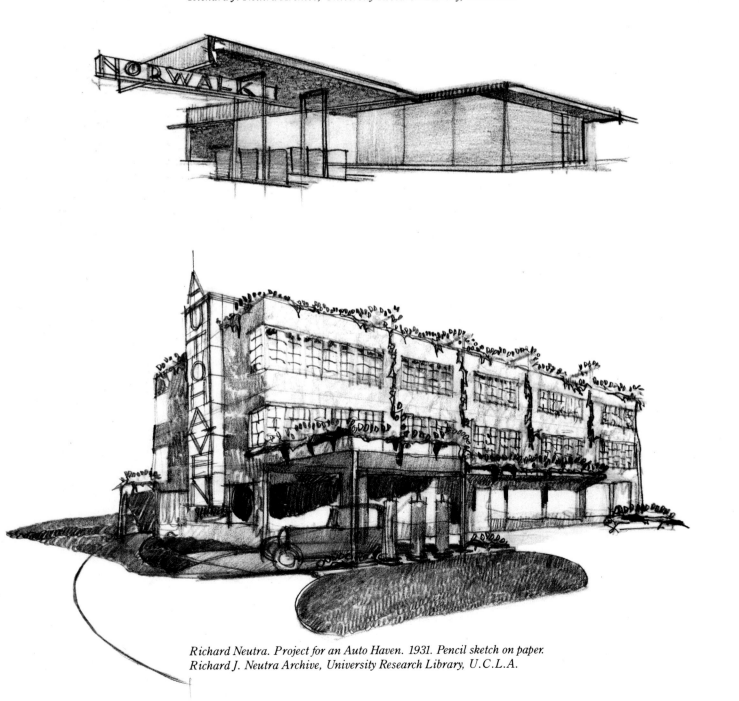

Richard Neutra. Project for an Auto Haven. 1931. Pencil sketch on paper.
Richard J. Neutra Archive, University Research Library, U.C.L.A.

THE DRIVE-IN CULTURE

Lloyd Wright. Yucca + Vine Market, Hollywood. 1928. View from Yucca Street. Flower shop on left, open market for meat, produce, and groceries in back, sun curtains on far right

T he impact of the automobile on American culture is particularly evident in the buildings that were developed to meet the changing needs of a motorized society: gas stations, motels, parking garages, car washes, drive-in restaurants, drive-in movie theaters, and shopping centers. The exact origins of these vernacular building types remain largely undocumented, though many evolved as drive-in adaptations of buildings that existed before the automobile was made available to the mass public. Beginning in the 1920s, many well-known architects such as Richard Neutra and Lloyd Wright, Frank Lloyd Wright's son, began experimenting with proposals for these then novel automotive structures, which were designed to accommodate both the individual and his automobile. Although many of these projects were never built, their concepts bear strong relationships to the vernacular drive-in and "drive-thru" buildings that now line urban and suburban roadways.

Richard Neutra, architect and planner of the motorized Rush City Reformed, explored the impact of the car on a new class of structures; he designed car showrooms, gas stations, drive-in markets, and other experimental drive-in buildings while residing in Los Angeles, the epitome of an automobile-infatuated society, even in this early period. For Neutra, the car symbolized modernity; automotive design paralleled his own architectural ideals of modernism, precision, and efficiency. In photographs of the buildings he designed, he often used automobiles to highlight the conceptual design correlation between the structure and the car.

Although few of Neutra's car-related structures were actually built, their design concepts influenced the subsequent evolution of vernacular building types. Neutra's Norwalk Service Station, built in 1947 in Bakersfield, California, incor-

porates pitched roof slabs and glass in the International Style to create an archetypal modernist gas station. His 1931 study for an Auto Haven explores the idea of combining a motor-hotel with a service station and garage, complete with large-scale signage. Neutra's 1929 project for the Dixie Drive-In Market was heralded as a new architectural form, though Lloyd Wright's Yucca + Vine Market had actually been built a year earlier in Los Angeles. Neutra's integration of parking facilities, motorized access, and signage scaled to the motorist's viewpoint were seminal developments in the evolution of drive-in structures. In the early 1960s, Neutra designed the world's first drive-in church in Garden Grove, California. Based on the idea of a drive-in movie theater, the Garden Grove Community Church broadcast sermons over hi-fi speakers to a congregation seated outside in its cars—"pews from Detroit"— in the church parking area.

In 1924, Frank Lloyd Wright and Richard Neutra collaborated on the design of an automobile observatory for Sugarloaf Mountain, in Maryland. Although the project was never executed, it represented a visionary treatment of auto access and streamlined form. Lloyd Wright also created city plans and building designs shaped by the needs of a motorized society. His 1928 Yucca + Vine Market in Los Angeles, and a 1965 project for the First Christian Church of Conejo Valley, California, incorporated ideas similar to those proposed in the Dixie Drive-In Market and the Church at Garden Grove. Lloyd Wright's First Christian Church project integrates a spiral parking structure that allows access to each of the church's three levels, rather than orienting the building toward a single, ground-level parking lot.

By 1930, the automobile's impact on human activities such as shopping and church-going was growing across the

201

1. Richard Neutra. Garden Grove Community Church, California. 1962. 2. Lloyd Wright. Rendering of project for First Christian Church of Conejo Valley. 1965. Eric Lloyd Wright, Los Angeles. 3. Gilmore Gas Station, corner of Wilshire and La Brea, Los Angeles. c. 1920. 4. Atlantic Richfield Service Station. c. 1932. 5. Armét and Davis. Wich Stand Drive-In, Los Angeles. 1958

country. The first drive-in movie theater, for example, made its appearance in Camden, New Jersey, in 1933. Most drive-in facilities were built as commercial structures rather than as exercises in experimental design. The earliest service stations were usually adapted to existing structures, a technique that resulted in strange hybrids of form and function. By the thirties, new service stations were built, and many were designed in simplified Art Deco or streamlined modern style. In the fifties, Neutra's Norwalk Service Station emerged as a typological form that persists to the present day.

Drive-in restaurants and diners first emerged in the thirties, and became important cultural products of a motorized society. Several of these businesses evolved into fast-food chains that now dot the American landscape. The coffee shop as a new building type developed in the fifties in southern California, inspired in

part by the dynamic linear forms and extensive use of glass and metal common to automotive styling of the period. When illuminated at night, fifties eateries such as the Wich Stand in Los Angeles beckoned to the passing motorist.

As commercial architecture and signage directed at the passing motorist began to visually transform the American roadside, the country witnessed the rise of "the strip." In the western sections of Los Angeles in the twenties, professional planners had laid out such commercial road strips as Pico and Lincoln boulevards over transportation axes that remained from earlier railroad lines. In general, however, the strips developed arbitrarily along urban and suburban roadways from the thirties through the fifties, inexorably linked to the growing use of the automobile. Along these strips, which exist today, commercial enterprises vie for visibility using large-scale signs,

directional motifs, and imagistic symbolic forms.

Early roadside architecture of the commercial strip epitomized popular culture of the mid-twentieth century, although these vernacular forms were later viewed with increasing disfavor by architects, planners, and the general public. In recent years, the opinion that road architecture blights the American landscape has been questioned. The architect Robert Venturi has been instrumental in encouraging a shift of taste from general condemnation to appreciation of the vitality of the commercial strip. In his highway-oriented showrooms for the Best Company and the Basco Corporation, he successfully employed design elements like massive signage and brightly colored decorative patterning, which are easily perceived by and attractive to the motorist. Venturi's more recent explorations of the urbanscape include "Signs of Life:

Symbols of the American City," a 1981 exhibition at the Renwick Gallery in Washington, D.C., organized by his Philadelphia architectural firm. The collagelike celebration of the icons of the American roadside landscape, from the glittering neon lights and signs of Las Vegas to golden arches and gas station emblems, was sponsored in part by a major advertising company.

American fifties drive-in culture and the automobile environment inspired Archigram, a British group of planners and architects, to create visionary drive-in schemes in the mid-sixties. Expanding upon Le Corbusier's dictum that the house was a machine for living, Archigram's Living Pod developed out of the idea that the car was a completely self-reliant mobile environment, a satellite unto itself. Between 1964 and 1966 the project evolved into a larger proposal for drive-in housing by Michael Webb and David Greene. Related to the popular custom of setting up house in motorized campsites, the drive-in housing concept became the foundation of later Archigram schemes for entire instant mobile cities, not unlike Buckminster Fuller's Dymaxion experiments of the thirties. But whereas Fuller proposed a utopian, functionalist revolution in environmental design through a coherent program integrating vehicles and single-family houses, Archigram planners based their conception exclusively on the self-sufficient mobility of contemporary automobile culture.

Louis I. Kahn's 1952–53 Plan for Midtown, Philadelphia, exerted seminal conceptual influence on Archigram's programs. Kahn's rational studies of movement patterns and their implications led him to create new architectural forms by incorporating the functions of the street

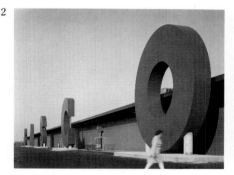

1. The Las Vegas Strip. 1978–79. 2. Robert Venturi. Basco Corporation, Philadelphia. 1976.
3. Installation view of "Signs of Life: Symbols in the American City." 1976. Exhibition at the Renwick Gallery, Washington, D.C.

into large circular parking towers meant to surround the city. Archigram's Michael Webb designed a "Sin Centre" complex between 1959 and 1962, a popular Times Square-type entertainment center, designed around a drive-in parking galleria system. The access to Sin Centre is dependent upon distribution of vehicular traffic as a feature that defines the principle layout and planning of the entire scheme.

The multilevel shopping/entertainment center and parking garage has developed as a common feature of the contemporary urbanscape. Characterized by drive-in access and parking facilities, this building type has succeeded in luring the motorist away from retail establishments situated on the street. In recent years, these contained and inwardly designed complexes have proliferated, contributing to the demise of the traditional roadside environment. Drive-in movies, restaurants, and churches have diminished in importance

as part of the cultural fabric and social experience, though drive-through bank windows, cleaners, and other service establishments of convenience are now more frequently patronized. The romance of the mid-century automotive environment has been undermined by the public's need to move quickly and economically from point to point. In fact, a certain nostalgia now pervades our comprehension of the roadside and its monuments, because much roadside architecture, the expressions of vernacular Americana, is rapidly vanishing. Contemporary photographers attempt to preserve visual records of drive-in and roadside culture, and architectural historians now consider the strip worthy of documentation and study. A campaign is presently under way to give landmark status to the earliest existing McDonald's hamburger stand, which is located in Downey, California.

—ELIZABETH A. T. SMITH

HENRY FORD'S BETTER IDEA

enry Ford's invention of the assembly line inspired a production system that catalyzed the explosion of American automotive production in the early part of the twentieth century. In the spring of 1913, Henry Ford and his managerial force devised the first moving assembly line for the production of small automotive parts for the Ford Model T. Over the next year, the system was developed to incorporate all aspects of car production, and by April 1914 it could be used to assemble a Model T every twenty-four seconds. The moving assembly line became an integral part of the mass-production process, which depended on the division of labor into specialized tasks, the use of standardized interchangeable parts, and mechanical preeminence in the workplace. As the economic advantages of the mass-production system began to assert themselves, other industrial production methods began to experience radical transformation.

Ford's endless-chain conveyor belt put an end to the practice of hand-pushing the vehicle from point to point on the assembly line, but production methods remained primitive in the early years: an outdoor ramp served to lower auto bodies onto the completed chassis. Nonetheless, by 1915, the Ford Motor Company could produce one thousand Model Ts in a single day at Highland Park in Detroit. Rising levels of productivity increased output and dramatically lowered the cost of the Model T, from an average price of $950 in 1908–9 to $360 in 1915–16. The assembly-line system, hailed as a revolutionary industrial improvement, inspired worldwide admiration of Henry Ford, whose decision to double his employees' wages and shorten the workday in 1913 was viewed as an extremely unconventional labor practice.

The ideas motivating Henry Ford's pursuit of rapid, efficient production of well-

Opposite: Assembly line at River Rouge plant, Michigan. 1928
Above: Stationary assembly line at Highland Park plant, Michigan. c. 1910–12

constructed, affordable automobiles also led him to commission the architect Albert Kahn to build the Ford Company factories at Highland Park in 1908 and at River Rouge in Dearborn, Michigan, in 1917. Kahn's industrial architecture was characterized by functionalism and precision, emphasizing technique and economics of factory design rather than external or decorative appearance. Kahn's industrial structures are acclaimed for the effective placement of utilities, aisles, ramps, and well-ventilated open spaces, which he combined with optimum fenestration and natural light sources to completely eradicate associations with sweatshop factories of the early industrial age.

In 1903, Kahn built the first American

reinforced concrete factory for the Packard Motor Car Company, and by 1938 the volume of his work comprised nineteen percent of all architect-designed industrial construction in the United States. Anticipating the self-conscious adaptation of the machine aesthetic to multipurpose building design characteristic of modern architecture in the 1920s and 1930s, Kahn had earlier recognized and applied effective mechanical principles in his architectural designs. For Kahn, form was a natural outgrowth of function. The design evolution of his Ford Motor Company buildings paralleled the growth and refinement of mass-production techniques; as the assembly line at Ford became increasingly sophisticated, so did the technical and organizational

1. Portrait of Henry Ford. c. 1915. 2. Moving assembly line at Highland Park plant, Michigan. c. 1914. 3. Assembly line outdoor body drop at Highland Park plant, Michigan. 1914

4. Elevated conveyor system at River Rouge plant, Michigan. 1924. 5. Ford Motor Company River Rouge plant, view from Dix Bridge. 1934. 6. Assembly line Ford Model A body drop at River Rouge plant, Michigan. 1931. 7. Employees outside Ford Motor Company, Highland Park, Michigan, January 5, 1914

development of Kahn's industrial environments. Reinforced concrete as the major factory building material gave way to steel, and the requirements of space, flexibility, and expansion inherent in modern industrialism were met.

Kahn revamped the River Rouge plant, which had been originally constructed as a facility for wartime submarine production in 1917. It became the largest industrial plant in the world, composed of fourteen plant structures encompassing 1,096 acres. The manufacturing buildings covered more than 9,650,000 square feet. The new Ford Model A was introduced to the public in late 1927, and coincided with the beginnings of production at River Rouge in 1928. Raised conveyer belts carried automobile bodies smoothly and

precisely through specially designed directional systems onto the chassis—a vast improvement over the laborious manual outdoor ramp system in operation at the Highland Park factory. The assembly line made rapid advances in the 1930s: a body lift and turnover device at the end of the chassis line automated a previously manual portion of the system, and by 1931 all manual lifting was eliminated by power cranes which set auto bodies in place on the moving chassis. At this time, the Ford Motor Company ceased production of the Model A and replaced it with the new model Ford V-8, and the River Rouge plant was canonized in photography and painting as the epitome of American industrial might and precision.

—ELIZABETH A. T. SMITH

207

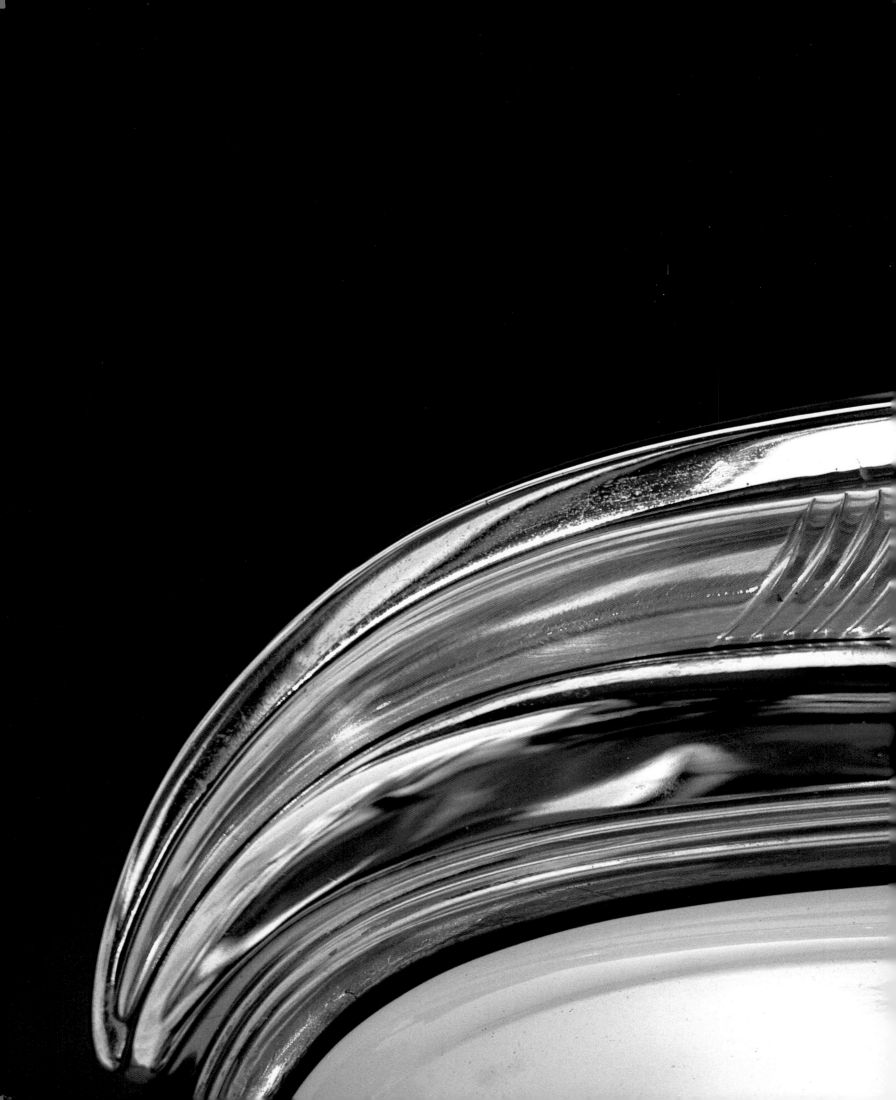

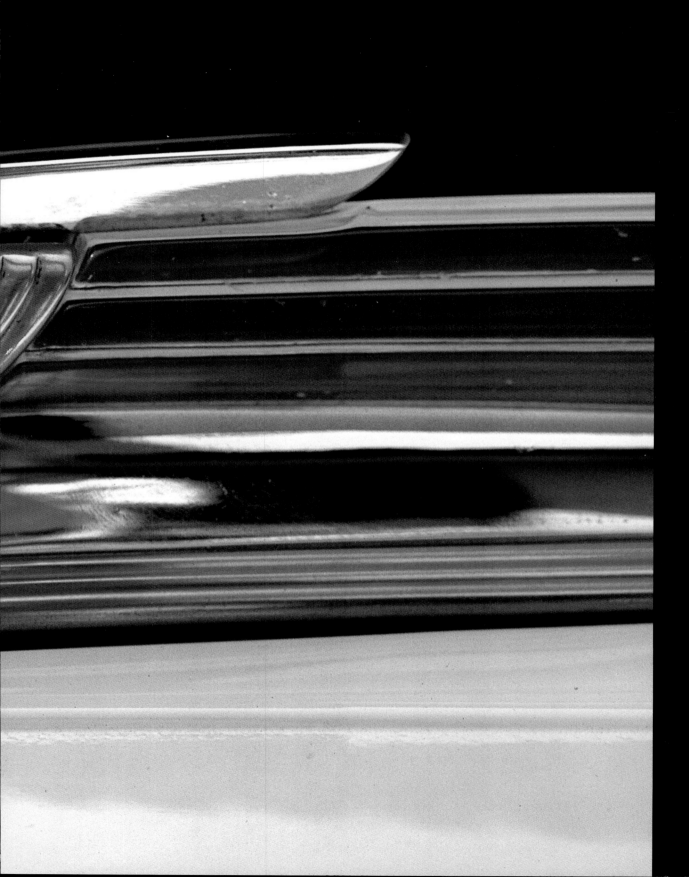

Detail of a 1939 *Packard Darrin Convertible Victoria,* Model 120

FROM CUSTOM COACHBUILDING TO MASS PRODUCTION

As soon as it was dark, they brought a horse around to the rear of the machine shop and hooked it up to the buggy that had been lowered from the second floor that afternoon. Pulling it quietly past the business district, they stopped at the horse and buggy barn on the west end of town, unhitched the horse, and left it for the night. The next morning, four men pushed the buggy out into the September sunshine, and waited while the young man in charge climbed onto the seat, checked some levers, and signaled for a push. No horse. As the helpers began to run, the rider moved a control. There was a dramatic explosion from the rear of the buggy, which continued forward to the pulsing beat of its hidden motor, moving about two hundred feet until brought to rest by a high curb. It was September 20, 1893, in Springfield, Massachusetts, and J. Frank Duryea, twenty-three-year-old toolmaker and machinist, had just driven the horseless carriage built following the plans developed by his older brother, Charles. As far as any of the men present knew, it was the first time in history that such a vehicle had moved under its own power.

Historians agree that it was not the first time that a gasoline-powered vehicle had operated successfully, but it was the pioneering effort of two young Americans who would continue to refine their idea and later make the first sale of a United States-built motorized vehicle.

The next major event in this historical drama was a driving contest sponsored by the *Chicago Times-Herald* newspaper. Originally scheduled for July 4, 1895, it was postponed twice and finally run on Thanksgiving Day in a snowstorm. Frank Duryea won in a car that traveled at an average speed of seven miles per hour. (It was doubtful whether a horse and buggy could have covered the distance at all under such difficult conditions.)

A race in May 1896, sponsored by *Cosmopolitan* magazine, included four Duryea "Motor Wagons," and netted Frank the $3,000 first prize; Charles came in second against formidable opposition from a German Benz. While staving off an assault by foreign manufacturers to dominate the American market, the Duryeas were achieving formalized motorcar production and sales. J. Frank Duryea then took two new cars to England, and, astonishingly, won the first London-to-Brighton race over the best English and

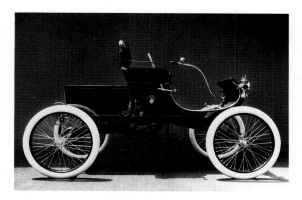

Above and opposite: Oldsmobile Curved Dash Runabout. *1902. Model R. Engine 1 cyl., pushrod, 4 h.p. Wood body, leather seats. Designer Ransom E. Olds. Manufacturer Olds Motor Works, Lansing, Michigan. Collection Joel Naive, San Diego, California.*

Continental cars. His margin of triumph over the second car to finish was a full hour.

At about the time that the Duryea brothers were developing their adapted buggy, at least four other United States inventors had built and run gasoline-powered, self-propelled vehicles, but the inventors knew nothing of each other's work. Steam and electric propulsion systems dating from the 1890s also had advocates, who built and demonstrated operable prototypes, but gas-powered cars were simpler and had greater range.

Elwood Haynes, a superintendent for the Indiana Natural Gas and Oil Company, drove a horse and buggy to supervise the company installations and supply facilities around Kokomo. Haynes was an engineer, and it occurred to him that he could cover more ground in less time if he motorized his buggy using one of the small marine gasoline engines manufactured by the Sintz Machinery Company of Grand Rapids, Michigan. He drew up plans and contracted the Apperson brothers to build a vehicle in their machine shop. He celebrated July 4, 1894, with his first trial run, and began to consider building duplicates on a custom basis.

The turn of the century was an era of incredible enterprise, and witnessed unprecedented progress in the development of communication systems and personal transportation. Samuel Morse had perfected the telegraph in 1844, and messages could be flashed across continents and oceans to be read by anyone with access to a newspaper. The telegraph provided the essential link that bridged the barrier of isolation, and inspired conquests of inquiry, education, and progressive development.

There remained, however, a problem with personal mobility. Seventy percent of the population still lived on farms in the rural areas and plains, although the great migration to the cities had begun. The purchase and maintenance of the prime mover—the noble horse—represented a capital investment that placed ownership in a necessary but minor luxury category.

The urban man either walked to work or took a trolley. If from the upper levels of professional society, he might live in the suburbs and commute to town by steam train. When the chain-driven safety bicycle first appeared, its appeal was so unanimous that it fostered a bicycle "craze." Hundreds of thousands of them were in use within a few years. Bicycle sales and repair shops sprang up in every city and town, focusing interest on skills related to bicycle maintenance and precision machinery. Bicycles were practical, affordable, and fun, and bicycle racing became a major sport.

With possibly three exceptions, all of the automobile pioneers in the United States came from humble origins. They were less inclined to speculate idly, and were able to perceive and pursue their goals with imagination and professional pride. Although individually different, they all shared an insatiable appetite for hard work, and were also able to collaborate in their efforts. To do an honest day's work, to be adaptable, and to profit from one's skill was the emancipated American democratic ideal.

Historian Richard Crabb clearly cites Eli Whitney's early nineteenth-century idea of machines designed to produce identical parts as the inspiration for the development of mass production. Five great men and a spellbinding organizer commanded Whitney's vision into reality at the beginning of the automobile era.

Henry Martyn Leland, through dynamic persistence bordering on fervor, wedded Whitney's theory to precision quality control in order to achieve production-part interchangeability. Born on a farm near Barton, Vermont, in 1843, Leland began his apprenticeship as a machinist at age sixteen and eventually worked his way up through the country's most prestigious machine and tool manufacturer, Brown & Sharpe, in Providence, Rhode Island. This company developed and produced the vernier calipers, hand micrometers, and precision gauges that permitted machining to tolerances of one-thousandth of an inch. In 1890, when Leland opened a Detroit machine shop in partnership with lumber magnate Robert C. Faulconer, Leland's son Wilfred gave up his studies in medicine to join the firm, and the pair became an insuperable team.

John and Horace Dodge were the sons of a Niles, Michigan, blacksmith, whose fortune was so meager that the boys went to school barefoot and did odd jobs to get through. In the early 1880s, their father moved the family to Port Huron, where he ran the Dodge Machine Shop. The young men learned the precision art of machining while working on marine engine repair. Eventually setting out on their own, the brothers worked in Detroit before moving across the river to Canada, where they set up a bicycle business. When they sold it, they netted enough cash and machinery to open the Dodge Brothers Machine Shop in Detroit in 1901. With their combined experience, they were able to engineer and produce nearly any kind of metal part or assembly. Their timing was perfect, though a stroke of fate brought real success to their door within a period of weeks.

Also born on a farm, Ransom Eli Olds worked in his father's machine shop in Lansing, Michigan, when he graduated from high school. They began manufacturing and selling a range of gasoline engines for farm and marine use, and eventually reached national distribution. When he was twenty, Olds built a steam-powered three-wheeler, and drove it regularly around the area. In 1897, he formed the Olds Motor Vehicle Company and built a pilot car; confident of the automobile's future, he found $500,000 in backing to build a brand new, self-contained factory in Detroit. The Olds Motor Works built several different cars to test the market. One of these was an economical light runabout that could be sold for about $650. On March 9, 1901, the factory burned down, but a timekeeper, James Brady, pushed the little runabout out of the burning building to safety. This curved-dash prototype was all that Olds had left, but with the help of friends in Lansing he set up a production assembly facility there. Forced to look elsewhere for component supplies, Olds contracted with Leland & Faulconer for an initial run of two thousand engines, and with the new Dodge Brothers Machine Shop for the companion transmissions. The Curved Dash Oldsmobile was a success from the start; 2,500 were produced in 1902, 4,000 in 1903, 5,508 in 1904, and 6,500 in 1905, when differences with his management about future product policy caused Olds to leave the company.

Henry Ford's ascent from humble beginnings to notoriety as the most celebrated individual in the history of the American automobile is both fact and legend. His home workshop-built quadricycle inspired such professional confidence in his abilities that he was named chief engineer of the Detroit Automobile Company in 1899. His first move was to build and drive a race car that beat Alexander Winton on its first time out. Excited

Ford Racer. *1902. Model Type 999. Engine 4 cyl., L-head, 80 h.p. Wood body, leather seat. Designer C.H. Wills. Manufacturer Henry Ford, Detroit. The Henry Ford Museum, Dearborn, Michigan*

stockholders then formed the Henry Ford Company, and a production car was partially developed before Ford left the Detroit Automobile Company. The directors approached Henry Leland for advice on liquidation, but he recommended that they proceed with what they had, and advised them to include the improved one-cylinder engine that Leland's engineers had developed for Olds. The new company was renamed Cadillac Automobile Company, and went into production of chassis and bodies, with Leland supplying engines, transmissions, and steering gear.

In the meantime, Ford built his "999" race car, which he named after the New York Central locomotive that set a world speed record of 112.5 miles per hour on May 10, 1893.

Henry Ford and Tom Cooper persuaded Barney Oldfield, a bicycle racer, to drive the monster, and Winton was beaten again. Alexander Malcomson, a coal merchant, had catalyzed the funding for the Ford Motor Company in 1903, and the twelve original stockholders included the Dodge brothers, who then supplied everything but the bodies and wheels. Ford Models A through N were increasingly successful, with the possible exception of the big, six-cylinder Model K.

No vehicle in history has made a more important contribution to cultural advancement via affordable mobility than the Model T, which went into production in 1909. The Model T was the product of one man's philosophy directing an extraordinary team of men who knew, from the start, that the car was absolutely right for the times and their purpose.

If Ford's single-minded approach was through one door, William C. Durant's concepts of power and productivity went through many doors that led to one office. In 1883, at age twenty-two, he and Josiah Dort started building and selling road carts. By 1895, the Durant-Dort Carriage Company had become the largest carriage and buggy manufacturer in the country. Durant's first move in the automobile business was to turn the failing Buick Motor Car Company into the leading car manufacturer in the United States by 1908. That same year, he organized General Motors as a holding company, and quickly absorbed Buick, Oakland (Pontiac), and Oldsmobile. Durant paid $4,500,000 in cash for Cadillac in 1909; his entrepreneurship was irresistible.

It was most fortunate that the automobile was born during the romantic period of art and design described as Art Nouveau. Its graceful, flowing rhythms, subtle colors, and high precision were handsomely echoed in the fine craftsmanship of carriage styles that had evolved over more than one hundred fifty years. The Curved Dash Olds was the most innovative reflection of this aesthetic; its scrolled footboard was pure artistic invention, and gave substance to the front end so it no longer resembled a carriage missing a horse. When the seating was increased to accommodate four passengers in an optional rear tonneau, it was romantically christened a phaeton, the name being derived from the Greek word *Phaethon,* which denotes Prometheus's sun-chasing chariot, *ergo,* an open vehicle for sunny days.

In 1905, American manufacturers moved the engine to the front of the car and established the firewall or "dash" behind it—the point where the chassis ended and the body began. When the gauges and controls mounted on the firewall were eventually moved rearward to a separate panel, the name "dashboard" persisted. The all-season popularity of automobile

Henry Ford and race car driver Barney Oldfield (seated) with the Ford "999" in 1902

Race car driver Ralph de Palma and Dorothy Lane in the 1912 Mercer 35 Raceabout. (The 1912 Mercer could be distinguished from the 1913 because it had six wheel bolts instead of twelve)

Cadillac Touring. *1912. Model Thirty. Engine 4 cyl., L-head, 48 h.p. Wood and steel body, leather seats. Designer Charles F. Kettering. Manufacturer Cadillac Motor Car Company, Detroit. Collection Thomas Cadillac, Los Angeles*

Below and opposite: Mercer Raceabout. *1913. Model Type 35-J. Engine 4 cyl., L-head, 58 h.p. Aluminum and wood body, leather seats. Designer Finley R. Porter. Manufacturer Mercer Automobile Company, Trenton, New Jersey. Collection William Evans, San Diego, California*

use encouraged the development of enclosed bodies that took styling cues from carriages, but compromised the carriage curved bottom sill to conform to flat automotive frames.

The determined drive to expand production and build products that could meet the accelerating demand for transportation characterized automobile history in the decades between 1910 and 1930. Competitive cost, inventive engineering, and visual enchantment became the tools in the war of mass production. Reliability was still a strong point in salesmanship, but body design was becoming a decisive factor.

As more motorists began to venture farther into the country, they encountered the widespread problem of poor roads. Turnpikes and toll roads were scarce, and many roads that were little more than wagon tracks became virtually impassable during wet weather. The developer of the Indianapolis Motor Speedway, Carl G. Fisher, proposed the development of the Lincoln Highway Association. Its objective was to build a coast-to-coast highway that would, by its example, stimulate improved road building throughout the country. The association was formally organized during the summer of 1913 in Detroit, and many of the first contributions came from automobile company executives who felt that improved roads would expand their markets. A route was laid out from New York to San Francisco, construction of segments began in 1914, and the highway was completed in 1925. In 1916, the United States government appropriated seventy-five million dollars for comprehensive road development. A second Federal Highway Act followed and provided that the federal government would share costs on an equal basis with the states to build a 175,000-mile network of improved roads.

Even as late as 1917, it was estimated that there were still thirty million horses and mules in the United States. The transition from horse and buggy to motorized vehicle was well under way, but a fundamental competition still existed, as evidenced by a 1911 Buick advertisement: their price of $485 was "about the cost of a good horse and buggy."

Ford's massive new factory in Highland Park, Michigan, opened on January 2, 1910. The complex of buildings, designed by the architect Albert Kahn, covered sixty acres. Although it included a foundry, it was primarily an assembly plant that put together components supplied by the Dodge brothers and others. Kahn also designed the Dodge manufacturing plant, which was built on another sixty-acre tract in nearby Hamtramck.

A friend of Henry Leland's had died as a result of injuries sustained in an accident while hand-cranking a car. As Leland was already concerned with the problems of starting engines, he pressed his engineers to complete a mechanical system, powered by a small electric motor, that could be installed on Cadillac cars. Charles F. Kettering, of the tiny Dayton Electric Laboratory Company, developed the motor and agreed to produce it and all of the mechanical components—a complete assembly. Since the system required a generator and battery, Leland and Kettering introduced electric lighting circuits on the 1912 Cadillac, the first car to standardize a self-starter and fully independent electrical system.

Ford's profits had been accumulating from ever-increasing production. By the end of 1913, Clarence W. Avery had installed the world's first moving assembly line at Highland Park. Anticipating the one-thousand-

per-day output, Ford shook the commercial community by raising the minimum daily wage of his employees from $2.30 to $5.00 on January 5, 1914, in the middle of a business recession.

John Dodge gave a one-year notice when he announced his retirement from the Ford Motor Company's board of directors in the summer of 1913. True to expectations, he and his brother Horace began planning a car that could compete directly with Ford. The first Dodge rolled out of the plant on November 14, 1914, and featured a thirty-five-horsepower, four-cylinder engine; sliding gear transmission; and an all-steel body built by the Budd Company—improvements that had been suggested to and refused by Ford.

While general manager of Hale, Kilburn & Company, Philadelphia, Edward G. Budd developed expertise in welded sheet metal body construction, producing pressed steel panels for the Hupp Motor Corporation about 1909. He established his own firm in 1912, and the contract with the Dodge brothers was his first major quantity production. His later work included mass production of steel disc wheels based on a Michelin patent, and unit body construction techniques used by Citroën. He also participated in the formation of Ambi-Budd in Germany, and the Pressed Steel Company, Limited, in England.

On the other end of the market spectrum, the battle of the titans was about to be waged. Leland thought carefully about his options, and acting on excellent advice from his son Wilfred, set Scottish-born engineer D. McCall White to work in secret on a new engine. The resulting Type 51 Cadillac V-8 was announced in September 1914, and marked the first use of a V-8 engine in a mass-produced automobile. Jesse G. Vincent mesmerized Packard's board of directors with his incredible Twin-Six, a twelve-cylinder engine of great flexibility and smoothness. It was introduced in May 1915.

As production increased on all cars, so did the size and strength of body suppliers. The Briggs Body Manufacturing Company and the Murray Body Company supplanted such earlier firms as Seavers & Erdman and the Wilson Body Company. The role of the body draftsman, who could not only evolve and communicate complex compound shapes to pattern- and diemakers, but also evolve forms in faultless style, had reached a respectful rank. The production car designers of the late teens and early twenties gradually smoothed out the abrupt differences between engine hood and cowl, domed the fenders and roof panels into graceful curves, and carefully managed the proportions of windows and doors within limits set by the body builders. Their meticulous "working drafts" were done with india ink and ruling pens on tracing cloth. Many of the designers were graduates of the Carriage and Automobile Body Drafting School in New York, and had been taught by Andrew J. Johnson. Johnson had mastered the art of surface geometry by attending a similar trade-sponsored coachbuilder's school taught by M. duPont in Paris. DuPont had discovered and brought into the carriage industry the special surface development techniques used by shipyards in Bordeaux for laying out the individual iron plates of ship hulls. These "keys" and systems are still the basis for body surface development practiced today.

Machines catering to the sport of driving were the brass ring on the new industry's carousel. Enthusiasts agree that the most advanced car of this type was conceived by Finley Robertson Porter, chief engineer of the Mercer Automobile Company. There may have been only five hundred or so Type 35-R Raceabouts built between 1911 and 1914, but they responded to driver's commands better than anything to come for several decades. The cars were architecturally honest, and were little more than a bare chassis with bucket seats and a cylindrical gasoline tank behind. They were low slung and close to the ground compared to other cars of the period, a feature that gave them amazing stability and a rakish appearance. Harry C. Stutz produced his Bearcat at about the same time and established the car as a symbol of romantic flair and dash. The Simplex Speed Car was a stripped version of the very expensive, high-quality luxury car built by Simplex for affluent sportsmen. Built in the same format as the Mercer and Stutz, it towered over them like a yacht.

Henry Leland left Cadillac in 1917 to build Liberty aircraft engines and, following the armistice, converted his factory to build a precision luxury car, naming it Lincoln. Unfortunately, his conservatism showed in the car's rather plain and pedestrian styling: it was high enough to enter while wearing a tall hat, and the squarish body forms were devoid of any characterful ornamentation. The car was introduced during the postwar depression, a period that discouraged the sale of luxury cars. The firm finally fell into receivership, and Ford bought the company in June 1922, naming Edsel Ford as president.

In 1923, Ford's Model T reached a peak production of 1,817,891 cars, utilizing both the Highland Park and the new River Rouge plants. Part of the formula for success was the simplicity of the body design—but it did have a style of its own. Even its bare necessities possessed a sense of grace and logic that endeared it to its loyal customers. The windshield on the roadster and touring car was raked back at a snappy angle, and the cowl that preceded it made a graceful transition to the hood. The Fordor and Tudor sedans had rather refined-looking curved rear quarters that wrapped around to the back. The rear side windowsill curved up toward the roof line from the horizontal belt molding that ran completely around below the glass areas. There was even a sun visor above the windshield. These elegant touches were all features of the "new" Model T introduced that year.

When Walter P. Chrysler "retired" from the General Motors Corporation in 1919, he joined Maxwell-Chalmers to help revitalize that company's production. In 1924, he produced a very advanced car bearing his own name and designed by three inspired consultants, Fred Zeder, Owen Skelton, and Carl Breer. Its high-compression, six-cylinder engine developed sixty-eight horsepower; the car had a top speed of seventy-five miles per hour. It could also accelerate from five to twenty-five miles per hour in 7.5 seconds—very lively for a middle-priced car. Its looks matched the performance: the cap on top of the smoothly rounded and plated radiator shell was decorated with a pair of wings. Bodies came in one, two, or three tones of paint. What normally would have been called a two-door coach became, instead, the five-passenger brougham with a dummy landau bar on the rear quarter panel, step plates on the running board, side-mounted spare tires, and a brightly plated trunk rack above the rear gas tank. The cars were smart looking, quick, and smooth, and the buying public responded favorably from the very start. The rather dowdy-looking, low-priced Maxwell was

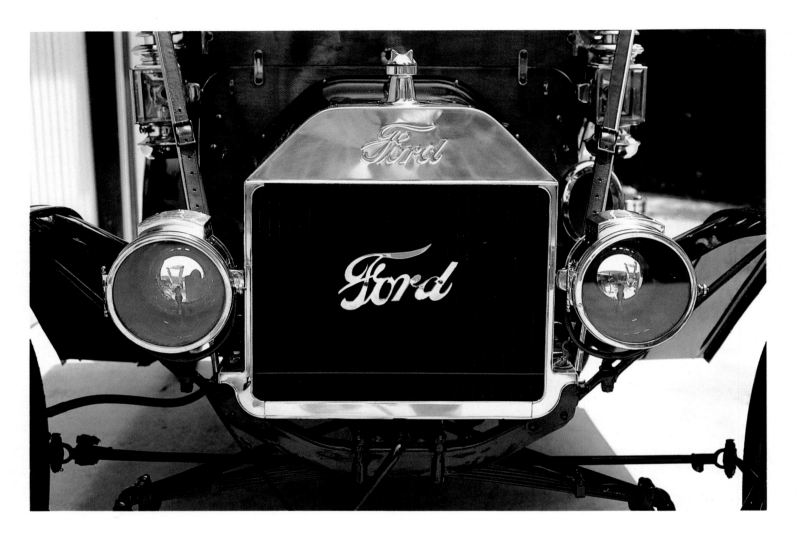

Above and opposite: Ford Touring. *1910. Model T. Engine 4 cyl., L-head, 20 h.p. Wood body, aluminum hood, steel fenders, leather seats. Designer and manufacturer Ford Motor Company, Detroit. Collection Gordon Howard, Burbank, California*

phased out in 1925 and replaced by a sportier, four-cylinder Chrysler. In June, Maxwell was reorganized as the Chrysler Corporation.

The established culture of the carriage trade formed guidelines of taste and architecture for automobile bodies, which gradually evolved into direct statements of purpose relative to commercial reproduction. Independent carriage builders were located in every major city from New York to the West Coast, and many easily translated their craft to custom bodies erected on high-grade automobile chassis. In the process, they created the utmost refinements in the new state of the art. Brewster & Company, founded in 1810, was foremost among them. The company's standards in quality of materials and craftsmanship became the ultimate statement by which all similar products were judged. William Brewster was a third-generation member of the founding family, and had studied design in Paris. Under his direction, the company developed new ideas in windshield construction for improved night visibility, distinctive body molding treatments, and convenient interior refinements. These features were executed with such finesse that when ordering a custom-built body, customers were able to select the optional ideas that conformed to their tastes, rather than attempting to dictate requirements. The final tribute to the company's excellence occurred in 1925, when Rolls-Royce of America acquired it to design and build their standard and custom body lines for the United States market.

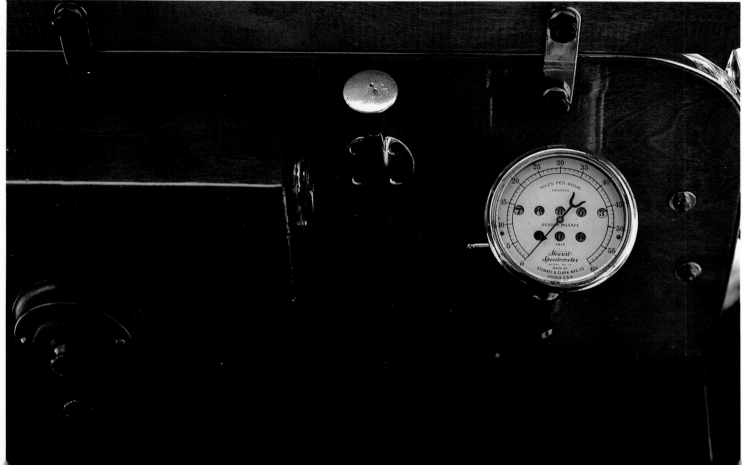

Cadillac Touring Sedan. *1920. Model Type 59. Engine V-8, L-head, 70 h.p. Custom body, aluminum or steel, leather seats. Designer Harley Earl. Body built by Don Lee, Incorporated, Los Angeles. Manufacturer General Motors Corporation, Detroit*

LaSalle Roadster. *1927. Model 303. Engine V-8, L-head, 75 h.p. Steel body, leather seats. Designer Harley Earl and Art & Color Section, production body by Fred Fisher. Manufacturer General Motors Corporation, Cadillac Motor Car Division, Detroit. Designer Harley Earl (seated) and Fred Fisher*

Don Lee, the West Coast Cadillac distributor, bought the Earl Automobile Works in the early twenties, and, along with the company, acquired the design services of the founder's son, Harley J. Earl. He had noted (as he proudly observed years later) that in Los Angeles Brewster coachwork at the curb commanded proper respect, but that the Cadillac sedan, executed with new and fluid ideas, really caught people's attention.

The distinctive feature, a broad molding that curved smoothly from the base of the windshield to the body side just below the windows, formed a continuous belt line, an effect requiring a curved glass corner window between the sloping windshield and the door pillar to give a full, wraparound effect. In the rear quarter panel of his sedans, Earl placed an oval window that would frame the face of the car's rear seat occupant in a most complimentary way, when seen by an outside observer. Earl's dramatic design philosophy was celebrated so frequently by products from Don Lee's custom shop that it attracted the attention of General Motors President Alfred P. Sloan, Jr., who had become concerned about the mundane appearance of the corporation's cars. On his invitation, Harley Earl moved to Detroit. His first assignment was to create an entirely new image for a smaller Cadillac, the La Salle, which would be developed to appeal to women drivers. Earl's design directly imitated the Hispano-Suiza, the most respected and expensive luxury chassis then available. The sharp edges of the radiator shell implied precise craftsmanship, and its front profile curved quickly from top surface to side, creating a firm shoulder that was carried horizontally back to the windshield. Ventilation louvers in the hood side were large and coarse, suggesting the imperative need to carry heat away from the powerful engine. All the body style visual features were associated with carriages and fine coachwork: a vertical molding extending down from the windshield and curving forward at the bottom resembled the sill line of a carriage; inset window moldings borrowed from the same source. On the open bodies, Earl used parallel moldings that curved gracefully from the top of the cowl around the cockpit and rearward on the body to give a flowing effect. The entire ensemble expressed grace and dignity, an image that women of culture would appreciate. In 1926, Earl began organizing a body design department at General Motors; it was called the Art & Color Section.

It was coincidental that the country's largest auto body builder, Fisher Body Corporation, was bought and assimilated into General Motors just as Earl was beginning his new career there. It was necessary that a healthy alliance be established between the Fisher brothers and Earl.

In February 1921, two former Brewster designers, Raymond H. Dietrich and Thomas L. Hibbard, went into business to form a custom body design service, LeBaron, Incorporated. With the addition of Ralph W. Roberts, and the illustrator Roland P. Stickney, they evolved body designs of careful proportion and distinction, and soon had an important list of clients, including all suppliers of luxury automobile chassis in New York City, where their office was located. As a result of these contacts, their fame spread to the manufacturers, and eventually each of the founders became a separate consultant to a major firm. Dietrich Incorporated created custom designs for Packard and Lincoln, Hibbard joined Howard "Dutch" Darrin on a European venture, and Roberts carried the LeBaron name to the Briggs Body Company, where it served Chrysler as an expression of its finest products.

THE STREAMLINED DECADE TO THE FABULOUS FIFTIES

I n the 1930s, the parallel explosions of production technology, quality control, and craftsmanship, all done with tremendous style, produced a grandeur accompanied by innovation that cast the automobile as a true artform. It was all the more remarkable that this clear advance was accomplished during a period of severe economic depression. The momentum and inspiration developed in the late twenties carried through, and entire organizations felt that the dynamics of their combined skills could revitalize the market. Every designer treated the period as one of challenge and opportunity; optimism and progress were the bywords.

To an engineer or financial comptroller, a straightforward product that makes its case without any superficial embellishment is a thing of beauty. It must have mystified Henry Leland, whose convictions on quality, work, and behavior were so puritanical, that cultured customers responded so unemotionally to his Lincoln. It was clear to Alfred P. Sloan, Jr., however, that the urge to purchase responded well to a dramatic statement of style, especially if it was fresh. Enter the designer.

Automobile body and appearance design has been the province of men and women who have a profound enthusiasm for the particular subject. The imagery of an automobile as a total concept is unique, and its design is unlike any other profession, though it shares concerns for human factors—safety, comfort, structure, and maintenance. The sense of style that embraces these factors and expresses itself in an artful manner is often an enigma to management minds, because style follows a broad range of interpretation. It is subjected to continuous rationalization by managers and planners, who would like to formulate the elements of success and the essence of good design. Progressive design blends art and logic, and follows a variable path toward the elusive, ultimate expression. It contains endless compromises.

Designers working for the most productive coachbuilders had latitude to develop new styling ideas, and became influential leaders in the industry. LeBaron, Incorporated, had been successful in producing both

Pierce-Arrow, Silver Arrow. *1933. Model 1234. Engine V-12, flathead, 175 h.p. Steel body, broadcloth seats. Design concept Philip Wright. Body engineer James Hughes, body manufacturer Studebaker. Manufacturer Pierce-Arrow Motor Car Company, Buffalo, New York. Harrah's Automobile Collection, Reno, Nevada*

Cord Westchester Sedan. *1936. Model 810. Engine V-8, 125 h.p.. Steel body, cloth seats. Designer Gordon Buehrig. Manufacturer Auburn Automobile Company, Connersville Indiana. (right) Cord Town Car. 1930. Model L-29. Engine 8 cyl., L-head. Aluminum body, leather seats. Designer Philip Wright, body by Walter M. Murphy Company, Pasadena, Calif. Manufacturer Auburn Automobile Company, Connersville, Indiana*

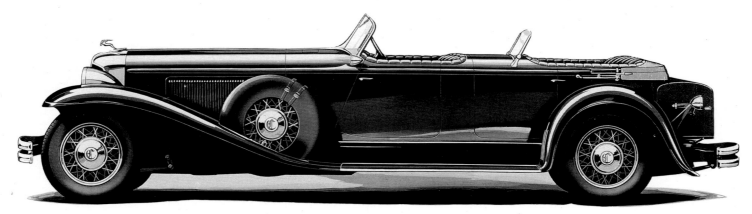

Chrysler Imperial Eight. *1931. Model CG. Engine 8 cyl., L-head , 125 h.p. Steel body, leather interior. Designer LeBaron, Incorporated. Manufacturer Chrysler Corporation, Detroit*

custom and semicustom designs for Lincoln and Packard, when Allan Sheldon, president of the Murray Body Company, lured Ray Dietrich away to set up his own custom design firm as an in-house design service. Murray was a major production body supplier to Ford. Dietrich had personal contact with Edsel Ford, president of Lincoln, and proposed designs that would freshen that automobile's dignified visual posture.

There is no question that the precision of this work was of great assistance to Joe Galamb, as he worked out the body designs for the Model A Ford, which closely echoed Lincoln in styling. The fenders curved close to the wheels, the shape of the radiator and hood, and the overall proportions of the body forms had a direct resemblance to the standard Lincoln. The subtlety of this corporate image was intended to subliminally present the Model A as a member of a distinguished and cultured family. In no way did the car look cheap.

Ever since the engine had been moved to the front of the chassis, the shape of the hood and radiator had become a major identification feature. In some self-conscious way, the majority of American manufacturers had adopted the shape of the 1901 German Mercedes Simplex radiator, and imitated it with only minor modifications. The most radical exception was Packard, which invented and patented its own radiator design, and maintained the theme. When Harley Earl styled the La Salle radiator, he chose for his motif Hispano-Suiza, with its ultimate reputation for quality and performance, though he scaled it down slightly. It was such a success that the theme was carried over to all General Motors products by 1930.

From 1930 to 1932, long hoods and lower bodies were the trend, and the most exciting car to hit the American market was the L-29 Cord. Cornelius Van Randst directed the chassis design and John Oswald took credit for the bodies, but it was Alan H. Leamy's peaked race car radiator, lean hood, and exotically swept fenders that gave the car its romantic stance. Leamy's designs for Auburn were first-class, especially his rhythmic refinement of their speedsters. But the Cord Corporation's ace was the Model J Duesenberg, the fastest and most prestigious chassis one could drive across the continent. The bodies were custom built, many of them designed by the factory's official designer, Gordon Buehrig, and constructed by the finest coachbuilders. The majority were products of the Walter M. Murphy Company in Pasadena, California, from designs by Franklin Hershey, Philip Wright, and George McQuerry, Jr.

Fred and August Duesenberg introduced their first production car in 1921 with the intention of capitalizing on their strong reputation as race car designers and builders. Conservative body styling and a depressed economy led to failure. E.L. Cord acquired the company, and directed the two brothers to design a chassis and engine that would be faster and more powerful than any other American car on the road.

The result was dynamic: the straight eight, 420-cubic-inch displacement engine had twin overhead camshafts, and could produce 265 horsepower at 4,200 revolutions per minute. The chassis came in two wheelbases: 142.5 inches and 153 inches, so the custom body builders had ample room to execute well-proportioned bodies, which ranged from full luxury to sports roadsters and convertibles.

LeBaron, Incorporated, was commissioned to design the

Ford Deluxe Phaeton. *1931. Model A. Engine 4 cyl., L-head, 40 h.p. Steel body, vinyl seats. Designer and manufacturer Ford Motor Company, Detroit. Collection Gunnar Gluckman, Encino, California*

Above and opposite: Duesenberg Boattail "French" Speedster. *1931. Model J (supercharger added later to make an "SJ"). Engine 8 cyl., double overhead camshaft, supercharged, 320 h.p. Aluminum body, leather seats. Designer and body by Figoni. Manufacturer Duesenberg Incorporated, Indianapolis. Black Hawk Auto collection, San Ramon, California*

dual cowl phaeton body for introduction at the Chicago automobile show. The body was narrow and lean astride the powerful chassis. The two cockpits, each just wide enough to hold two passengers each, had separate windshields; and a raised panel separated the red and black areas of the exterior paint. The "swept panel," as it was called, started at the front of the hood, just behind the radiator cap, and traveled diagonally along each side of the long hood, swept across the cowl and down the body side in a graceful arc. Engine heat ventilation louvers in the side of the tall, imposing hood were curved to follow radii that centered on the side-mounted spare wheel. The long, tapered clamshell fenders swept smoothly over and down the front wheels and met the running boards in a continuous curve. The taillight was almost as large as an ordinary headlight and included a built-in stoplight. Nine gauges on the instrument panel communicated everything from road speed to the time of day and height above sea level. The automatically controlled warning lights, two on each side, informed the driver when various parts of the chassis required service. The LeBaron represented a dazzling and dramatic design concept, and captured the fantasies of automotive enthusiasts across the country.

One of the most innovative designers in the industry, the head of production design at the Murray Body Company, was Amos Northup, who made proposals to many of Murray's clients as a way of keeping their business. Reo built a good-quality car, but the design appearance was dated and common. The popularity of flying had infused everyone with an appreciation of applied aerodynamics, so Northup skillfully softened all the edges, and sharply pointed the radiator on what was otherwise a conventionally proportioned design. The resulting Reo Royale was so sensational that it started a snowball in styling. It was advertised as an aerodynamic concept, and was the first public evidence of the trend in aerodynamic-type design that was to follow.

It seems incredible that a mere two years after the Wall Street crash, America's prestige automobile manufacturers involved themselves in a multicylinder race for what they described as the ultimate refinement in luxury automobiles. There was no hedging on quality. Cadillac offered a V-12 in addition to the V-16 and "normal" V-8, while Packard revived the Twin-Six name for a magnificent new V-12 that capped the eight-cylinder lines. Marmon, breathing its last, courageously offered up its aluminum V-16 that was, in many ways, the best of the lot technically, and featured beautifully proportioned bodies designed by Walter Dorwin Teague. Lincoln's 1932 KB V-12 reached the absolute pinnacle of that make's production with a full line of both standard (Murray) and custom-built bodies.

These automobiles were the noble profits of a thoroughly refined society. And then Amos Northup did it again, this time for Graham, which was almost lost anyway, and had everything to gain. Heeding the wind even more seriously, Northup used a decorative grille in *front* of the radiator, leaned the windshield back, rounded everything, and, in a final coup de grace to the carriage style, added skirts to the fenders to solidify the form and hide the muddy underside from view. Although Graham was not a major volume threat to the rest of the industry, the car did make everything else on the market look suddenly obsolete. *Everybody* had to make a fast change and add skirts to the fenders—even Duesenberg offered an updated design that could

be bolted on in place of the lithe, lean, sweeping originals, though their cars were at the end of the run.

Forty years after the great Columbian Exposition, Chicago reasserted itself as the hub of the civilized world with its Century of Progress World's Fair in 1933. The car manufacturers gave it their very best. Cadillac's four-passenger, fastback coupé by Fleetwood on a Cadillac Sixteen (designed under Harley Earl's close supervision at the Art & Color Section) was a brilliant pacesetter, while Packard displayed the ultimate formal sports berlin designed by the LeBaron studio. Its hood stretched all the way back to the windshield, and the lavish use of polished, burled walnut on the garnish moldings and fine broadcloth in the interior earned it the title of the "dome" car, taken from "pleasure dome" of course. Duesenberg knew how to impress the hungry masses best, even on its last stand. Gordon Buehrig designed, and Rollston built, an intimate, four-passenger sports sedan on a long wheelbase supercharged chassis with a name derived from the no-holds cost of "Twenty Grand." It was the hit of the show—the fabled fantasy of power, riches, and speed come to life.

The Ford exhibit had something more to offer, though, in the form of two *very* advanced and streamlined *running* prototype cars designed by a brilliant young Dutch engineer and designer, John Tjaarda, who was working at the Briggs Manufacturing Company studio. On the primary car, the Ford V-8 engine was in the rear of the unitized body. Briggs, like Murray, was a body supplier to Ford and Chrysler, and this display of design advancement held out temptation for public acclaim.

In the history of automobile design, the 1930s stand out as a perpetually innovative and exciting period. The famous Chrysler trio of Zeder, Skelton, and Breer were way ahead when they introduced the biggest gamble of their careers: the Airflow and De Soto in 1934. They caught the spirit of progress completely, but the execution was as blunt as an equation which, in its own world, was right. Sales dropped while the public paused for adjustment and read Alexander Woollcott's testimonials to the ease of writing in the backseat at fifty miles per hour.

The very best was yet to come: Gordon Buehrig's masterpiece and E. L. Cord's ultimate engineering breakthrough, the magnificent front-wheel drive 1936 Cord Model 810. Not just another pretty face, the car reflected a philosophy in concept from every point of view. In 1937, the engine received a supercharger, so the Cord 812 went even faster, but the ads cautioned owners that the car itself was sufficient evidence of superiority.

Buehrig's body design reflected his admiration for the French architect Le Corbusier's uncluttered sense of proportion. The car resembled a fuselage with pontoon-shaped wheel enclosures attached. The squarish engine hood tapered backward to meet the wider passenger capsule, which ended in a downward-sloping fastback. Air entry for the radiator at the front of the hood and air exit from the engine compartment at the sides were managed by a continuous series of horizontal louvers that wrapped back to the cowl. The wheels were covered by large, plated discs with oval perforations around the outer edges to encourage airflow to cool the brakes. There was no superficial decoration anywhere on the car. The manufacturer's badge, located on top of the front-wheel drive housing, contained a coat of arms and the word "Cord"; there was no other product identification needed.

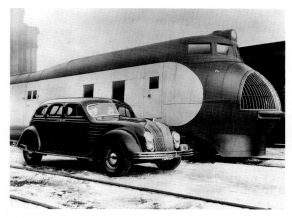

Chrysler 4-Door Sedan. *1934. Model Airflow. Engine 8 cyl., L-head, 122 h.p. Steel body, broadcloth seats. Designer Chrysler Styling Section. Manufacturer Chrysler Corporation, Detroit. Chrysler Airflow 1934 parked next to the Union Pacific Streamliner introduced in 1934*

Opposite: Packard Sport Phaeton (Dual Cowl). *1934. Model 1108. Engine V-12, flathead, 160 h.p. Steel body, leather seats. Designer and body by LeBaron Incorporated. Manufacturer Packard Motor Car Company, Detroit. Harrah's Automobile Collection, Reno, Nevada*

Inside, the instrument panel was the focal point. The bank of aircraft-style gauges was mounted on a central, damascened panel; four vertical throw levers that controlled headlights, instrument lights, choke, and throttle were positioned below it. The Bendix "electric hand," the most ingenious control of all, was mounted on a shaft that projected to the right from the steering column. Just below the wheel, a tiny lever could be moved in a miniature gate to shift the transmission.

In the thirties, Harley Earl emphatically established styling as a dominant factor in automobile marketing, and he never lost sight of any opportunity to advance in a new direction that might build greater prestige for General Motors' products. He initiated design contests within the staff at the Art & Color Section to encourage concept development, and brought forth great results—though not always for General Motors. Philip Wright, a member of Art & Color in 1932, took his rejected proposal from the first contest and executed it, with refinement, at South Bend in 1933. His design concept became the Pierce Silver Arrow. Frank Hershey's Art & Color design concept included a band of chrome strips that went from bumper to windshield and became Pontiac's Silver Streak. The two most ingenious design inventions to emerge from Earl's Art & Color contests were the 1934 La Salle, with its narrow, vertical radiator grille and art moderne hardware details, and the 1938 Cadillac Sixty Special. Earl anticipated the appeal of a medium-sized, formalized sports sedan that could add vitality to Cadillac's image. He turned the theme over to the head of the Cadillac studio, William L. Mitchell, who executed it as an instant success. In April 1937, Art & Color changed its name to "Styling Section."

The thirties wound up with a succession of innovatively styled aerodynamic automobiles. Young Rust Heinz, member of the famous Pittsburgh family, commissioned Bohman & Schwartz of Pasadena to build his design for an amazing, aerodynamic coupé that used the engine and front subframe from a 1936 Cord sedan, and named it the "Phantom Corsair."

John Tjaarda's skill with aerodynamic form and body engineering succeeded with the 1936 Lincoln-Zephyr where Chrysler's formula had lacked contemporary grace. Its twelve-cylinder engine was really a flathead Ford V-8 with four cylinders added for smoothness and torque. The car made a strong impression on the market.

Beginning in 1932, Ford countered the Chevrolet Six, introduced in 1929, with the incredible V-8, steadily improving the concept until it became the standard low-cost, high-production power vehicle, which was really fun to drive. Chevrolet had taken the sales lead in 1931, lost it to Ford in 1935, and recaptured it until 1945. Apparent luxury combined with such progressive features as independent front suspension and controlled ventilation gave Chevrolet a definite advantage.

Above and opposite: Phantom Corsair Six-Passenger Coupé. *1938. Experimental model. Engine V-8, 190 h.p. Aluminum body, leather seats. Body designer Rust Heinz. Manufacturer Bohman & Schwartz, Pasadena, California. Collection The Harrah Automobile Foundation, Reno, Nevada*

Cadillac, Lincoln, Packard, and even Chrysler offered such refined luxury line products that little market was left for made-to-order auto bodies. As most of the great coachbuilders quietly slipped away, the era of individualized craftsmanship gave way to the age of mass refinement.

Massive automobile production facilities and sophisticated engineering techniques gave America its triumphant edge in World War II. The incredible transition from consumer goods to wartime equipment was

accomplished under the direction of William S. Knudsen, the chairman of the National Defense Council, who mobilized the automobile industry almost overnight. Each manufacturer took its specific responsibilities seriously, and with patriotic fervor. Ford's Willow Run plant was symbolic of the entire effort: built up from scratch, it turned out 8,685 B-24 Liberator bombers at the rate of one per hour. All military trucks and armored cars, fifty-seven percent of the tanks, and about half of all hand and machine guns were produced by the automobile industry.

The Jeep remains as the dominant legacy of military automotive production. Willys-Overland, Ford, and Bantam produced 1,500 original prototypes for field testing, and the Army adopted the quarter-ton 4 × 4 foot truck, whose name was derived from Ford's designation "GP" for General Purpose. Its responsive and "go anywhere" character opened the door to an entirely new kind of automotive market in the postwar period. Willys took advantage of the momentum by continuing production of commercial variations on the Jeep for civilian use, and, in 1948, introduced the Brooks Stevens-styled "Jeepster."

After the war, the industry returned to consumer goods production with all possible speed. Because auto production had halted in 1942, a tremendous demand for new cars of all kinds had been steadily growing. New automobiles were introduced from every direction, though most of the promoters were aiming at the basic transportation market.

Henry Ford II became president of the Ford Motor Company, and acceded to an infusion of efficiency experts, collectively referred to as the "Whiz Kids," to help reorganize the company's financial structure. Credit for the turnaround, however, went to Ernest R. Breech, Lewis D. Crusoe, Del S. Harder, and Harold T. Youngren, automobile men with vast, accumulated experience. Like everyone else, Ford revived production of its prewar cars as the quickest way to meet consumer demand, but planned for new models immediately. George Walker, a local industrial designer, was hired as a styling consultant and invited to present proposals in model form. Holden Koto, an experienced designer who worked with great facility in three dimensions, made a scale clay model for a friend who worked on Walker's design staff, and Ford executives chose it for the revolutionary 1949 model. Koto later worked as a design executive for Ford, but never received credit for his early contribution.

Henry Kaiser turned his incredible reputation for World War II shipbuilding toward postwar auto building in company with Joseph Fraser. Under the aegis of the Kaiser-Fraser Company, they leased Ford's Willow Run facility and had two brand new cars ready for production in 1948. Howard "Dutch" Darrin was hired as styling consultant. With his typical far-sighted flair, he evolved a very clean, continuous-sided body form with no separate fender projections.

Engineering had been Chrysler's trump card from the beginning, and it was reflected in the corporation's huge war effort. President K. T. Keller dominated postwar product direction with a down-to-earth dictum of size and efficiency, which was stated in advertising campaigns as "bigger on the inside, smaller on the outside." Such good common sense was not what the deprived public craved, but it continued to buy because new cars were still in short supply.

LaSalle. *Styling prototype for 1934 Model 6330-8. c. 1933. No engine. Wood and metal, hand finished. Designer Art & Color Section. Manufacturer General Motors Corporation, Detroit*

Opposite: Cord Cabriolet Sportsman. *1937. Model 812. Engine V-8, supercharged, 175 h.p. Steel body, leather seats. Designer Gordon Buehrig, body by Central Body Company. Manufacturer Auburn Automobile Company Incorporated, Auburn, Indiana. Collection Chris Cord, Beverly Hills, California*

The Hudson Company knew that it needed a good start to compete with the giants, and plunged in with a new body design that featured unitized construction. Its lower floor and higher doorsill earned it the name "step-down" model. Holden Koto had worked at Hudson before the war under Frank Spring, the director of styling, and one of his models was used as a basis for postwar styling. Spring, along with his assistant, Arthur Kibiger, executed the design and further enriched the concept by selecting upholstery materials of a very high quality.

Studebaker had been using Raymond Loewy as a design consultant since 1936, and Clare Hodgman and Virgil Exner had designed the company's prewar models under Loewy's direction. As the war was ending, Loewy assembled a remarkable group of designers in South Bend, Indiana, at the Studebaker plant. Gordon Buehrig initially headed the team, with Virgil Exner as his assistant. The 1947 Studebaker was principally Exner's work; it represented a complete breakthrough in precision surfacing and consistent character, and was almost architectural in its tapered definition. The large wraparound rear window on the Starlight coupé had even more glass area than the windshield, a feature that earned some facetious remarks about what direction the car was traveling in, but it was generally well received.

Robert Bourke took over when Buehrig left, and directed the design of the sensational 1953 Studebaker. The Starliner hardtop coupé, the pacesetter of the line, was actually designed as a supplemental idea for a personal coupé that could be built on the old Land Cruiser chassis left over from previous model production. Its long wheelbase and low frame presented an opportunity to stretch the body shapes dramatically.

Werner Gubitz was responsible for the careful and tasteful development of Packard's "look" from 1925 to 1947. Under his direction, Philip Wright had helped evolve the excellent Clipper series, which was continued after the war. In 1947, John Reinhart was named chief designer. He was forced to deal with limited modification techniques because company policy resisted major expenditures in new body die forms.

Nash saw the postwar market as an opportunity to continue with the economical compact cars that had become its hallmark. In 1949, the Airflyte series was introduced. In appearance, these cars seemed designed around aerodynamic principles, with their covered front wheels and softly rounded body forms. In 1950, Nash revived the Rambler name and used it to identify the compact car line.

General Motors viewed the postwar period as an opportunity to accelerate the seller's market by dramatizing its future automobiles in a series of previews used to display the corporation's new technical advances. Alfred P. Sloan, Jr.'s, special luncheons for friends in the business community were held each year during National Auto Show week at the Waldorf-Astoria hotel in New York. For 1949, General Motors decided to expand the show, called it "Transportation Unlimited," invited the public to attend, and the Motorama was born. The theme—product research—naturally included some advanced thinking on auto styling, represented by a special range of "dream cars." A full-blown, thirty-five-minute musical extravaganza set the whole thing off. The Motorama became an almost annual affair, and traveled to many principal cities around the country. General Motors stated

Above and opposite: Ford Convertible Coupé. *1955. Model Thunderbird. Engine V-8, overhead valve, 193 h.p. Steel body, vinyl seats. Designer Franklin Hershey. Manufacturer Ford Motor Company, Detroit. Collection George Watts, Villa Park, California*

Above: Willys Jeep. *1944. Model GPW. Engine 4 cyl., L-head, 40 h.p. Steel body, canvas seats. Designer Karl Probst. Manufacturer Willys Overland, Toledo, Ohio. Collection Bill Barker, Los Angeles*

Top: Studebaker Hardtop Coupé. *1953. Model Starliner. Engine 6 cyl., L-head, 85 h.p. Steel body, vinyl seats. Designer Raymond Loewy and Associates. Manufacturer Studebaker Corporation, South Bend, Indiana*

that its objective was to familiarize the public with new styling ideas, but it also hoped to overwhelm the market with new excitements faster than the competition could keep up. The idea worked, but the feast of new, experimental designs proved beneficial for the competition, so the last Motorama was held in 1961. It drew over a million visitors in New York, San Francisco, and Los Angeles.

In 1938, Harley Earl and his friend Harlow Curtice, the head of the General Motors Buick division, had cooperated in producing an experimental car called the "Y" job. The "Y," with its small, thirteen-inch wheels, disappearing headlights, high compression engine, and special transmission, was a very advanced test bed for new design ideas. Dramatic styling guaranteed international publicity. The technique was so successful that two new supercars loaded with skillfully assembled stylistic themes, the Le Sabre and the XP-300, were built and shown in 1951. Technical inventions included an aluminum block, a supercharged V-8 engine, and a transaxle at the rear. The cost in dollars seemed astronomical, but even this helped strengthen General Motors' image as a corporation striving toward the future for the benefit of its customers.

One of Earl's great inspirations derived from his appreciation of the dramatically profiled twin tails on Lockheed's P-38 World War II fighter. Small fins housing the taillights appeared on the 1949 Cadillac, and, in subsequent years, these appendages became a dominant styling theme. Both the Le Sabre and the XP-300 used the fin theme to great advantage.

By 1958, even the journalists were appalled by the proliferation of applied decoration on all car makes. Some were using two distinctly different schemes on the side panels alone. Earl theorized that repaired collision damage on sheet metal was seldom perfect, and would greatly depreciate a used car's value, whereas bright appliqué could be easily replaced. The shiny, new trim would attract a prospective buyer's eye away from the subtle defects. Almost every strategy that Earl's designers developed was deliberately made difficult to imitate. Wraparound windshields, extensive die-cast ornamentation, deep-drawn bumpers, and lavish interiors all cost extra money to make. It was a competitive dilemma. The best things to come out of this styling era were the sleek, fastback sedanets in 1949, and the graceful, hardtop coupés and sedans in the middle fifties.

Virgil Exner's move to Chrysler in 1949 offered him the perfect opportunity to redirect the corporation's design section. The corporation's blunt, practical production cars were out of step with the more exciting styling then offered by other makers. Aware of this difference, Chrysler's management had commissioned the Italian coachbuilder, Ghia, to build a Plymouth styling prototype sedan, which cost a mere $10,000. Exner realized that he could persuade corporate management to accept his new designs by building a series of different prototypes and exhibiting them publicly. If they were well accepted, it would reinforce his opinions. It would also give the corporation a progressive posture in the public eye. Over the next eleven years, twenty-one design exercises were built and shown with such success that corporate advertising began to stress Chrysler's "forward look." Exner himself was a man of impeccable taste with a consuming passion for the field of genuine automobile design. His work helped to restore stature to his profession and brought Chrysler's products back into the competitive market.

Ford also made several important contributions in the fifties. The retractable hardtop was a mechanical miracle, and the evolution of the 1956 Lincoln-Continental Mark II represented discretion and care. The most outstanding contribution, though, was the 1955 Thunderbird two-passenger personal car, designed by Bill Boyer and a top team of designers under Frank Hershey's direction. Bob Maguire directed the interior design and made the general design presentations to the company's management.

Initiative for developing the project was stimulated by rumors that Chevrolet was planning to introduce a sports car. Ford very wisely decided not to compete head-on and chose instead to pursue the broader market for "sporty" cars. The cars sold very well when they were new, and they added a youthful flair to the company's personality. Today, the 1955, 1956, and 1957 Thunderbirds have appreciated to many times their original values and are highly prized by collectors.

Chevrolet, on the other hand, took the long road and gradually built the Corvette into a true driving enthusiast's machine. The first model in 1953 had a six-cylinder engine and came in white with a red interior. By 1955, it had a 195-horsepower V-8 engine option and three exterior color choices. The 1957 models could be had with a 283-cubic-inch V-8 engine that would propel the car from zero to sixty miles per hour in 5.7 seconds. In 1958, many private owners were racing their Corvettes against 300SL Mercedes-Benz and Jaguar XK-150-S sports cars, and the serious image of a competitive sports car was established in the enthusiast's world.

The fifties was an era of flamboyant styling exploration and serious engine performance development. Appearance design may have taken a detour, but recovery toward a sense of grace and refinement was in sight by the end of the decade.

Above: Chrysler Sports Sedan. *1951. Model K-310, experimental prototype. Engine V-8, 310 h.p. Steel body, cloth seats. Designer Virgil Exner. Body built and assembled by Carrozzeria Ghia, Turin. Chassis by Chrysler Corporation, Detroit*

Top: Cadillac LeMans Convertible. *1953. Model experimental prototype. Engine V-8, 250 h.p. Fiberglass body, leather seats. Designer Harley Earl and General Motors Design Staff, Cadillac Studio. Manufacturer General Motors Corporation, Detroit*

A NEW SENSE OF STYLE

If the fifties were flamboyant, the sixties could best be described as a period with strong character and a sense of style. Automotive engineers and designers participated in development and exchanged ideas; product planners became aware of the psychological forces that were expressed in popular lifestyles. The general economy was good, and consumers possessed disposable income, which, in turn, encouraged the manufacturers to pursue bolder and more competitive ideas.

European automotive products began gradually intruding on the American domestic market, and as volume percentages increased there was some cause for alarm. Foreign sports cars were tolerated because they added interesting flavor to the market, and the Corvette won often enough to sustain a comfortable balance in competitive events. The unmatchable Volkswagen, which inched its way up the sales charts past the tolerable ten-percent limit, bothered domestic manufacturers the most. They interpreted the car's appeal to be economy, so, when Volkswagen sales reached fourteen percent of the total market, American manufacturers fired off a triple salvo of "compact" sedans to halt the Teutonic tide.

Ford's Falcon grew out of a straightforward formulation of what a small car ought to be. It seemed plain and obviously inexpensive, and although it lacked personality, it sold reasonably well. Virgil Exner gave Plymouth's Valiant and Dodge's Lancer a distinctive touch of character, which journalists liked to call "European." Chevrolet's Edward N. Cole started with a clean sheet of paper and invented what he thought might make an interesting economically competitive car. Like the Volkswagen, it had an air-cooled rear engine, but with six cylinders instead of four. The styling featured a sculptured, horizontal peak that ran all the way around the car just above the wheel arches and tended to make the car look longer than it really was. Uninterrupted lines on a form always create the illusion of greater dimension. Unfortunately, low pricing eliminated decorative details, and each of the cars had a frugal look that newness could not overcome. A buyer could pay the same amount of money for a one- or two-year-old highway cruiser, complete with luxury details, and not look as though he had lost his job.

Above and opposite: Chevrolet Corvette (Split Window Coupé). *1963. Model Sting Ray. Engine V-8, overhead valve, 300 h.p. Fiberglass body, leather seats. Designer and manufacturer Chevrolet Motor Division, General Motors Corporation, Detroit. Collection Bob McRae, Los Angeles*

The manufacturer's answer was to add a little makeup. The Chevrolet Corvair shown at the Chicago auto show in March 1960 had full wheel covers, a bright molding below the doors to emphasize a low part of the body, and a bright molding around the side windows of its coupé upper body. The colorful interior had pleated, vinyl seats, and the final touch was a glamorous new model name: Monza. Chevrolet began falling behind while filling orders.

After pondering the Falcon platform with Chevrolet's revelation in mind, Ford designers and planners came up with a better idea: a special model of the Falcon that could use either the standard six-cylinder engine or the small V-8. By moving the engine toward the rear and compressing the seating area, they developed a new, basic body design that had a longer hood and an intimate passenger cabin resembling a sports car. In its basic format, it could be advertised at a low and attractive price. Buyers could then customize their cars according to taste, by selecting from a long list of options. The result was the Ford Mustang. The nameplate portrait of a young horse in full gallop helped to suggest the generic term for this racy compact, thereafter known as a "pony car."

Chevrolet and Pontiac shared General Motors' market response to this new image by introducing the Camaro and the Firebird in 1967. The unit construction bodies carried the engine and front suspension forward on a bolt-on subframe, which allowed for subtle variations in hood and fender design, and gave great rigidity to the whole assembly.

The idea of placing a big engine in a small chassis to achieve a high power-to-weight ratio and dynamic performance is almost as old as the industry itself. It has appeared on the market in manufactured form as often as planners have felt that there was a large enough demand to justify the cost and ensure a profit. With the advent of "compact" cars on one end of the maker's range, and large cars on the other, it was natural to put the big engine, a tough transmission, and powerful brakes in the little car, and gain incredible performance at a low cost. The possible variations on a manufactured hot rod with bucket seats, a radio, and air-conditioning seemed almost endless.

In the fifties, the National Association of Stock Car Auto Racing had gone a long way to develop prestige for the manufacturers who could show a good percentage of victories. Racing specialists did most of the development work on the big, rugged V-8 engines, converting luxury-oriented chassis to high-speed racing capability. The manufacturers viewed this development work as a two-way street, and began under-the-counter support programs to bolster competitive superiority. The end result was over-the-counter, bolt-on equipment that the consumer/enthusiast could buy and install, or order as original equipment. It was also a high-profit business, and cruising and drag racing became a major sport for anyone who could afford it.

As a result of the performance image appeal, the majority of production cars gradually converted from softly sprung "insulated" cars to become vehicles that could be driven with greater precision. Responsive handling and a smooth and stable ride were achieved through close attention to shock absorber control, quicker steering ratios, and power-steering units that allowed some inertia feedback from the front wheels to the driver's hand on the steering wheel. Improved suspension geometry with a higher roll center helped to cut down body roll on corners.

The most difficult refinement occurred in chassis balance. The big V-8 engines were heavy, and required a fair amount of room. Moving them rearward would impose on the seating area, but the advent of the sporty two-passenger plus small occasional rear-seat cars allowed the engine to be located far enough aft to put some weight on the rear driving wheels and give them traction.

The resulting impressively long hood made the sporty compacts look "normal" to the forward-looking driver and became an important factor in helping previous large car owners adjust to short wheelbase cars. Both the Mustang and the Camaro had long, flat hoods whose width was emphasized by peaks on either side, an effect that made the cars look massive enough to seem safe in large-car traffic. The addition of an air intake that projected through the hood was visual evidence of a muscular hybrid. Rumbling, dual exhausts and an erratic engine idle at the stoplight were also indications of high-performance potential.

Plymouth created a compact personal car at the same time the Mustang appeared, calling its Valiant variation a Barracuda. Its fastback styling was sleek and handsome, and it was available with either the smooth and economical six-cylinder or more powerful, small-block V-8 engine.

The merger of Nash and Hudson in 1946 resulted in the formation of American Motors Corporation. Both of the previous firms had been active in the compact car market long before it became a necessary element in the sales race. The Rambler name was retained to identify the corporation's strongest-selling model. Richard Teague, the vice president for styling, enthusiastically promoted the idea of a derivative that could compete in the new, light personal car field. It was called the Javelin, perhaps to symbolize a sharp penetration into the active part of the market.

The Corvette had gone through many changes since its first model in 1954, all of them aimed at making it a serious road and track car. Both Harley Earl and his successor, William L. Mitchell, were strong performance car enthusiasts, and the Corvette's development had received close attention since the beginning. The cars were now winning in the amateur racing events against formidable opposition from much more expensive European sports cars. Perhaps the ultimate compliment was the team of Corvettes entered in the new GT class at Le Mans in 1960. Briggs Cunningham entered three, and one of them came in eighth place overall against competition from Ferraris, Jaguars, and Maseratis—a remarkable achievement.

The rapidly advancing technologies in American business produced an increasing number of self-made young executives who frequently wore a coat and tie but played golf and tennis regularly. A full-scale Lincoln or Cadillac was more of a banker's family car to them, and Ford's four-passenger Thunderbird was the closest thing to a medium-scale, quality car that had a lively personality. Remembering his experience in developing the 1938 Cadillac Sixty Special as a young executive's car, Bill Mitchell proposed an intermediate-sized, high-quality four-passenger coupé to enliven the

Buick division's image. The 1964 Riviera fulfilled that objective. Oldsmobile's management was enthusiastic about the results, and agreed to share the development costs for a new model to appear in 1966. Under Assistant Chief Engineer John Beltz, Oldsmobile's engineers worked out an ingenious front-wheel-drive power train that permitted a lower floor with no driveshaft tunnel. By this time, Cadillac's Eldorado special series had become little more than a trim option in the standard Cadillac lineup. The Oldsmobile-developed front-drive platform for the corporate "E" body made an ideal foundation for Cadillac's revival of the Eldorado image.

Chrysler also participated in this executive express market with their "300" letter series four-passenger coupés. Their special advantage had been the famous "hemi" (hemispherical combustion chamber) high-output engine, but when it was taken out of production in 1965, the substituting 300-series had much less exciting performance to offer.

Studebaker continued its Hawk coupé series, using the 1953-style body with numerous face-lifts through 1964. Raymond Loewy's final performance for the corporation, the 1963 Avanti, did so well that it survived its sponsor and is still manufactured today. Loewy had, again, managed to gather a small group of excellent designers together, and, with his usual flair and encouragement, brought out their best. Tom Kellogg developed the theme of sensuous shapes and slightly raked posture, while Bob Andrews worked on the interior and finishing details.

Lincoln reflected on the growing interest in compact size, and introduced an entirely new Continental in 1961. The wheelbase was shortened from 131 inches to 123, but the quality of its styling was extraordinary. The theme consisted of two deep side pontoons that stood up slightly above the continuous hood to rear deck central form. A well-contoured, trapezoidal upper was placed on top of that. The front door was hinged conventionally at the forward edge, but hinging the rear door at the rear pillar gave a much more convenient access to the rear seat. The simplicity and refinement of the design made its own unique and elegant statement. The four-door convertible, introduced in 1962, had a top that disappeared completely under a section of the rear deck, and is still considered to be one of the handsomest luxury cars ever offered. Throughout its history, the American automobile industry has demonstrated its resilience and ability to meet new challenges. Product refinement to improve the existing state of the art and development of new trends to suit the changing market continued smoothly until 1973. Most consumers *expected* that a new car, given reasonable maintenance and care, would run for well over 100,000 miles without needing a major overhaul; brakes, tires, and paint excepted. Accelerated corrosion from the salts used to melt snow and ice was controlled to some degree by undercoatings, automatic flushing, and drying channels around structural areas and the use of plastic inner wheelhouses. Electronic ignition and fuel injection systems added efficiency and longer life to engines. Automatic transmissions became virtually foolproof, and helped to lengthen engine life through better torque/speed management. Reliable air-conditioning not only made cars habitable in all climates, but also became a normal accessory. Power steering virtually became standard. Automatic cruise control helped drivers maintain economical average speeds on long trips. The improvement in automobile cassette recording sound systems may have been one of the greatest advances in helping to control the driver's emotional stability during periods of tension.

The supplemental industries that perfected and supplied these desirable accessories added employment for thousands of skilled workers. On the other hand, such refinement and luxury added to the cost of the vehicle and occasionally made it more vulnerable to deterioration, but most consumers were swept along with the tide and felt it was worth the risk.

For years, geologists have been predicting that the world's fossil fuel supplies were limited, and that it was only a matter of time before warfare erupted over ownership of the precious remains. Americans, like most inhabitants of the civilized world, heard no sputtering from the engine to tell them that a change was needed until it happened. Suddenly, the supplies to local outlets began to run dry and there were lines at every gas pump. The news media was quick to raise every flag of alarm, and there was talk of rationing.

Cadillac Fleetwood Eldorado. *1968. Model 69437. Engine V-8, 375 h.p. Steel body, leather or vinyl seats. Designer General Motors Design Staff, Cadillac Studio. Manufacturer General Motors Corporation, Detroit*

The frustration was many-sided. Car owners were stuck with what they had, and simply had to cut back on the luxury of free movement. The situation was worse for the auto manufacturers, who were unable to provide more economical substitutes without years of development and reorientation. The federal government felt pressure from consumer groups and began developing and issuing regulations. It has been argued that the process of conforming to the increasingly stringent regulations added more than twenty percent to the vehicle cost. In the bumper area alone, one could criticize the industry for drifting into a cosmetic myopia, and for ignoring the fundamental requirements for daily bumps and crunches, but then the government's firm stand on energy absorption suddenly created enormous cost and manufacturing problems. As manufacturing costs were going up, sizes and weights were coming down, and it became difficult for the consumer to understand why a less powerful and more crowded small car should cost more than the glamorous beauty he bought several years ago. Consumers started keeping their old cars longer because the cost of repairs was minor compared to the accelerated depreciation of big cars, and the resulting increase in the price gap of new car purchase. Gasoline was plentiful again, but it cost a lot more.

Europe and Asia had been living with high fuel costs for decades and had refined the art of small, lively, and economical cars. Some American manufacturers had developed successful compact models, and were able to improve and market them while they researched and developed for the future. For most, though, the big profit-makers died, and there was little cash flow to divert into new research and development. The Ford Motor Company had a well-established international manufacturing and marketing system, and could lean on its European establishment for balance. General Motors took massive loans and retreated from some of its dispersed assembly plants, which had suddenly become liabilities. The success story of the seventies and the eighties belongs to the Chrysler Corporation, whose apt management, under the stewardship of President Lee Iacocca, reshaped its new corporation into profitability from the brink of bankruptcy in a few short years.

The products of the early seventies reached a stage of proliferation that was difficult to comprehend. The technique involved developing a minimum number of basic assemblies that were made up of a drive line (engine, transmission, axles), suspension components, auxiliary units (gas tank, electrical system, frame ends), cowl box, and floor pan. It was then possible to erect on these foundations a number of variations in body and trim structure. Inner body structures that included hinge and lock pillars, sills and halos, glass drops, and control assemblies could accept different outer skin assemblies. The Camaro and Firebird are good examples of variation on a common structure.

Reduction of tooling costs is the key to competitive price structuring. An apparently large number of models was created as a marketing tool, to appeal in detail to the American assumption of individuality. The real problem in restructuring the products for the new market of the late seventies and early eighties has been to reduce the complexity of the combinations in order to reduce the cost of all-new development, while continuing to offer appropriate products, to compete with all potential obstacles. The expedient "join 'em if you can't beat 'em" has meant absorbing some imported products within the domestic distribution and service network—captive imports. Absorbing foreign products has enabled domestic manufacturers to take advantage of their international statuses. General Motors' "T" car, which was the Chevrolet Vega, was developed internationally and marketed on four continents. Sharing costs in this way can obviously accelerate the future development of automotive design, as long as the basic design is, in itself, international.

Most people close to the process of American automobile design feel that the industry is poised on the threshold of a brilliant renaissance, and that the products of the eighties will supersede, in efficiency and artful refinement, anything experienced before. Superior products will be needed to compete with the high-quality foreign vehicles that have enjoyed a commercial penetration. The contemporary field of automobile design is working with a vision of personal mobility and communication that relies less heavily on the automobile, and includes potential systems of movement management that can be segmented or combined. The transition into these various and selected modes is the province of free enterprise. The major transportation manufacturers have anticipated this gradual change, and have diversified while supporting free research and maintaining commercial growth. Each of the world's major car manufacturers has established a series of research and design think tanks in southern California. Relatively removed from hierarchical interference, the organizations are developing feasible new ways to solve future transportation problems and to improve their parent corporations' products in international competition.

The application of high technology to contemporary products is another example of the rapid development in auto design. Emission control via on-board computers is one. The little black box that measures air and fuel mixtures to the power plant is far more efficient than yesterday's common meter adjustment. Instrumentation that can anticipate problems and inform the driver before they occur is the present state of the art. Aerodynamics is one of the most variable and logical arts presently applied. The results of its application are fundamentally beautiful and truly exemplary of profound cultural reflection.

Opposite: Chevrolet Corvette. *Sting Ray*

BUCKMINSTER FULLER'S DYMAXION CAR

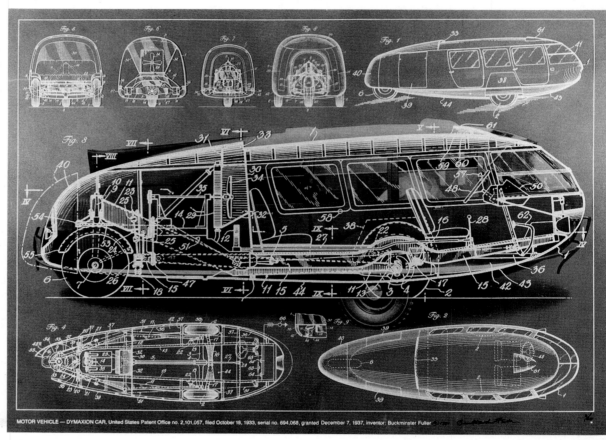

MOTOR VEHICLE — DYMAXION CAR, United States Patent Office no. 2,101,057, filed October 18, 1933, serial no. 694,068, granted December 7, 1937, Inventor: Buckminster Fuller

Buckminster Fuller. Motor Vehicle Dymaxion Car. *1981. White ink on clear polyester film on a screenprint on Lenox paper, 30 × 40". After patent application drawing filed October, 1933, granted December 7, 1937. Carl Solway Gallery, Cincinnati*

hree Dymaxion cars, designed and built by the architect-engineer R. Buckminster Fuller in 1933 and 1934, form part of his visionary scheme for complete reform of the human environment through revolutionary design. In addition to the vehicles, Fuller's Dymaxion world was based on completely prefabricated houses, dwelling units, and geodesic domes. The Dymaxion concept represents Fuller's interest in functionalism, efficiency, engineering innovation, and the geometric principles of nature, which he applied to daily living systems. The word Dymaxion, a fusion of "dynamism," "maximum," and "ions," implies doing the most with the least, or maximum performance with minimum materials.

The Dymaxion world was to be constructed around a mass-produced, factory-built, energy-efficient house that was conceived to exist as a tensile structure capable of suspension in remote places. The Dymaxion house, an entirely self-sufficient single-family dwelling, utilized a centralized living core that incorporated plumbing, cooking, and sleeping quarters. Meant to provide optimum shelter at minimum cost, it was developed according to available production technology and the price scale then current in the automobile industry—approximately twenty-five cents per pound, or fifteen hundred dollars. Fuller's idea for a vehicle to transport people to and from these living cells evolved into the Dymaxion car, first proposed in 1927 as a four-dimensional flying auto-airplane apparatus, or "omni-directional transport."

In 1933, Fuller rented a Locomobile factory in Bridgeport, Connecticut, to develop an earthbound version of the Dymaxion car. His collaborator and chief engineer on the project, airplane designer and naval architect Starling Burgess,

shared Fuller's conviction that technical innovation and design should remain responsible to social issues. Under Fuller's supervision, his friend, the sculptor Isamu Noguchi, built plaster scale models to define the unconventional aerodynamic hull structure of the projected car. On July 12, 1933, crowds gathered to watch the car's first road test on the private speedway of the Bridgeport plant. Innovative even by today's standards, the Dymaxion car boasted front-wheel drive, rear steering, and a rear engine. Its three wheels, each capable of ninety-degree turns, allowed the vehicle exceptional maneuverability; the steering wheel could be turned full circle. A submarinelike periscope protruded through the roof

above the driver's seat, designed to permit maximum rear visibility. With the lowest center of gravity of any road vehicle of its time, the car seated eleven passengers. Its Ford V-8 engine was capable of speeds up to 120 miles per hour and the vehicle consumed fuel at the rate of only 30 miles to the gallon.

Perhaps the most remarkable feature of the Dymaxion car was its aerodynamic form. Fuller's studies of airflow effects led to the streamlined shape of the aircraft-steel chassis that encased most of the running gear. The triangular frame and rear steering were derived from models of airplanes and boats, rather than the horse-drawn vehicle, the immediate predecessor of the conventional automobile.

Opposite: Buckminster Fuller. Early study of airflow effects around a conventional car contour and around contour of an ideal streamlined form. 1930. The Buckminster Fuller Institute, Philadelphia

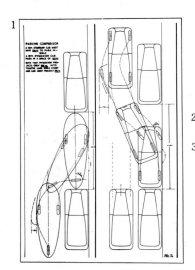

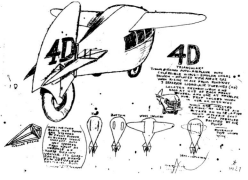

1. Buckminster Fuller. Sketch showing the parking path of the Dymaxion car compared with that of a standard 15-foot car. 1933. The Buckminster Fuller Institute, Philadelphia. 2. Buckminster Fuller. Sketch of early 4-D version of omni-directional transport. 1927. 3. Fuller's Dymaxion car No. 3 (restored) next to a Republic Seabee amphibian plane, also owned by Fuller. Wichita, Kansas, 1945. 4. Fuller's Dymaxion car No. 2. 1934. 5. Fuller's Dymaxion car No. 1. 1933

The completely drivable Dymaxion car caused much excitement when it appeared on the roadway, particularly on the streets of New York City. After riding with Fuller, author H. G. Wells described futuristic cars very similar to the Dymaxion in his book *The Shape of Things to Come*.

A second Dymaxion car prototype with a lighter three-frame structure and recessed headlights that doubled as air intakes was built later in 1933 as a refinement of the first car, which had been damaged in an accident and restored by Fuller to its original condition. Fuller presented a third and final Dymaxion car prototype at the 1934 Chicago World's Fair in the American transportation pageant "The Wings of a Century." In the

1940s Fuller regained ownership of the car after it had passed through the hands of several owners and disappeared from view. He restored the car, which had been driven some 300,000 miles over a nine-year period, to its original condition. It is currently housed in Harrah's Automobile Collection in Reno, Nevada.

Fuller designed a fourth Dymaxion car with a retractable wheel tail boom and a seven-foot driving divan that converted into a bed, but it never went beyond the planning stage. A 1933 application for a motor vehicle patent on the original Dymaxion car was granted in 1937, but Fuller's visions of mass-produced Dymaxion cars were never realized.

—ELIZABETH A. T. SMITH

Opposite: Fuller's Dymaxion car No. 3 at the 1934 Chicago World's Fair

Detail of a 1965 *Citroën*
Saloon, Model 2CV

TOWARD THE CULTURE OF THE AUTOMOBILE

Has the automobile as a cultural product earned its place in official aesthetics, does it still belong to a separate domain, or has it merely gained acceptance within official culture by dint of constant visual repetition? In other words, can the automobile be made to obey the canons of "good design," or is it irretrievably savage and refractory to the functionalist theories generally held in design criticism?

Is the car destined to become a tool like any other, or will it continue to be loaded with metaphoric significance? To seek answers to these questions is in itself a controversial undertaking. To inquire into the "cultural status" of the automobile today retains a provocative flavor, though, to be fair, some of the question's thunder has been stolen in recent years. The ranks of cultural organizers have been broken by those who choose to honor and study the automobile on its own terms, in such venues as the "Carrozzeria Italiana" exhibition in Pasadena in May 1981, or with the June 1984 "Automobile and Culture" exhibition connected with this book at the Museum of Contemporary Art in Los Angeles. There remains the nagging thought that the "and" in "Automobile and Culture" may be there to separate the two terms, as well as link them.

The gradual rise of the automobile as a respectable cultural by-product has been quietly happening for over a century, and will probably end only with the unlikely demise of individual transportation. By contrast, the controversy over the "decency" of automobile aesthetics is a product of the mid-fifties, when designers and architects, having failed to annex automotive design, decided instead to ostracize it.

In those days, European industrial designers (all trained as, and some practicing as, architects) began to evolve a group self-consciousness, postulated the artistic dignity of their vocation, and adopted, not unexpectedly, a professional ethic largely inspired by the rigorous morals and functional approaches of the Modernist movement.

The famous judgment attributed somewhat imprecisely to Adolf Loos, "Ornament is crime," became (rather late and with some loss of subtlety), the centerpiece of an aesthetic meant to be necessary and suf-

Benz Patent Motor Car. *1886. Model Three-wheeler. Engine single-cylinder, L-head, 0.9 h.p. Wood body, leather seat. Designer Karl Benz. Manufacturer Benz & Co., Mannheim, Germany. Deutsches Museum, Munich*

ficient to any honest and culturally aware industrial designer. In some ways, this aesthetic was a scaled-down replica of the great holy war waged by the Modernists against eclecticism and formalism in architecture.

In a manner analogous to what happened in architecture, the social and production aspects of industrial design were emphasized to the point where they began to dictate a largely abstract and inapplicable aesthetic norm. No one in Europe could muster the candid courage that enabled James Marston Fitch to state, in his lecture "The Critic's Shifting View," that he objected to Adolf Loos's vision on the grounds that implicitly "he was, by extension, calling beauty itself a crime." There have been many people who still earnestly deceived themselves into thinking that simple geometric shapes agreed with the constraints imposed by manufacturing tools, and that simplicity and linearity of form were an intrinsically moral approach to beauty.

This thesis was nothing more than an abbreviated, indeed mutilated, version of Gropius's Bauhaus manifesto, which in this portable form became the true faith of an entire generation of architects and visual arts creators, almost all of whom were altogether ignorant of industrial production methods. As a result, their greatest impact was exercised on the area within their reach—namely, the design of domestic appliances. It appears that no one succeeded in getting across to them, either during school years or in the course of professional practice, the fact that machine tools are impartial executors, capable of making *most any* shape with equal ease. Indeed, the machine aesthetic would in some respects benefit from a modicum of ornamentation, which often comes in handy to disguise the bareness of mass-produced objects. To quote J. M. Fitch again, out of time but not out of place: "Science and technology appeared to that generation as much safer paragons than human passion." This attitude was largely an act of faith rather than knowledge, and its propounders were almost wholly ignorant of the complexity of technology and its own laws of organic form.

The automobile, the epitome of industrial production methods and the prime candidate for the supposed design constraints of mass production, somehow slipped from the moralistic grip of industrial design and was declared to exist in a fringe area outside official art. (We use the terms "industrial design" and the equally arbitrary "good design" not in their literal senses, but in the allusive connotation that made them reign over ideas in their day.)

These were days when Detroit's output was heavily symbolic, and it comes as no surprise if European appreciation of these cars, on aesthetico-moral grounds, was less than enthusiastic. Some United States critics shared these strictures; again, J. M. Fitch wrote: "The stylistic distance between the Platonic geometry of the new Seagram Building in New York and the absurd vulgarity of this year's automobile is a measure of the crisis in American design today." And a little later he stated: "Anyone who has watched the migration of tail-lights and brakelights over the rear end of American cars or the ever-changing size and shape of the radiators knows that this kind of change is completely divorced from objective progress."

Aside from the brilliant defense expressed in a number of essays by Reyner Banham from 1955 onward, European criticisms of automobile styling, indeed of the idea of styling itself, were no less sharp and authoritative.

Tomás Maldonado, then member of the Council of the Hochschule für Gestaltung (Academy of Design) in Ulm, Germany, vented his displeasure at "the huge circulating dinosaurs of Detroit" in the course of a lecture given at the Brussels World Fair in 1958. He went as far as to name explicitly, and none too politely, Virgil Exner, who was then responsible for styling at the Chrysler Corporation, and to articulate the problem in terms of social responsibility: "I am not convinced that the aerodynamic fantasies ... coincide with the artistic needs of the man in the street."

Maldonado deftly turned the tables on those who claimed that planned obsolescence was the unavowed aim of yearly novelty, and suggested instead that the change was illusory, and that no deep structural progress was under way, at any rate no leap comparable to that between the Ford models T and A. Maldonado resorted to the utopian *a priori* judgments of the "Machine Aesthetic," setting forth the following proposition: "If, in the past, the product to a certain extent determined the operative behavior of the machine, then in the future it will be the operative behavior of the machine which will determine the product." This view is none other than the ancient myth of the "production machine" as a sufficiently inflexible stiffener of "aesthetic and moral rigor," which by its presence alone precludes any hankerings toward mere styling. (For Maldonado, it was no longer the machine tool pure and simple, but instead something in operational research and automation—two elements then new on the scene—in which he was particularly interested.)

This thesis is worth refuting at once. Much as Le Corbusier and his friends of the periodical *L'Esprit Nouveau* were wrong in their estimations that simple objects were most easily made by machines and were hence "better" aesthetically, Maldonado's guess that the automation of the production process would dictate the shape of the product has been disproved by events.

In the twenty-five years since the Brussels lecture, the automobile industry has vastly improved and increased its automated production capabilities. Enormous and enormously complex robot machines now take care of body assembly and painting without human intervention. But as far as we are aware, the only alteration in the car itself to be produced by this revolution has been a minor, and by no means universal, change in the connection between roof and sides. The robots themselves have become increasingly accommodating. A robot of the most recent generation can determine which type of car will be brought to it by the conveyer, select its own program, and thus tolerate work on a fluctuating assembly line.

Maldonado could hardly be expected to have foreseen these developments, but he was active at the time in discouraging the use of the automobile as a didactic subject in industrial design courses at the Hochschule für Gestaltung on the grounds that it was too emotionally loaded a product. It is of anecdotal interest to recall that one of the most gifted students to attend that course in 1958, Pio Manzù, was later to prove an innovative and talented automobile designer. He made his first drawings of automobiles in his spare time and, so to speak, did them in a clandestine manner.

This situation was by no means the result of an isolated manic attitude on the part of Tomás Maldonado or his colleague Hans Gugelot, who was then in charge of the industrial design department. The vast majority of Modernist European architects held similar views on the automobile, particularly if it had been made in Detroit. As for a European automobile, well, a hopeful posture could still be adopted, but only along the following lines:

A. Strong reprobation of its opportunist design, its anthropomorphic and/or spatial symbolism, all naturally concerned with a distasteful will to power.

B. Exclusion of the automobile from any form of cultural dignity, and in any event from the world of "good design."

C. Attempted annexation and reform along reductive schemes. A good example might be the Diamond project produced by Gio Ponti in 1954. This design, by a master of Italian postwar architecture, featured a faceted bodywork impossible to make by steel press methods, but equally fiendish to realize in then-promising fiberglass.

D. Confident use of the "wisdom of hindsight" method to incorporate cars already in production along functionalist lines. This happened with the Citroën DS 19, which was exhibited in the Industrial Design section of the XI Milan Triennale (1957) with the following caption: "The car's shape was...arrived at from purely technical requirements. It is nowadays no longer surprising to find beauty where there is only technical excellence. This is yet another illustration of a well-known fact: the search for a scientifically coherent solution is often rewarded, as if by miracle (sic!) by an unlooked for aesthetic success. And it is deeply satisfying, even on a moral level, to find that an object exquisitely fit for its intended use is also beautiful to look at, and that functional efficiency is but another road to beauty."

This vapid rehash of functionalist credos lay in a direct line of descent from the prescriptive statements of the Bauhaus manifesto (1919), but it was stripped of the moral and political tensions that help to explain, if not altogether justify, many similar utterances made in the first quarter of this century. Undoubtedly, the pseudo-functionalist culture that lazily held sway until the end of the fifties received invaluable assistance from Herbert Read's *Art and Industry*: for a long time, this was the only elementary text on these problems.

In fact, at the time, several far more stimulating alternative ideas were already at large. Two essays written with great acumen by Reyner Banham had appeared a few years earlier, constituting in 1958 a largely unexploded time bomb. "Machine Aesthetic," and "Industrial Design and Popular Art" put forward an innovative thesis that was echoed by the article "Le colpe dei padri" in *Casabella-continuità,* and by Gillo Dorfles, one of the most authoritative Italian students of visual communications and industrial design.

Under the heading "Machine Aesthetic," the first of his two essays, Banham sought to define and refute the idea of justifying simple bare shapes on the grounds that they were easier to make by machine. As Banham stated this dictum: "maximally useful, minimally priced objects take on geometric shapes." This central tenet adopted by the Modern movement pioneers was restated later by Herbert Read and Max Bill. Banham then found it easy to prove that this assumption had not influenced industrial production, and to suggest instead that the "machine aesthetic" was a kind of defensive apparatus enabling architects to pass supposedly competent aesthetic judgments, while hiding their inability to contribute to technological progress.

Banham's attack was fierce and accurately aimed: "Architects are frightened of machinery, and have been so ever since engineering broke loose from the back pages of Vitruvius and set up on its own." This is a fitting description of the situation of automobile design. The architects who established themselves as critics of industrial design had no objections to automobile aesthetics while it was still cast in the established "Vitruvian" mold, i.e., in the neoclassical nineteenth-century engineering tradition and the equally academic horse-drawn carriage. Problems began when the automobile developed its own formal code distinct from anything around it; in other words, when it became an automobile proper.

Banham's idea, the intellectual kernel of both his essays, proposed an aesthetic of the transient, typical of industrial products and mass media, in contrast to the durable aesthetic of fine arts. This proposal was no doubt understood correctly by his audience, but his conclusion appears to have escaped almost everyone: if the design of mass-produced objects is part of popular art and must make use of mass media, then its aesthetic can, indeed must, be different from that of fine arts. This distinction makes it pointless to criticize the design of mass-produced objects on moral or other grounds for its lack of conformity to visual schemes belonging to architecture, and, in particular, to the bare, linear rationalist school.

As an immediate corollary of this theorem, Banham daringly went on to defend and justify the "Borax" approach—the device of increasing the visual impact of a product by overloading the symbolism of its design. In his own words: "Like the tree, the building is a long-standing investment. Compared with it the motor-car is, like the fruit, a deciduous affair. Its season is the four or five year retooling cycle of the big manufacturers, and like the fruit it must have an appetizing exterior. In this situation Borax is entirely proper.... Basically, its propriety to automotive design lies in its symbolic content, which is concerned, more than anything else, with penetration."

Banham expanded and refined this theory four years later in an article published in *Stile Industria*. He meant it to serve as a comment on Maldonado's Brussels lecture, but did not succeed, perhaps through misunderstanding and lack of publicity, in rehabilitating the automobile in the eyes of cultural spokesmen. European purist critics and United States collectors continued to prefer automobiles that recognizably belonged to an ill-defined, continuously shifting but unsinkable ideal of permanent aesthetic worth.

Banham's defense was undoubtedly correct and penetrating, but his justification of transient aesthetics retained a sense of incompleteness, because it failed to account for a fact of which he seems not to have been aware: the automobile, or indeed the product of any other industry, can

Steam-Driven Vehicle *(Fardier à vapeur). 1770–71. 2 cyl., steam-powered engine. Wood chassis and seat. Designer and manufacturer Nicolas-Joseph Cugnot.*
Musée du Conservatoire National des Arts et Metiers, Paris

occasionally escape the treadmill of transience to give birth to an object still prone to practical obsolescence, but which is perennially beautiful. Some of these objects were in fact produced in significant numbers, and were markedly successful with the public.

This escape from "aesthetic consumption" is at odds with Banham's thesis: in March 1959, he wrote: "The aesthetics of expendability, as revealed in the products of the communications industry, as manifested in the products of Detroit or of the leading fashion houses, may not be the kind of thing that the European tradition in aesthetics can easily accommodate— so much the worse for the European tradition."

So much the worse, indeed, except this is not what happened. Twenty-five years later, Detroit dinosaurs have given way to smaller, leaner species, far closer in looks to the controlled sobriety of the European tradition. Meanwhile, European automobile production has gone the way of rationalization, and its production process now leaves very little room for

Fiat City Mini Taxicab. *1968. Model 850. Engine 4 cyl., overhead valve, 52 h.p. Steel body, imitation leather seats. Designer Pio Manzù. Manufacturer Fiat, Turin. Fiat Styling Center, Turin, Italy*

purely provocative prototypes and dream cars. Some European manufacturers, despite occasionally disastrous results, draw upon the expert knowledge of industrial designers originally educated, so to speak, in the other camp—i.e., architects.

There has been a measure of intermixing between two previously separate worlds: automobile designers on one hand, and university-trained architects and designers on the other. There is as yet no school capable of teaching automobile design at the graduate level in Europe. The automobile world has seized upon the innovative content of "good design," not without a measure of risky opportunism, and it remains to be seen who will be the hunter, and who the prey.

The cultural establishment has also brought its rules up-to-date, and has taken stock of the obvious novelty and force embodied in ninety years of automobile design. The term "material culture" has come to denote an area just as fertile and dignified as official culture. At long last, a serious attempt to understand car design as it is practiced has been made, and it has become self-evident that as far as expressive design and formal composition are concerned, there never were two entirely separate cultures, as was once thought.

It would be inappropriate to offer a purely aesthetic judgment on a few exceptional automobiles, along the lines of the excellent "Eight Automobiles" exhibition organized by Arthur Drexler in 1951 for the Museum of Modern Art in New York. Today, the genesis of a production automobile is interesting insofar as it combines technological requirements and visual syntax.

This happened only very recently, and we may be too close to perceive the tortuous interdisciplinary path that has brought us at last to this long-awaited critical vantage point. Instead, I shall attempt in the second half of this essay to sketch the evolutionary strategy of that most emotional object, the automobile.

An attempt to determine historical priority in the invention of the automobile always leads to failure, and eventually compels one to accept that it may be the brainchild of a collective endeavor spread over two centuries. The so-called "centenary of the automobile," scheduled under the aegis of Daimler-Benz AG with great pomp for May 1986, is a purely conventional affair, and largely a tribute to Mercedes's enduring industrial muscle.

There will no doubt be Italian connoisseurs to recall the priority of Barsanti and Matteucci over Otto and Langen, and that of Enrico Bernardi (born in Verona 1841, died in Turin 1919) over Karl Benz and Gottlieb Daimler. Equally, French historians will legitimately claim that Édouard Delamarre-Debouteville allegedly built, in 1883, a gas-powered vehicle with four wheels and an internal combustion engine. Despite solid documentary proof, these claims will no doubt remain unheard because of a lack of a public relations impetus matching that provided by Germany's oldest manufacturer.

This small distortion of history should not cause us to despair: six or twelve months lead by Bernardi over Benz is a matter for specialists to settle. Proof that Delamarre's machine actually worked must be compared with actual production in numbers afforded to Benz and Daimler's creations.

By contrast, it is interesting to inquire about the background of the emergence and definition of an automobile culture, and into the field of influences it has been subject to. Research in automotive vehicles was always carried out in one of three environments: military engineering, applied physical science, or the fragmented, small-scale world of the artisans, precision mechanics, and instrument makers.

As always, military engineering benefited from an abundance of funds, and was the first to produce mechanical vehicles propelled by men or animals. Machines, such as those designed by Roberto Valturio or Agostino Ramelli, were meant to be used to assault fortifications during sieges, and their living power sources had to be adequately protected from enemy fire. Their propulsion mechanisms made the first use of elementary mechanical devices compatible with wood: the straight-toothed gear and the screw. As befits military engineering, their exterior aspects were altogether devoid of frills. The first truly automotive vehicle—that is to say, a vehicle propelled by a mechanical energy source—was also military: the steam-driven car built by Nicolas-Joseph Cugnot (1769–1770) was intended for gun transport. Though clumsy as a carriage, its mechanics have the grace of a magnified clockwork and belong squarely in late-eighteenth-century mechanical culture.

Research, pure and applied, in the motive potential of fluid state changes was carried out at the time principally in monastic circles, which were then invaluable repositories promoting knowledge. During a stay in Peking in 1861, the Belgian Jesuit missionary Ferdinand Verbiest demonstrated an automotive carriage driven by a rudimentary steam-driven paddlewheel. It is also worth recalling that Eugenio Barsanti (1821–1864) was a monk.

On the manufacturing side, exceptionally able precision mechanics, instrument makers, and rectifiers were in some way connected, usually through family ties, to arms manufacture, the first steel-based industry in most countries. It is no accident that cities with great automobile traditions, such as Turin, were originally military arsenals where arms production was run by the state and set standards of discipline, coherent planning, and, most of all, standardization of components built with greater precision than ever before.

Some would go so far as to attribute the panelbeating excellence of French and Italian craftsmen to a hereditary transmission of their ancient legendary skill in shaping lightweight suits of armor and helmets that weighed little more than a top hat. It is more likely that professional education, the major means of cultural self-improvement in the late nineteenth century, played the decisive role.

Mechanical engineers, university physicists, and chemists (many connected with the Catholic church), teachers, and students of professional schools, were all proficient at employing technical draftsmanship and engineering calculations as part of the solution to mechanical or structural problems. But they also used a common ingredient derived from their humanist educations: the practice or, at any rate, the habit of using classical proportions and ornaments in the Vitruvian tradition.

They also shared a degree of distance, either by design or by accident, from the artistic avant-garde. The aesthetic world, the "taste" of engineers, churchmen, and craftsmen, was antiquated and out of step with its time. Their understandable artistic conservatism may explain why the automobile ceased borrowing from convention only after it succeeded in gaining autonomy.

Let us take as an example the official F.I.A.T. car bodies: they were the most modern of their time, yet they waited until 1911 and 1912 to reveal the first signs of any Art Nouveau influences. Even the improbable supposition of a complete communications breakdown between the Piedmontese capital and the rest of the world (Liberty's opening in London in 1875, S. Bing's shop Maison de l'Art Nouveau in Paris in 1895) explains nothing, for Turin itself in 1902 organized the "Esposizione di Arte Decorativa Odierna" ("Exhibition of Today's Decorative Arts"), which included the much-vaunted Scottish exhibit and the famous "Rose Boudoir" designed by Charles Rennie Mackintosh's group. We still have to account for the ten-year delay before a major manufacturer would take up these new stylistic suggestions, despite the international success and acknowledged elegance of Art Nouveau. We must conclude that the automobile world was artistically "airtight" when it began to break free from the artistic and mechanical tradition of the horse-drawn carriage.

THE FUNCTIONAL
AUTOMOBILE

Early automobiles, whether just imagined or actually built, whether powered by hand cranks, springs, or sails, had often borrowed their decorations from royal carriages, church pulpits, and Renaissance or Baroque decoration. All this fortunately ended with the advent of the petrol engine. The engine itself would eventually lose its monumental aspect, and with it the decorative architectural elements that it had been given by academic engineers. (To be fair, most of the early engines were static and stood on workshop floors.) Freed from the supercilious university laboratory, the lightweight engine showed its exceptional practical vigor by becoming a plain, unadorned industrial product. (De Dion-Bouton sold 26,000 single-cylinder engines in the first half of 1902.)

The automobile found itself at a crossroads: it could go the way of cycles (tricycles and quadricycles with tubular steel frames), or follow the "heavy" engineering approach, with reinforced wood, and, later, steel frame struts. The extraordinary efficiency of the 1901 Mercedes Simplex was to tip the scales in favor of the latter.

Both schools made sparing use of ornament: the overall proportion and whatever else could be plausibly borrowed from carriages was used; the task of carrying five or six people in relative comfort over awful roads remained the same, and speed had not increased over that of horses. But this resemblance was dictated by practice and habit as much as by function, for the early car was compelled to borrow techniques and models from practicing coachbuilders. Something as audacious as an automobile could either look like a sporting vehicle—according to Barney Clarke, like "cars that were fabricated out of sheer excitement"—or could opt instead for the reassuring lines of the horse-drawn carriage. In the early years of the century, the engine hood was the only innovative element in front-engined cars (in a minority of small cars, and almost all large ones). The hood acquired its first distinctive style with the "alligator-nosed" Renault of 1901, which later became a trademark of the firm, until the end of the twenties. (The conceptual origin of this shape probably goes back to the 1898 Panhards.)

Above: Renault Runabout. *1901. Model Type D. Engine 1 cyl., L-head, 6 h.p. Wood body, leather seats, 56" × 8'2". Designer Louis Renault. Manufacturer Renault Freres, Billancourt, Boulogne, France. Regie Nationale des Usines, Renault, Paris*

Opposite: Renault Town Car. *1910. Model AX. Engine 2 cyl., L-head. 10 h.p. Wood body, aluminum hood and fenders, Scottish leather front seats, English broadcloth rear seats. Designer and manufacturer Renault Freres, Billancourt, Boulogne, France. Hillcrest Motor Company, Beverly Hills, California*

Within the next few years, the frontal honeycomb radiator, seen for the first time on the 1901 Mercedes, was used by all automobile manufacturers except Renault. The frontal radiator made the engine hood a continuous sectioned box, a device used until 1908. This solution accentuated the separation between engine cover and body; from a frontal view, the automobile, in a striking, evocative configuration, acquired two headlight "eyes" on either side of the radiator. The automobile thus developed a snout, in some cases a face, whose features were deliberately used by manufacturers to identify particular makes. The effect only works in full-face view: from the side or the rear, most cars of the period are hard to identify, because *baquet* (cockpit) seats (deep and padded, used in the open types like tonneaux and double phaetons) all look alike, as do the closed bodies of landaulets and coupés.

It must be remembered that horse-drawn carriages had little or no maker's identity and were instead specialized according to their intended use. The first automobiles adopted this ritual typology of shape and color, following social usage rather than function. The late-nineteenth-century carriage is arguably a functional vehicle, and what ornament it has arose from the natural curves of structures and surfaces (for instance, the curved blades of the suspension springs). Similarly, the first automobiles, with their honest, open mechanical design and their variously styled body types, must be considered functional.

Since automobiles of this period were principally meant for fun, and actual journeys were made by train or tramway, they often looked very much like tools, albeit highly refined ones, with the natural tendency of tools to become stylized rather than decorated (consider, for instance, axes, bicycles, or carriages, all hard to differentiate by make). Yet while the bicycle consistently rejected grafts of style for over a century, the automobile soon became a spectacularly fertile ground for styling. This process began in earnest during the first ten years of car production, as the automobile moved away from the horse-drawn carriage; it became faster, more aerodynamic, lighter, and stronger. Since it was built on a greater industrial scale, it was less complicated to assemble. The automobile ceased to be a hybrid and became a full-fledged, independent entity.

Despite this newfound independence, the next ten years did not witness the appearance of much superimposed styling. The automobile remained highly functional, and the industrial drive due to the Great War helped it along, bringing with it the first indication of aerodynamic design.

The emancipation of the automobile from the canons of horse-drawn carriages was a necessary prerequisite for its industrialization, but the process remains unfinished to this day. In its early stages, the transformation was retarded by several factors.

The existing tried-and-tested constructional techniques of horse-drawn carriages had to be replaced by others, for which machines and factories were entirely lacking. In the early years of the century, automobile factories were small workshops without tradition, while carriage coachbuilders were large, influential, long-established concerns, equipped with adequate tooling and machinery to deal with repetitive tasks.

Industrial bodywork failed to achieve the dignity and aesthetic perfection of the coachbuilt automobile, particularly as regards detailing, choice of materials, and finish. As a result, coachbuilding survived as a luxury trade until the forties, and lives on to this day.

Automobile factories, then principally chassis manufacturers, drew exclusively on experience in mechanics, largely obtained in such other fields as small arms and textiles. This enabled the coachbuilding establishment to become the suppliers of bodies or, at any rate, of body designs and prototypes for the automobile factory. The latter could then build them in its own body department, often assembled by acquiring small coachbuilding firms or by hiring managers and workers from the large ones. The independent designer only surfaced in the later twenties, and very few existed; more usually, the designer was a full-time employee of the firm or a member of the owner's family, as was the case, for example, of Emilio Castagna.

Clearly, these factors contributed powerfully to technological lag and aesthetic conservatism because they discouraged interaction between creative talent and new technology. The decisive break came from two new elements that were often associated: the need to make aerodynamic or "streamlined" bodies, and the rise of pressed-panel technology for bodywork.

The commingling of these new ingredients signaled the beginning of a dialogue that continues to this day between the aesthetic and manual excellence of the great coachbuilding tradition and the innovators. The innovators need not be outsiders: they often belong to the same school, they can be junior members of a coachbuilding family (Pininfarina *vs.* Giovanni Farina), or can be young collaborators gradually acquiring independence. Despite their impending doom, the long-term strength of the great coachbuilders lay in their ability to mediate, subdivide, temper, and finally

Opposite: Automobiles were still conversation pieces in 1909. This French single-cylinder car has a Renault-type "crocodile nose" hood over the engine, which was moved up to the front of the vehicle. The body is a strictly functional open four seater of the tonneau type with a rear entrance to the back seats.

Renault Town Car. *1910*

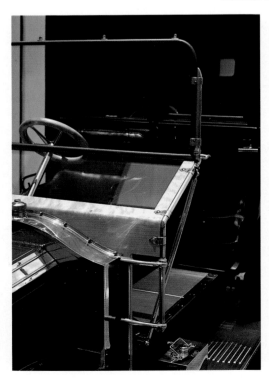

render socially acceptable what was in essence an aesthetic, technological, and behavioral revolution ("descending" into a car rather than climbing into a carriage, etc.).

It would have been difficult for any of the great firms representing the coachbuilding tradition in France, England, or Italy, to break with the canons of *savoir faire,* on which their status by appointment to the establishment depended. The break became possible only with the birth of the sports car, which was less restricted by social rules and belonged to the realm of novelty and provocation in which new rules are made.

This phenomenon transpired, first within, and later outside the great coachbuilders when new ones appeared, so to speak, by budding, as in the case of Pininfarina, Touring, and Zagato in Italy, and Figoni and Falaschi in France. The working groups were led by a new generation of men, who were the same age as the automobile itself. They created a new, increasingly independent culture, yet were never forgetful of the arts and crafts tradition, as they had constantly to deal with the "good taste" of their rich customers.

Among the "complete" automobile designers, Ettore Bugatti's story is emblematic: his creative family background and his connection with the artistic milieu around the Brera Academy in Milan were at once helpful and restrictive contributing factors. As a designer, however, he succeeded in "forgetting" all that surrounded him, and designed both engines and bodies along new "clean" lines. Ironically, his son Jean exemplified the force of tradition: his body designs of the twenties were less than revolutionary and very much in a line of direct and respectful descent from such men as Jean-Henri Labourdette.

The long road toward an integral, monolithic body design reached its avowed aim in the forties but started in the last years of the previous century; aerodynamics can fairly be said to be as old as the automobile itself.

A clean shuttle-shaped intent was obvious in the record-breaking electric vehicle Jamais Contente (1899) built in light alloy by Rothschild Coachbuilders for Camille Jenatzy. Wedges and inverted hull shapes are frequently seen on record-breaking racing machines of the early years of the century. In some of his cars, Amedée Bollée, Jr., even tried to give a wedge shape to the big radiators at the prow of his cars, while his 1899 Torpilleur probably sports the first inclined windscreen in automobile history.

In its early days, aerodynamics remained the aesthetic expression of the idea that the machine must somehow cut through the air. Early aerodynamic shapes, however, did not exert the powerful pull that appeared in the thirties, but failed altogether to have any influence on "normal" body design, which remained bound to the carriage form—enormous vertical windscreens behind a flat *coupe-vent* (windshield) at right angles to the engine hood, and very tall bodies.

During the second decade of the century, aerodynamic form appeared only on exceptional, high-performance machines: the barrier between a socially acceptable automobile, such as a town car or opera coupé, and a sporting machine remained insuperable. Even sports cars had to wait until 1912 before being allowed to borrow ideas from record breakers, the dream cars of yesteryear.

Jenatzy Special Torpedo. 1899. Model "Jamais Contente." Rotary electric engine. Partinium (aluminum alloy) body, leatherette seat. Designer Camille Jenatzy. Manufacturer Rothschild & Fils, Coachbuilders, Paris and Rheims. Nicknamed the "Jamais Contente" (Never Satisfied), this electric-powered racing vehicle sported one of the first shuttle-shaped, fully aerodynamic bodies, and on April 29, 1899, became the first land vehicle to break the 100 kilometers-per-hour speed limit

S.T.A.R. Rapid Submarine Coupé. 1908. Engine 4 cylinder, two block, 10–12 h.p. Steel body, wool seats with silk borders. Designer unknown. Manufacturer Diatto-Garavini & Company, Coachbuilders, Turin. On the continent, the search for a design with low air resistance and the influence of military engineering produced sporadic body designs with rounded corners (note rounded windshield) and little exterior ornamentation

Below: F.I.A.T. Racer. 1911. Model S.76. Engine 4 cyl., two block. Aluminum body, leather seat. Designer F.I.A.T. Aviation Staff. Manufacturer F.I.A.T. Body Department, Turin. Built by appointment of the Russian Prince Boris Soukhanoff, this record-breaking race car was perhaps the first Italian example of an ovoidal aerodynamic body form

Below: F.I.A.T. Touring. 1913. Model 501 (Brooklands Type Zero). Engine 51A, 4 cyl., monobloc, 12–15 h.p. Steel body, leather interior. Designer and manufacturer F.I.A.T. Body Department, Turin. This early prototype was built in the torpedo body shape on a Type Zero chassis. The shape of the radiator reflects the influence of the 1911 F.I.A.T. S.76 racer

In 1912–13, F.I.A.T. commissioned from the Turin firm of Locati & Viarengo a new type of touring car that was built on a batch of modified type Zero chassis. Its tall, narrow, and rounded "bull-nose" radiator (as it was to be christened after its appearance on the mass-produced 1913 Morris Oxford and 1915 Cowley) had made its first appearance on the big speed-record car type S.76 300 HP built in 1911 by F.I.A.T. at the behest of the Russian Prince Boris Soukhanoff.

An event of greater importance also took place roughly at the same time. A new type of body appeared in industrial production: the streamlined tourer, whose lines stretched from nose to tail, replaced the earlier, segmented double phaeton shape. The streamlined tourer was the first type of body that owed nothing to the horse-drawn carriage, the first in which the automobile was intended as a complete object. Its invention is attributed to the Frenchman Lamplugh, who designed it in 1908 to 1909. Its aerodynamic tendencies are implicit in the name "torpedo."

The strength of this new body type lay in its simple, unified conception, which made it suitable for industrial and, therefore, standardized production methods. Until the mid-twenties, it was the most popular body type in the western world, as it was vastly cheaper and more durable than the fully enclosed automobiles.

The Lancia Lambda may have been aesthetically jarring, but was undoubtedly structurally coherent: it was the first automobile to arise from a concerted study of body and chassis. The industrial drive of the war effort had expanded the horizons of the automotive industry, while its potential customer market was expanding, thanks in part to the driving experience acquired by many young men during military service. Production demands stimulated the search for alternatives to wooden bodywork, which was still beholden to carriage coachwork. The rapid increase in automobile performance, propelled in the early twenties by new, more powerful engines, showed up the poor structural behavior of some mixed wood/metal constructions, particularly in the connection between chassis and body.

The Lambda project was formally launched on March 15, 1921, at a meeting during which Vincenzo Lancia suggested to a working party headed by Giovan Battista Falchetto an idea that had been patented three years earlier, on December 7, 1918. The story that Lancia himself liked to tell may be apocryphal, but it is supposed to have come to him while he was taking a walk along the seacoast in Liguria. In essence, the body was to be *monocoque,* along the lines of a boat hull, and thus do without frame members that were separate from the body.

The Lambda, which was developed during tests in 1921, had a round body cross-section, and a horseshoe-shaped radiator grille reminiscent of the Bugatti. Bugatti had his reasons for using it, but Lancia was merely quoting an earlier success.

The true test of the shape came during attempts to press the body panels, which proved impossible. The smooth hull was abandoned and replaced by a faceted box that was easier to build and also in keeping with the wave of pseudo-rational design that overtook car design in 1921. This angular look was a distant echo of Cubist and Art Deco influences in reaction to the unexpected longevity of Art Nouveau forms during the rapidly receding Belle Epoque (1911–1914).

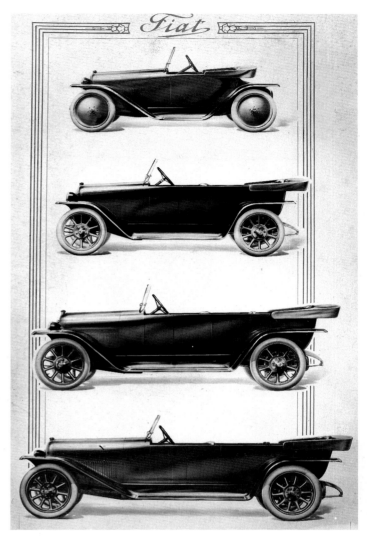

Unfinished advertising artwork representing the Fiat 1918 and 1919 family of models. The body shapes of these mass-produced phaetons were clearly influenced by the rounded radiators of the 1911 S.76 racer and the F.I.A.T. 1913 Brooklands. The two-seater prototype 500 on the top was never produced; the 510 on the bottom had a six-cylinder engine

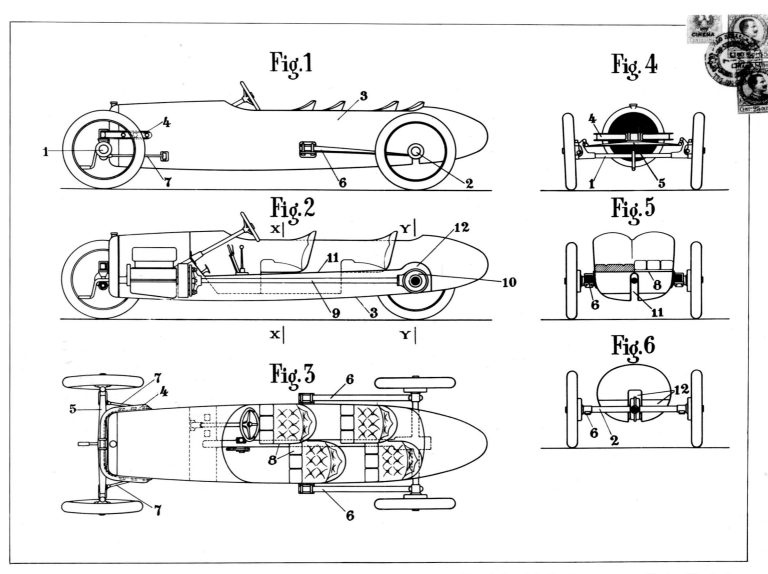

The patent drawing for a tubular body design without a frame as conceived for the 1918 Lancia Lambda Touring prototype. The boatlike hull was originally conceived by Vincenzo Lancia himself, who collaborated with G. B. Falchetto to design this prototype.

Lancia Lambda Touring. 1923. Engine 67 V-4. Steel body, leather or leatherette interiors. Designer G. B. Falchetto and staff. Manufacturer Lancia & Company, Fabbrica Automobili, Turin, Italy

The year 1918 witnessed the appearance of a new wave still based on oval shapes that were simple and easy to manufacture; it lasted in some isolated cases until 1925. There had been a peak of rationality in car design, a style common to both Europe and the United States, a situation never to be repeated.

The smooth forms had met with a cool reception; the same conservative opinion now welcomed the new boxy shapes and their flattened, separate surfaces. The lines connecting these facets were used as a new design element, and the overall shape of the car became essentially two-dimensional, like an elevation view of a palace facade.

Engine covers became boxlike once again, but their new-found height made them follow naturally from the body waistline, itself a stylistic innovation of the period. Hoods became part of the car itself: engine and cabin had merged altogether, emphasizing high, flat radiators, primarily by increasing the length of the engine cover to balance the rest of the body. This was to some extent a cosmetic fashion: only a small proportion of these new engine covers were fortunate enough to hide from view one of the splendid straight-eights that everyone wanted to transfer to his small, dumpy town car.

The origin of this fashion, in some ways a regress or at any rate a pause on the road to industrially pressed bodies (flat panels flex easily, and curved ones are preferable for strength), probably arose from a context of style and taste more congenial to simple, classical architecture than to volumes modeled along elusive and complex rules.

This approach offered a number of practical advantages: design and construction of car bodies (particularly those of cheap automobiles, a postwar invention) were greatly simplified whenever the wooden body frame members could be retained. Wood was often used and was easy to upholster. Even Fiat, despite the scale of its production, retained this idea until 1935. There was also an aesthetic by-product in the novelty of the new "coffin" shape, whose tautness and forward drive immediately made the ovoidal bodies, introduced as early as 1914, look tired and static.

If the Lancia Lambda was not the inspiration of this design tendency (it appeared in public in final form only in early November 1922, and faceted shapes had appeared at the Paris Salon the previous year), it was perhaps its clearest and happiest expression. Other coachbuilding and automobile firms borrowed its low, lean shape, which was accurately suggestive of its superlative efficiency. However, they did not retain the pathbreaking, rigid one-piece structure responsible for the qualities that had made it a symbol.

The Lambda shape became an aesthetic "must," an unavoidable fashion that obliged Fiat, like other European manufacturers, to redesign its entire 1925 range of medium-sized cars, in the first great industrial face-lifting in history. This fashion was also perfectly suited to the Weymann construction system, which made use of wooden frames covered in leatherette, and became widespread at about the same time. The Weymann system made use of "architectural" rules in designing enclosed car bodies, which were to become the dominant form of body even for customers of modest means. In the wake of the Lambda, aerodynamics appeared to have been forgotten altogether.

Above: F.O.D. Saloon. 1925. Model 500. Engine 4 cyl., monobloc. Leatherette body (except bonnet), wool seats. Designer unknown. Manufactured by a Weymann licensee in Turin. The tiny 1925 F.O.D. Saloon was constructed with a Weymann-type enclosed body. Except for the bonnet covers, all exterior sheeting was made of leatherette instead of metal. The underframe, a conventional ladder type, and body frame were made of wood

Top: Frontal view of the Lancia Lambda prototype with hull-shaped touring body without underframe, as tested in 1920–21. Independent front suspensions were of the later mass-produced type. Many engines were tested before production. Body was steel, with leather interior. Designed by G.B. Falchetto and staff, built by Lancia & Company, Fabbrica Automobili, Turin, Italy

THE SPECIALIZED
AUTOMOBILE

In the second half of the twenties, the luxury automobile matured and settled down; its forms became somewhat fuller in volume and clearer in proportion. The mechanical skeleton underlying the body remained roughly constant, and the great European coachbuilders, between 1925 and 1930, succeeded in producing what is known today as the classical automobile.

The great compositional skills of the masters of the craft combined with a very accurate execution of detailing that was no less impeccable than in the first decade of the century. Lean, hungry shapes, and a certain excess of dour but interesting sobriety, now gave way to a new, controlled opulence. During this period, overall visual balance and precision in painting and upholstery reached an all-time high. The best of European coachbuilders became full-time members of the subset of European culture that finds favor in the United States: this was the time when Hibbard & Darrin, or LeBaron (Dietrich), helped by the lean and fast United States luxury chassis, successfully imitated the Isotta Fraschinis, Rolls-Royces, and Hispano-Suizas built by Castagna, Sala, Mulliner, and Labourdette.

This period also witnessed a progressive specialization of the automobile along different types. On one hand, the requirement for a minimal car for middle-class users arose for the first time. On the other hand, the great road races, the opening of the first motorways, and the temporary decline of circuit races helped define a new type of high-performance race car that doubled as an elegant sports vehicle. Everyday, medium-priced cars became more reliable, and were expected to function properly, even in foul weather. As a result, fully enclosed bodies became the norm, and the industry was forced to redesign its production tooling for all-metal bodies, the only method compatible with mass-production.

These new car types gradually acquired recognizable national characters: French cars of the period look very French, and English ones English. Cyclecars, ultralight vehicles powered by engines derived from or inspired by motorcycles, covered with spartan, rudimentary bodies, were a typical French and English phenomenon. Cyclecars may have been ephem-

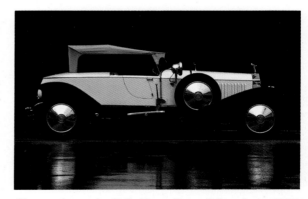

Above and opposite: Rolls-Royce Boattail Speedster. *1925. Model Phantom I. Engine 6 cyl., overhead valves, 40/50 h.p. Aluminum body and fenders, leather seats, 75" × 16' 10". Designer and body by Barker and Company, Ltd., London, England. Manufacturer Rolls-Royce, Ltd., Crewe, England. Hillcrest Motor Company, Beverly Hills, California*

275

Right: The luxurious passenger compartment in the rear of a 1925 Fiat type 519 limousine was upholstered with a rich, custom-designed woven fabric. Custom-made perfume bottles were fitted in the wood fascia behind a courtesy clock. The microphone was part of an acoustical system designed for communication with the driver. The car was designed and manufactured by Fiat

Bugatti Berline de Voyage. *1931. Model Type 41 (Royale). Engine 8 cyl., single overhead camshaft, 300 h.p. Wood body, aluminum fenders, leather front seat, broadcloth rear seat. Designer Ettore Bugatti. Manufacturer Bugatti, Molsheim, France*

Hispano Suiza Coupé. *1931. Engine 6 cyl. or V-12. Aluminum and steel body, leather interior. Designer Felice M. Boano and Pinin Farina staff. Body by Carrozzeria Pinin Farina, Turin; chassis by Hispano Suiza, Paris. Classic coachbuilders never forgot the influence of horse-drawn carriages. This exceptional coupé, with its passenger compartment reminiscent of the formal carriage coupé, was a two-seater built for the famous race car driver Carlo Felice Trossi by Pinin Farina, in 1931*

276

Volkswagen Two-Door Limousine. *1948. Model Type I.
Engine 4 cyl., overhead valve, 25 h.p. Steel body, vinyl
seats. 60" x 13.' Designer Ferdinand Porsche. Manufacturer Volkswagenwerk AG., Wolfsburg, West Germany.
Chick Iverson, Inc., Newport Beach, California*

Above: The Bugatti T-35 at the British Grand Prix, Brooklands, in 1927, leading a Delage

Top: Fiat Topolino. *1938. Model 500. Engine 4 cyl., L-head, 13 h.p. Steel body, cloth seat. Designer Dante Giacosa. Manufacturer Fiat, Turin. Collection Sergio Montorsi, Hasbrouck Heights, New Jersey*

Above: Alfa Romeo Two-Seater Sporting. *1929. Model 1750GS. Engine 6 cyl., in line monobloc, supercharged. Aluminum body, leather interior. Designers Ugo Zagato and Luigi Fusi. Manufacturer Carrozzeria Zagato, Milan. The hard face of sports car racing in the twenties: Princess Dorina Colonna waiting for the check-in at the Mille Miglia, on April 12, 1930. The man at her side is Formenti, the co-driver, and one of the best Alfa Romeo testers of the time*

Top: Alfa Romeo Two-Seater Sporting. *1931. Model 1750SS (Flying Star). Engine 6 cyl., in line monobloc, supercharged. Aluminum body, leather interior. Designers Felice Bianchi Anderloni and Giuseppe Serregni. Manufacturer Carrozzeria Touring, Milan. This model represented the gentle face of the sports car in the early thirties. The styling, with its interlacing lines, was adopted for several type 8A and 8B Isotta Fraschinis, and by the type 1750 GS Alfa Romeo*

Opposite: Fiat Balilla Sport. *1934. Model 508S. Engine 4 cyl., overhead valve, 36 h.p. Steel body, leather seats, 55" x 11'7". Designer Ghia. Manufacturer Fiat, Turin.* Automobile Quarterly Magazine, *Princeton, New Jersey*

eral, but they were a very interesting answer to the continuing search for an autonomous style and shape for the small car.

In Italy, development of the cyclecar was hampered by a small, self-conscious market that feared ridicule, and it was strongly opposed by Fiat's maternal overbearance. Fiat, biding its time, realizing that the times were not yet ripe for the baby car, shelved one prototype after another until the surprise birth of the 500 Topolino in 1936. But even four-seaters for families of modest means only reached design maturity with the Morris Minor (built at the rate of one hundred cars per day in May 1929) and with Fiat's 508, influenced, like its big sisters, by the Detroit style.

Another European invention, culminating in the late twenties and early thirties, resulted in the fast sports car, powered not by large engines, as in the Bentley 4.5 liter, Mercedes 500 SSK, or Alfa Romeo RLSS, but instead with a new generation of lightweight, highly efficient engines (Ballot, Aston Martin, Lancia), occasionally supercharged (Bugatti, Alfa Romeo).

These cars were beautifully designed, right down to the smallest details; they became the standard-bearers for the old dream of speed and its aerodynamic necessities. Speed was no longer achieved with raw power alone—it had become more refined, easier to handle: a light, nimble Alfa 6C 1750 GS would accelerate strongly all the way to 90 miles per hour, yet was capable of winning a *concours d'elegance* in a woman's hands or of placing well in the Mille Miglia.

Maybach Aerodynamic Saloon. *1935. Model SW35. Engine 6 cyl., in line. Aluminum body. Designers Paul Jaray and Wolfgang B. Klemperer. Manufacturer unknown. Place of manufacture Friedrichshafen, Germany. The fully streamlined Maybach saloon body shocked the public at the Berlin Automobile Show in 1935. The turret-type passenger compartment with deeply curved windshield was designed in the dream-car style of the time*

Maybach Limousine. *1932. Model DSA (Zeppelin). Engine V-12. Steel body, wool seats. Designer Maybach staff. Manufacturer unknown. Place of manufacture Friedrichshafen, Germany. The Maybach 1932 limousine sported one of the first pontoon-type bodies. It was built on a Maybach chassis and exhibited at the Paris Automobile Show in 1932*

The aerodynamic idea became a general stylistic ingredient from the early thirties onward, but effective aerodynamism in current production, even of sports cars, is rather sparse—small sharply raked windscreens, flattened radiators, and flattened, lowered tails. The *bateau* (boattail) sunk without a trace, though it was no less efficient, only less fashionable. The vortices caused by the great winglike mudguards remained a problem, but a solution was discovered in 1934, with the appearance of ovoidal wraparound mudguards designed as individual wheel fairings.

Seen schematically from above, the shape of the period was made up of five ovals: one for each of the wheels and a big one for the body. The development of the connection between these separate shapes was a slow process, the long road to the "monolithic" shape. This last was for the time being only a dream car disobeying the rules of style, very far from cars in everyday production, which benefited from it only much later, through the filter provided by sports cars and "one-off" specials.

In the years between 1932 and 1936, touring cars struggled with the front mudguard that curved to meet the sideboard, though it was enclosed laterally as a supposed aid to airflow. Meanwhile, the cabin lost its perpendicular windscreen and angular shape. One leaned, the other became softer. The term "aerodynamic" was used primarily as a good sales point, or conversation piece, an excuse for rather modest style changes made possible by the advent of deeply pressed body panels.

Yet the Paris Salon of 1932 saw a revolution embodied by the Maybach "pontoon body" sedan on a chassis type DS 8 "Zeppelin" 12 cylinder. Maybach was a kind of German Rolls-Royce, and its novel design influenced production cars only after a twenty-year lag, though sports cars used it as early as 1936. The break between the paradigms of classical good

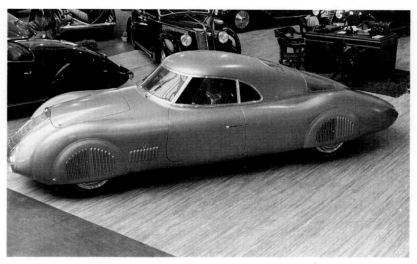

BMW Racing Berlinetta. *1939. Model 328 (Le Mans). Engine 6 cyl., in line monobloc. Aluminum body. Designers Felice Bianchi Anderloni and Aquilino Gilardi. Body by Carrozzeria Touring, Milan; chassis by BMW, Munich. This photograph was autographed by Fritz Husche von Hanstein and Walter Baumer, winners of the Mille Miglia race in 1940*

Lancia Two-Seater Racing. *1937. Model 97 (Aprilia). Engine V-4. Aluminum body, leather interior Designed by Pinin Farina staff. Manufacturer Carrozzeria Pinin Farina, Turin. Despite its dream-car appearance, the fully streamlined Lancia Aprilia built by Pinin Farina was often raced on the Italian roadside. It was one of four special streamliners built in 1937*

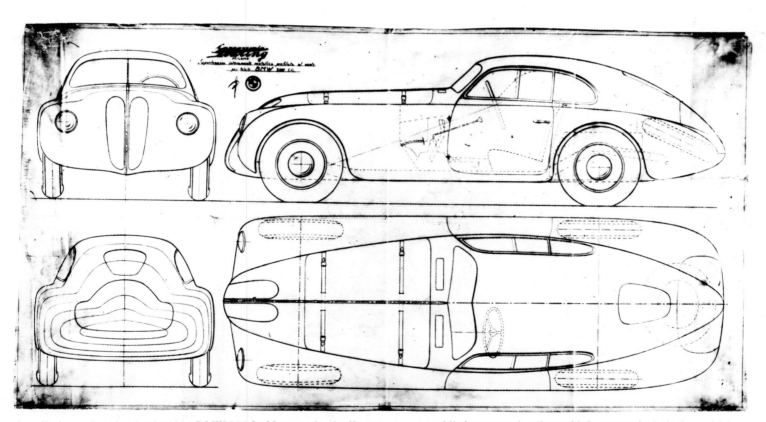

A preliminary drawing for the 1939 BMW 328 Le Mans racing berlinetta, an automobile incorporating the ovoidal-pontoon body design, which provided a very low air-drag coefficient. Built in the spring of 1939, it appeared well in advance of the celebrated 1947 Cisitalia

Mercedes-Benz Special Roadster. *1936. Model 500K. Engine 8 cyl., single overhead camshaft, supercharged, 100/160 h.p. Aluminum body and fenders, leather interior. Designer Sindelfingen. Manufacturer Daimler-Benz AG., Stuttgart, Germany. Black Hawk Collection, San Ramon, California*

Bugatti Berline de Voyage. *1931. Model Type 41 (Royale). Engine 8 cyl., single overhead camshaft, 300 h.p. Wood body, aluminum fenders, leather front seat, broadcloth rear seat. Designer Ettore Bugatti. Manufacturer Bugatti, Molsheim, France. Harrah's Automobile Collection, Reno, Nevada*

Lancia Two-Seater Racing Special. *1938. Model 97 (Aprilia). Engine V-4. Aluminum body, leather interior. Designers Felice Bianchi Anderloni and G. Belli. Manufacturer Carrozzeria Touring, Turin; chassis Lancia & Company, Milan. This fully streamlined roadster was built on a chassis tuned by Paganelli for Luigi Bellucci, an amateur race car driver from Naples. It won many road races in the 1500 class*

Cisitalia Granturismo Berlinetta. *1947. Engine 4 cyl., in line monobloc, tuned Fiat 1100S. Steel body, cotton velvet seats. Designers Giovanni Savonuzzi and Pinin Farina staff. Manufacturer Carrozzeria Pinin Farina, Turin. The post-World War II Cisitalia coupé, built by Pinin Farina in 1947, became the symbol of the "enveloping body" Italian granturismo berlinettas. Because of the bird-cage tubular frame, the entire body could be built low to the ground*

taste and genuine aerodynamism reduced the impact of the great German aerodynamics school, which was largely composed of engineers trained in Count Ferdinand von Zeppelin's industry at Friedrichshaven on Lake Konstanz, as was Maybach. The groups led by Paul Jaray and Wunibald Kamm were among the best of these engineers.

In 1935, Paul Jaray collaborated with Wolfgang B. Klemperer to design another aerodynamic prototype on a Maybach SW 35, which raised a storm upon presentation at the Berlin Motor Show, partly because of an unhappy two-tone paint scheme that split its accurately designed volume. Toward the end of the same year, the Berlin coachbuilders Voll & Rohrbeck used an Everling design (itself a descendant of Koenig and Kamm's studies), to build an appallingly ugly but doubtless very aerodynamic high tail body on a Mercedes chassis type 170 V.

The greatest impetus toward assimilation of these extraordinary shapes into normal production came from the Italian coachbuilding firms of Touring, Viotti, and Pininfarina, who used them, albeit diluted, in their many types of streamlined sports berlinettas, built between 1938 and 1940, and made famous by a spate of road and circuit race successes. Some of these cars, in particular the Alfa Romeo 2500 SS and BMW 328 Le Mans built by Touring, sowed the seed from which the postwar granturismo was to grow.

This sober, highly efficient school of thought was an important but minority phenomenon. The same period witnessed the appearance, first on "one-off" cars, later in production machines, of an aerodynamic style that was built around symbols rather than scientific calculations. The "prows," raked volumes, and cantilevered tails of some prototypes became truly pathological, particularly when built on modest, medium-powered chassis; in this case the overload was structural as well as visual. Such a fashion, intensively practiced in France by Figoni & Falaschi, by more traditional coachbuilders such as Chapron, and shamefully by Italian glories such as Stabilimenti Farina, was destined to a short life. In any event, it reached its end with the advent of World War II.

The "aerodynamic styling" period witnessed considerable United States influence on European styling. The Chrysler Airflow of 1934 spawned an entire family of Peugeots, in particular the 402 B limousine of 1937–38. But this impact, which developed in part from a transfer of the technology involved in body panel pressing and assembly learned during study visits by European designers, was a minor thing when compared with the widespread general influence of American culture and styling on postwar Europe. The Detroit cars lost the sobriety of the forties as they became a mass-media cliché and the driving force of a collective dream.

The much maligned whale-mouthed fashion for cars was in full swing in the United States, but Europe had to be content with ludicrous small-scale versions. Fashion and pressing technology required massive "soap-bar" shapes, which then begged for trompe l'oeil profiles and garish two-tone colors. This road was taken not only by European divisions of United States industries, such as Ford (United Kingdom) and Opel (Germany), but also by tradition-bound European firms, whose design philosophies simply had to be thrown overboard.

At the height of this apparent loss of direction in taste, the

M.G. Midget. *1948. Model MG TC. Engine 4 cyl., overhead valve, 54 h.p. Steel and wood body, steel fenders, leather seats. Designer and manufacturer MG Car Company, Ltd., Abingdon-on-Thames, England. Collection M. Howard Goldman and Moss Motors, Ltd., Goleta, California*

creative miracle of the Linea Italiana intervened. It was born in the heads of the great and vastly underrated Felice Mario Boano at Pininfarina, Felice Bianchi Anderloni at Touring, and in many smaller workshops in Turin. Together they succeeded in formulating and producing a uniquely sober formula, culminating in an altogether new product, the berlinetta granturismo: agile and potent but powered by a relatively small engine, and capable of providing comfortable, long, transcontinental journeys without compromising sheer driving pleasure.

The birth of Ferrari, and the rebirth of Aston Martin with David Brown at the helm, formed the archetypal export produced by the great European craftsmen. What matters here was the exportation of the very concept of an automobile whose supremacy lay in efficiency rather than in size. This idea influenced world automobile production through the sixties, and caused in its wake a return to sobriety on the part of the United States designers.

The granturismo movement, with its body conceived as a single volume, was directly descended from the research efforts epitomized by the precocious Maybach, and tended to integrate the mudguards into the body of the car itself. Ultimately, this slow merging required a change of concept: the body was thought of from the outset as a single volume rather than as a box made up of flat panels joined to enclose their contents.

It has since become customary to equate the greatest expression of this process with the berlinetta Cisitalia type 202 (1947) built by Pininfarina and purchased by the Museum of Modern Art in New York after its appearance there at the "Eight Automobiles" show in 1951. There can be no doubt that the functional and visual innovations of the Cisitalia, though impossible to transfer to normal cars, were a turning point in automobile aesthetics. The tendency it exemplified gained momentum in the fifties, particularly in the realm of high-performance cars, whose smoothly flowing volumes are most satisfying both to the eye and to the aerodynamic engineer.

Pininfarina itself was to reverse this tendency in 1957, when it returned to angular shapes, highlighted by sharp cutting edges meant to guide the eye over the composition. The project for the Lancia Florida, and even more that of the Lancia Flaminia four-door sedan, made plain a whole series of formal concepts and put an end to the idea of the touring automobile as a monolithic volume, with rounded shapes, bulbous rooflines, fat pillars, and small windows enclosed by gentle arcs.

The sleek flanks of the Flaminia were underlined, as it were, by the meeting of planes along sharp lines and the flat roof hovering on chromed pillars above the "empty space" of the cabin. These new elements became a conceptual model for the next twenty years, involving the world's makers in another great upheaval whose effects are still being felt, as, for example, in the Volvo sedan 760 GLE. It proved necessary to wait for the eighties to find attention given once again to aerodynamics, and to see touring cars again designed and built as one-piece solids. The Ford Sierra, with its rounded windows and fat pillars that give the overall shape a coherent character, exemplifies this tendency. The marked separation between glass area and hull, introduced by Raymond Loewy with his Studebaker Starlight, was later adopted and emphasized by the Flaminia as a neoclassical foil to the streamlined look.

Mercedes-Benz Gullwing Coupé. 1955. Model Type 300 SL. Engine 6 cyl., single overhead camshaft, dry sump, fuel injected, 240 h.p. Steel and aluminum body, leather seats. Designer and manufacturer Daimler-Benz AG., Stuttgart, West Germany. Collection Mike Blanton, Nevada City, California

Opposite: Ferrari Barchetta. 1949. Model Type 166MM. Engine V-12, 140 h.p. Aluminum body, leather seats. Designer Feliche Bianchi Anderloni. Body by Carrozzeria Touring. Manufacturer Ferrari, Modena, Italy. Collection John Bond, Escondido, California

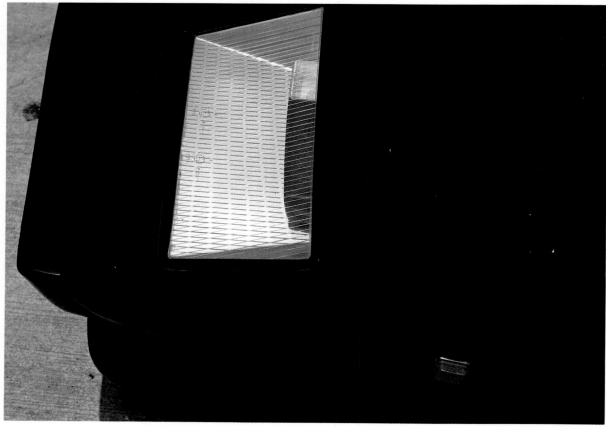

Lamborghini Countach. *1981. Model S. Engine V-12, dual overhead camshaft, 375 h.p. Aluminum body, leather seats. Designer Bertone. Manufacturer Lamborghini, St. Agata, Italy. Hillcrest Motor Company, Beverly Hills, California*

Alfa Romeo Sports Dream Car. *1968. Model 33 (Carabo). Engine 33/2 V-8. Aluminum and fiberglass body, leather interior. Designers Marcello Gandini and Bertone staff. Manufacturer Carrozzeria Bertone, Grugliasco, Italy. Introduced in 1968, this car's wedge shape encouraged an appreciation of low, apparently aerodynamic body profiles*

Lancia Four-Door Sedan. *1957. Model Flaminia. Engine 813.00, V-6. Steel Body, wool seats. Designed by Pinin Farina staff. Manufacturer Lancia & Company, Fabbrica Automobili, Turin. This car set a lasting, widespread fashion in continental automobile design. Smooth, flowing volumes were replaced with angular shapes, highlighted by sharp cutting edges meant to reflect light and guide the eye over the entire body*

Lancia Two-Door Sports Sedan. *1955. Model B 12 (Aurelia Florida Prototype). Engine V-6. Aluminum and steel body, leather interior. Designed and manufactured by Carrozzeria Pinin Farina, Turin. Conceived as a one-of-a-kind dream car, this automobile was eventually sold to a private party. It has recently been rescued and is undergoing restoration*

The sixties represented the last period of relative opulence before the oil crisis, and the Flaminia contributed to a differentiation among car styles according to purpose. Sports cars retained smooth shapes, while touring cars—even small ones—followed the Flaminia architecture to make maximal use of interior space and window area, acquiring an aristocratic new look in the bargain.

The meeting point between these two design approaches came in 1968 with the first wedge-shaped dream car. The wedge represented a new approach to aerodynamic problems and aerodynamic styling. The first example of this new breed of car was probably the Carabo, a wonderfully detailed Bertone prototype designed by Marcello Gandini. It contained, in embryonic form, many formal solutions that made their way into production cars only ten years later, for example in the Alfa Romeo Giulietta (1977) and the Ford Escort.

The wedge permitted the first use of flat or slightly convex surfaces and sharp connecting edges in high-performance cars, while it freed touring cars from the static "perpendicular" scheme of the Flaminia and introduced a new dynamic element that in time became an essential part of the message to the potential customer.

If one were to look for the origin of the wedge idea, it would probably be found in the tendency of Grand Prix racers to sacrifice some aerodynamic penetration in exchange for adhesion-promoting downward thrust, an effect achieved by making the car body slope forward like an inverted wing. This thrust is mostly unnecessary in road cars, and one is forced to conclude that its presence outside the racing world is merely suggestive and aesthetic.

The oil crisis that followed the policy change in Arab countries and the establishment of the Organization of Petroleum Exporting Countries (OPEC) has unavoidably helped revive a great deal of interest in the genuine aerodynamic efficiency of everyday cars. Today, ever-increasing use is made of wind tunnels and scientific measurement methods. One of the most interesting products of this scientific approach has been the study on the theme of the four-door, four/five-passenger family car, commissioned by the Italian National Research Council (CNR) from Pininfarina. The new dolphin shape, optimized by computer and verified in the wind tunnel, has made a substantial impact on car designers and has stimulated a new yearning for soft shapes. Pininfarina itself, breaking with its earlier wedge tradition, has taken something of a lead in the field, with its Jaguar XJ 12 roadster, unveiled only twelve months after the 1977 CNR prototype. S.I.R.P. Ital Design has also enthusiastically adopted this new tendency, no doubt to the great enjoyment of Giorgetto Giugiaro, who can now return to the art of flowing forms, of which he was a master in the sixties.

Good aerodynamic behavior, when transferred to a production car, can yield striking results (witness the Audi 100 and the Ford Sierra), but can also make the car harder to build, and more rapidly obsolete in the public eye. This poses a very serious problem to European manufacturers, whose panel-pressing machinery has a turnover time of ten or so years, as compared to the three to four years typical of Japanese manufacturers. The shape of the average car in the nineties remains very much an open question.

Above: British Leyland/Jaguar Roadster. *1978. Model XJ/12. Engine V-12 (current production). Aluminum body, leather interior. Designed and manufactured by Industrie Pininfarina S.P.A., Grugliasco, Italy. The rounded forms of this Jaguar prototype were a by-product of C.N.R. aerodynamic research. From 1979, all European automobiles have reflected more rounded and flowing forms*

Top: Aerodynamic Saloon. *1977. Model C.N.R. Prototype. No Engine. Plastic body. Designers Leonardo Fioravanti and Pininfarina staff. Manufacturer Industrie Pininfarina S.P.A., Grugliasco, Italy. This dolphin-shaped prototype was developed when wind tunnel research indicated that the design would maximize fuel consumption for a medium-size European four-seater. The shape influenced subsequent Pininfarina designs, notably the 1978 Jaguar prototype*

PASSENGER AND FREIGHT DIRIGIBLES AND AIRPLANES USING AIRPORTS ON ROOF OF BUILDING.

CITY OF FUTURE TO BE SINGLE UNIT OF REINFORCED CONCRETE FACED WITH BRONZE AND GLASS, ABOUT 1,000 FEET HIGH WITH 15 TIMES THE FLOOR AREA OF THE WOOLWORTH BUILDING. THIS STRUCTURE WOULD HOUSE ABOUT 150,000 PEOPLE.

BUILDING IN CENTER OF 20-MILE SQUARE METROPOLITAN DISTRICT, LAND BEING TAKEN UP WITH FARMS, FOREST AND PARKS. ALL EASILY ACCESSIBLE WITHIN FIVE MINUTES' RUN FROM BUILDING.

ALL ROOMS HAVE UNOBSTRUCTED VIEW OF SURROUNDING COUNTRY, BEING COLUMNATED WITH BRONZE-BUTTRESSED GLASS WINDOWS, REFLECTING LIGHT TO ALL PARTS OF STRUCTURE. BY MEANS OF SYSTEM OF BLINDS, LIGHT CAN BE SHUT OFF AT WILL

FORTY ACRE BUILDING ERECTED ON FLOATING FOUNDATION OF CAISSONS IN A RESERVOIR OF LIQUID MUD AS PROTECTION FROM TORNADOS QUAKES, ETC.

DIRIGIBLE MASTS

AIRPLANE LANDING FIELDS

RESIDENTIAL, ADMINISTRATION AND AMUSEMENTS

LANDING STATIONS AND DISTRIBUTION

INDUSTRIALS IN FOUNDATION AND LOWER STORIES.

LLOYD WRIGHT

TRAFFIC SYSTEMS AND THE VISIONS OF CITY PLANNERS

Throughout the twentieth century, the automobile has caused remarkable transformations in the built environment. The number of registered vehicles in the United States grew from four in 1895 to more than thirty million in 1939, propelling the automobile to the status of a mass phenomenon. Architects and urban planners, responding to the special conditions and needs of a motorized populace, began altering existing buildings and roads, and by mid-century were developing a new class of structures to meet the demands of a drive-in society.

Actual built traffic systems did not change significantly until the 1930s and 1940s, when the first parkways and freeways began to emerge across the United States. Modern urban street plans remained largely oriented to the nineteenth-century axial and grid systems imposed by planners such as the baron Georges-Eugène Haussmann in Paris and Pierre-Charles L'Enfant in Washington, D.C. Recognition of the motorcar's potential to transform urban circulation patterns was first expressed in visionary city planning. The utopian concepts of these early twentieth-century plans were rarely executed, but they did exercise a definite effect on the expressways and superhighways of the postwar period.

In the years before World War I, the Italian futurist architect Antonio Sant'Elia produced a revolutionary scheme in his designs for "La Citta Nuova" (New City). His projected Central City Station for Milan (1913–14) brings together seven levels of separated railway and motor traffic. Almost ten years later, the architect and city planner Le Corbusier used the same concept in his projected Contemporary City for Three Million People. Lloyd Wright's 1925 unbuilt plan for a Los Angeles Civic Center corresponds closely to Sant'Elia's vision of a single massive urban building complex oriented around many diverse traffic systems.

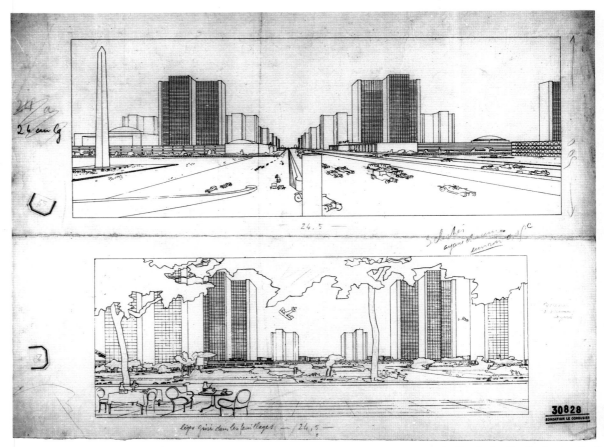

Le Corbusier. Project drawing for Contemporary City for Three Million People. 1921–22. Fondation Le Corbusier, Paris

Throughout the twenties, futuristic conceptions of skyscrapers and traffic bridges continued to develop on the drawing boards of such architects and planners as Le Corbusier, Auguste Perret, Mart Stam, Charles L. Morgan, and Hugh Ferriss. Charles Morgan's 1928 project for a skyscraper bridge in Chicago converts tall buildings, whose upper stories serve as garage spaces, into piers of a bridge. The entire structure is topped with a superhighway—a fascinating idea, but impractical for the technology of the time. Le Corbusier incorporated the elevated superhighway and unconventional roadway in many designs for city plans of

the twenties and thirties. His 1931–42 Plan Obus for Algiers proposes several kinds of traffic systems, which he conceived as "machines for transportation." The Algiers plan utilizes elevated road bridges envisioned to carry the surge of high-speed traffic out and away from the core of the city into massive superblock apartment structures with access roads, in the form of galleries, running through their middle stories. A regional highway, termed a "viaduct" by Le Corbusier, was meant to carry traffic parallel to the coast of the Mediterranean Sea at the imposing height of 350 feet. The superstructure supporting the highway was to

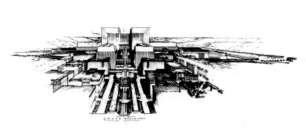

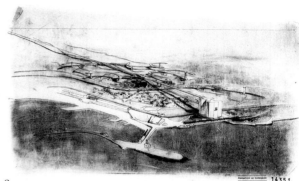

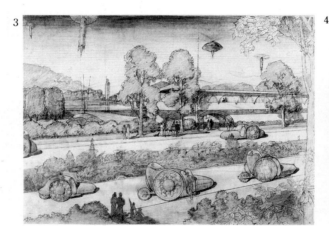

1. Lloyd Wright. Plan for Los Angeles Civic Center. 1925. Ink rendering. Eric Lloyd Wright, Los Angeles. 2. Le Corbusier. Project drawing for Obus Plan for Algiers. c. 1931–42. Fondation Le Corbusier, Paris. 3. Frank Lloyd Wright. Detail of Project for Broadacre City. c. 1932–34. Frank Lloyd Wright Foundation, Scottsdale, Arizona. 4. View of the Arroyo Seco Parkway (Pasadena Freeway). Completed in 1940

be gradually converted to new housing, according to the growth of the population.

While these futuristic city plans were never built, a practical adaptation of the elevated highway was realized on a modest scale in 1920–23 in Giacomo Matté-Trucco's rooftop test track for the Fiat factory in Turin. In the Soviet Union, visionary traffic planning was expressed in the towers and connecting traffic bridges of Serafimov and Kravetz's State Light Industry Center in Kharkov, which was constructed in the late twenties. On the whole, however, elevated superhighways and multistory circulation systems integrated with tall urban structures remained

paper projects until after World War II.

Greater suburban sprawl and lower urban density characterize the city plans designed by many American architects in the twenties and thirties. Frank Lloyd Wright's Broadacre City, circa 1932–34, was shaped by the American ideals of personal liberty and individualism or, as phrased by historian Vincent Scully, by "the uninhibited automobile road, the decentralized city, the endless horizontal expansion across the land." Wright used the car as an experimental design object as well as a conceptual tool in planning this vast, low-density suburban city. Although automobile suburbs had been emerging in the United States and Europe since 1910, Broadacre City prefigures the massive sprawling suburb as it was finally to develop in the postwar period, though Wright's plan proposes a completely self-sufficient city. Far removed from Le Corbusier's regularized vertical city planning, and communal ideals of superhighways and superblock highrises, Broadacre City's archetype was the individualized housing unit, the one- or two-car single-family home.

Rush City Reformed, Richard Neutra's major visionary town plan, was begun in Germany in the late 1920s, and continued in the United States in the 1930s. Its dramatically scaled transit systems and motor corridors closely approximate other visions and city plans of the period. In his detail studies for Rush City, Neutra rendered localized connecting traffic bridges and freeway on and off ramps, as well as individualized building types like drive-in markets, revealing his sympathetic understanding of the relationship between the individual and his car.

Motorways built in the first half of the century were actually quite modest when compared to the grandiose conceptions of the early modern planners. Parkways built between the twenties and forties in the northeastern United States were generally landscaped, localized, limited-access routes designed to save the motorist time and money in fuel costs. In 1940, the Pennsylvania Turnpike, a prototypical cross-country expressway that ran the length of the state, opened for public use, and enthusiastic motorist response produced a volume of traffic that far exceeded projected figures. In the same year, construction on the Arroyo Seco Parkway, later renamed the Pasadena Freeway, was completed in southern California, bringing the first modern road system to the western United States. These small-scale American state and local motorways contrasted dramatically both in

Norman Bel Geddes. General Motors Pavilion. 1939 New York World's Fair

form and function with the German *autobahn,* a massive roadway built primarily for military transport in the 1930s.

Extensive highway and freeway networks were not constructed in the United States until after World War II, when the country's economy shifted to peacetime production. The elevated superhighway systems, the most important legacy of visionary city planners to the postwar built environment, were conceived initially as a solution to traffic congestion on local roads and urban streets, though many highways and freeways produced adverse economic effects on the quality of life in bypassed neighborhoods and small town

centers. Many superhighway systems built in the late forties, fifties, and sixties are now considered to have had a dehumanizing effect, a sentiment that has catalyzed a resurgence of interest in the random, small-scale vernacular architecture on countless small-town Main Streets, commercial strips, and roadsides.

American world's fairs and industrial expositions delighted millions of visitors with imaginative and futuristic extensions of visionary city and traffic planning. The automobile industry's patronage of architects resulted in outstanding factory and technical buildings, which were designed

297

1. *Norman Bel Geddes. Detail of Futurama exhibition. 1939 New York World's Fair. 2. Giacomo Matté-Trucco. Fiat Lingotto factory, Turin, with rooftop test track. c. 1923. 3. Giacomo Matté-Trucco. Rooftop test track of Fiat Lingotto factory, Turin. c. 1923. 4. Giacomo Matté-Trucco. One of two spiral ramps leading to the rooftop test track of Fiat Lingotto factory, Turin. c. 1923*

and constructed by noted architects such as Albert Kahn and Eero Saarinen. The automobile industry exposition pavilions, forums where futuristic conceptions for urban centers and traffic plans could be tested and presented to the public, were also often created by major architects and planners. At the first major American world's fair, the 1893 World's Columbian Exposition in Chicago, only one automobile was on display, but subsequent world fairs featured increasingly elaborate participatory presentations of automobile travel in cities of the future.

At the 1939 New York World's Fair, the industrial designer Norman Bel Geddes

designed and constructed a "Futurama" for General Motors, and Walter Dorwin Teague, a "City of Tomorrow" for Ford Motor Company. Both schemes presented moving automobile systems as integral components of future city design, though Bel Geddes's conception of the American metropolis of 1960 was the more visionary of the two designs. The largest model of its time, the Futurama drew huge crowds to the "Highways and Horizons" exhibit in the GM pavilion at the fair. Viewers rode in moving chairs through the third-of-a-mile-long display of vast expressways, which had been designed to accommodate the projected traffic flow in

United States cities in 1960. Bel Geddes's Futurama expressway system, constructed to bypass outmoded and undesirable metropolitan slums, was close in spirit to the modernist ideal of social reform through architecture. Teague's "City of Tomorrow" exhibit for Ford, more modest in conception than Bel Geddes's, utilized actual cars to transport visitors over a model expressway and through a spiral-ramp traffic system.

The thrill ride automotive presentations in world's fairs continued into the second part of the century. For the 1964 New York World's Fair, the Ford Motor Company commissioned Walt Disney to build the "Magic Skyway," a fantasy ride through a constructed panorama of a "Space City," where high-speed automobile travel on giant expressways was meant to express the ultimate futuristic mode of transportation. GM's second Futurama at the 1964 fair represented outer space and deep sea as ultimate fantasy environments, alternatives to the world of high-speed automobile travel. The vision of the automobile as the transportation of the future spanned a fifty-year period, from 1910 through the sixties. Contemporary visions for future cities now focus on satellite stations in space, and space shuttle travel is envisioned to become the predominant mode of travel to and from the earth. The automobile today remains a reality of everyday life for the individual, but it is hardly an inspiration for progressive and efficient future living systems. With recognition accorded both to its beneficial utilitarian functions and its harmful ecological effects, the four-wheeled internal combustion vehicle can now be appreciated as a twentieth-century cultural artifact, as well as an object of aesthetic design.

ELIZABETH A. T. SMITH

Opposite: Walter Dorwin Teague. Road of Tomorrow at the Ford Pavilion. 1939 New York World's Fair

ACKNOWLEDGMENTS

This publication has been made in conjunction with an exhibition of the same title organized by The Museum of Contemporary Art in the summer of 1984. An exhibition as complex as the "Automobile and Culture" involves the work and ideas of many individuals. We first thank Pontus Hulten, Founding Director, for acting as Director of the exhibition, and Walter Hopps for proposing this idea to the Museum, and for serving as guest curator of the exhibition.

We thank the principle author of this publication, Gerald Silk, who first developed the idea of the automobile in art, and Strother MacMinn, Angelo Tito Anselmi, and Henry Flood Robert, Jr., for their essays on the various aesthetic manifestations of the automobile. We thank Ivan Chermayeff, of Chermayeff and Geismar Associates, for his design of the exhibition installation and poster; Henry Wolf, for his original photographs commissioned for the project; Paul Gottlieb, President; Sam Antupit, Art Director; Joan Fisher, Senior Editor; and Margaret Kaplan, Executive Editor of Harry N. Abrams, Inc., for bringing this book to completion. We thank Dr. Franklin Murphy, Chairman of the Executive Committee of the Board of The Times Mirror Company Corporation, for his assistance in establishing an initial relationship between The Museum of Contemporary Art and Harry N. Abrams, Inc. We thank Lord Montagu of Beaulieu for writing a foreword to this publication and for fostering interest in our project among the European automobile community.

For their generous contributions of time, advice, and special services, we are most grateful to contributing specialists in the fields of art, architecture, and automobiles. Above all, private collectors Terry and Eva Herndon; M. and Mme. Hervé Poulain; Joyce Ludmer, Librarian of the Elmer Belt Library of Vinciana at U.C.L.A.; Margo Leavin, Director of the Margo Leavin Gallery, Los Angeles; and Jack Rennert, who assisted in selecting and cataloguing posters for the book and exhibition are to be thanked for lending their expertise in refining the choice of the works of art that appear in these pages. We extend our thanks to Dr. Giuseppe Panza di Biumo for his assistance in obtaining photographs for this publication in Italy.

Kenneth B. Gooding, our primary liaison with the car-collecting community, was instrumental in coordinating the automobile selections and providing catalogue information. We also thank Phil Hill for his consultation on the automobile checklist. Also deserving of thanks for their parts in facilitating the photography of the cars, and for providing informa-

1931 *Bugatti Berline de Voyage,*
Model Type 41 (Royale)

tion, are Jim Duffie, Curator at Hillcrest Motors, Beverly Hills, and Clyde Wade, Director and General Manager, Transportation and Museum of Harrah's Automobile Collection in Reno. Otis Meyer, Librarian at *Road and Track,* patiently assisted us in obtaining and checking factual information. We are most grateful to Dean Batchelor, Executive Editor, Argus Publishers Corporation, for consulting with us in the area of customized cars and providing rare archival photographs with accompanying captions, and to George Barris, for generously making archival transparencies and information available to us.

Professor of History Thomas S. Hines, and Professor of Urban Planning Martin Wachs, both of U.C.L.A., and architect and historian Alan Hess, served as invaluable consultants regarding the impact of the automobile on our built environment. Others who assisted with photographs and clarification of information are Davira Taragin, Acting Curator, and Ruth Rattner, former intern of the Modern Art Department at The Detroit Institute of Arts; Cynthia Reed, Assistant Curator of Graphics at The Edison Institute, Henry Ford Museum and Greenfield Village, Dearborn, Michigan; and Nettie H. Seabrooks, Manager of the General Motors Public Relations Library in Detroit. To these and others too numerous to mention, we extend our sincerest thanks.

This project could never have been realized without the ongoing work of the staff of The Museum of Contemporary Art. Special thanks are due to Robert Sain, Director of Development; Sherri Geldin, Administrator; Julia Brown, Senior Curator; Kerry Brougher, Assistant Curator; Patricia Cleere and June Kino-Cullen, Curatorial Secretaries; and to those individuals particularly involved in the organization of the exhibition: Elizabeth A. T. Smith, Assistant Curator; Jacqueline Crist, Curatorial Assistant; and former Curator Marcy Goodwin, who laid much of the groundwork for the exhibition and publication. Additional assistance was provided by Ann Goldstein, Jane Hamsher, Norman Laich, Shelley Marks, Sandy Miller, and Carter Potter. Finally, Bridget Johnson, the museum editor for this publication, deserves our deepest gratitude for nurturing the embryonic book to the point of completion and delivery to our publisher.

Major funding for this exhibition and publication has been provided by the Los Angeles Olympic Organizing Committee, with special thanks to Robert J. Fitzpatrick, Director of the Olympic Arts Festival; to the Ford Motor Company, with special thanks to Henry Ford II, Chairman and Member of the Board, to Leo J. Brennan, Jr., Executive Director Ford Motor Company Fund, to Robert A. Taub, Vice President, and to Walter Hayes, Vice President-Public Affairs; to Renault, with special thanks to Bernard Hanon, Group General Manager, Former President Renault Inc., U.S.A., to Claude Renard, Chief of Research Service of Renault, and to Nadalette La Fonta, Public Relations, Renault; to Fiat S.P.A. with special thanks to Giovanni Agnelli, Chairman of Fiat S.P.A., to Furio Colombo, President Fiat U.S.A., Inc. and to Marco Pittaluga, Director of Public Affairs Fiat S.P.A. Initial support for the development of The Temporary Contemporary was provided by Citicorp/Citibank, with particular thanks to Walter B. Wriston, Chairman, Citibank, N.A., and Wilford M. Farnsworth, Senior Vice President, Citicorp USA, Inc.

Richard Koshalek
Director

I would like to acknowledge the late William C. Seitz, who first inspired me to address this subject, and whose perspicacious and provocative ideas continue to be inspirational. Many individuals have offered ideas and information throughout the history of this manuscript, and it would be impossible to mention them all. I do want to thank those who most recently provided assistance: Lee M. Edwards, Eugenie Tsai, Julia Plant, Timothy Burgard, Marguerite O'Brien, Susan Strauss, John Klein, Linda Downs, and Maria Morris Hambourg. Special thanks go to the museum editor of this book, Bridget Johnson.

Gerald Silk

Many individuals provided invaluable assistance during the research and writing of this essay. Special appreciation is extended to Miriam Roberts for her superb research and organizational work. Gratitude is also extended to Dean Batchelor, George Barris, and Gene Winfield, for their generously provided photographs and information. To Jane Barrett, Library Coordinator at Petersen Publishing Company, and to all those who shared their knowledge of and enthusiasm for the subject, sincere thanks. Finally, I am indebted to the museum staff, and particularly Bridget Johnson, for their support.

Henry Flood Robert, Jr.

Following pages: Interior detail
of a 1933 *Pierce Arrow, Silver Arrow,*
Model 1234

CREDITS

All original photography is by Henry Wolf.

The Angelo Tito Anselmi text was translated by Luca Turin.

Jon Abbott and O.K. Harris Works of Art, Inc., New York City: 146 (top)

Academy of Motion Picture Arts and Sciences, Beverly Hills, California: 172, 173 (top row, bottom left and right)

Archivio Anselmi, Milan: 266, 270 (top, center, bottom right), 271, 272, 273, 276 (top), 279 (right), 280, 281, 284, 292, 293

Arman, New York City: 160

Armét, Davis, Newlove, AIA Architects, Los Angeles: 202 (bottom right)

Corporate Archives, Atlantic Richfield Company, Los Angeles: 200 (top)

L. Scott Bailey, Princeton, New Jersey: 278

William T. Barker, Los Angeles: 238 (bottom)

Richard David Barnes: 1

George Barris, Los Angeles: 176–77, 192, 193 (top), 194 (top and center rows), 195

Dean Batchelor, Argus Publishers, Los Angeles: 180–85, 188, 190, 191 (top three), 193 (top two, bottom), 194 (top left, center left, bottom two)

Dean Batchelor and Sierra Photo, Incline Village, Nevada: 194 (center right)

Barbara Burden, Los Angeles: 163 (bottom right)

Rudolph Burckhardt, New York City: 136 (bottom), 163 (top left)

Rudolph Burckhardt and Leo Castelli Gallery, New York City: 134, 153

California Department of Transportation, Los Angeles: 296 (bottom right)

Center for Creative Photography, University of Arizona, Tucson: 92 (bottom)

The Edward Weston Archive, Center for Creative Photography, University of Arizona, Tucson: 110 (left)

Chrysler Corporation, Historical Archives, Detroit: 226 (bottom), 231

Chrysler Corporation, Press Information Service, Detroit: 239 (bottom)

Geoffrey Clements, Staten Island, New York: 70 (bottom), 106 (bottom), 115 (bottom), 146 (center right)

Eva Gluckman: 227

Foto-Studio-Grunke, Hamburg: 85 (top)

Foto Horst Hahn: 159 (bottom)

Dianne Hall, San Francisco: 161 (top left)

David Heald, New York City: 83

David J. Henry, Rochester, New York: 105

Thomas S. Hines, Los Angeles: 202 (top left)

Nancy Hoffman Gallery and French & Company, New York City: 146 (bottom left)

Pontus Hulten, Paris: 38 (bottom), 276 (bottom left)

Instituto Geografico de Agostini, Milan: 28, 29

Peggy Jarrell Kaplan, New York City: 163 (bottom left)

Giorgio Colombo, Milan: 85 (top)

John A. Conde, Bloomfield Hills, Michigan: 171

Daimler-Benz Aktiengesellschaft, Stuttgart: 254

Allan D'Arcangelo, Kenoza Lake, N.Y.: 140

Bevan Davies, New York City: 130 (bottom)

De Antonis, Rome: 60 (bottom)

D. James Dee, New York City: 156

Margaret D'Hamer: 163 (center, left)

Doyle Dane Bernbach, Inc., Detroit, and Volkswagen of America, Inc.: 143

Lee M. Edwards, New York City: 47

Eeva-Inkeri, New York City: 159 (top)

Don Emmons, La Mirada, California: 277

Ferretti: 58 (top), 59 (top)

Centro Storico Fiat, Turin: 298 (top, center, bottom right), 270 (lower left), 279 (upper left)

Henry Ford Museum, The Edison Institute, Dearborn, Michigan: 204–7, 214 (top), 215, 299

Brian Forrest and Billy Al Bengston, Los Angeles: 164 (bottom)

Buckminster Fuller Archive, Philadelphia: 251–52

Roger Gass Photography, San Francisco: 54, 110 (right), 133 (bottom), 148 (top)

General Motors Photographic, Detroit: 222, 235, 239 (top), 245, 297, 298 (left)

Monah Gettner, New York City: 48, 49, 50 (top)

Riccardo and Magda Jucker collection: 65 (bottom)

Kennedy Galleries, Inc., New York City: 72, 98

Galerie Samy Kinge, Paris: 167

Ute Klopliaus and Wolf Vostell, Berlin: 158 (bottom)

Lisson Gallery, London: 163 (top right)

Robert E. Mates, New York City: 91

Robert R. McElroy and Harry N. Abrams, Inc., New York City: 135

Strother MacMinn, Pasadena, California: 226 (top), 238 (top)

Wyatt McSpadden, Amarillo, Texas: 161 (right)

Meli-Color, Figueras, Spain: 116

Eric E. Mitchell and the Philadelphia Museum of Art: 84

James Monaco, New York City: 170, 173 (bottom row, center), 174, 175

The Photographic Library, National Motor Museum, Beaulieu, Great Britain: 212 (bottom), 260, 279 (bottom left)

Dion Neutra Architect, Los Angeles: 200

The Dorothea Lange Collection, The Oakland Museum, Oakland, California: 96, 111 (top center and right)

Edward Owen, Washington, D.C.: 150 (center)

Douglas M. Parker, Los Angeles: 142 (bottom)

Pelka/Noble and Metro Pictures, New York City: 144

Petersburg Press, Inc., New York City: 164 (top)

Archivio Pininfarina, Turin: 246

Eric Pollitzer, Hempstead, New York, and the Carus Gallery, New York City: 85 (bottom)

Eric Pollitzer, Hempstead, New York, and O.K. Harris, New York City: 146 (bottom right)

David Preston, Southampton, New York: 70 (top)

Jon Reis Photography, Ithaca, New York: 158 (top)

Renault Relations Publiques, Boulogne, Billancourt, France: 265

Jack Rennert, New York City: 36, 37, 40, 41, 45, 46

Road and Track photo by Joe Rusz, Newport Beach, California: 288

Rueger and Mary Boone Gallery, New York City: 166

Edward Ruscha, Los Angeles: 141

San Francisco Museum of Modern Art and Paul Strand Foundation, Millerton, New York: 93

Sandak, Inc., Stamford, Connecticut: 106 (top and center), 156 (bottom left)

Schenk & Schenk Photography and David McKee, Inc., New York City: 139 (top)

Security Pacific National Bank Photograph Collection/Los Angeles Public Library: 202 (center right)

© SIAE, Italy/V.A.G.A., New York City, 1983: 142 (bottom)

SITE Projects, Inc., New York City: 161 (bottom left)

SPADEM, Paris/VAGA, New York City: 38 (top), 39 (top), 87 (bottom), 88, 89, 295, 296 (top right)

Lee Stalsworth, Washington, D.C.: 152 (bottom left)

Allan Stone Gallery, New York City: 165 (top right)

Studebaker Corporation: 238 (top)

Summit Gallery Ltd., New York City: 73

Taylor & Dull, Inc., New York City: 43 (top)

Frank Thurston, London: 122 (top), 123 (bottom)

Michael Tropea, Chicago: 64 (top)

Photographic Service, University of California at Los Angeles and © ADAGP, Paris, 1984: 76 (top), 77, 87 (bottom)

Tom Van Eynde and Margo Leavin Gallery, Los Angeles: 156 (top)

Venturi, Rauch, and Scott Brown, Philadelphia: 203

Tom Vinetz, Venice, California: 142 (top), 152 (bottom right), 156 (bottom right), 168

Richard Walker, Schenectady, New York: 165 (top left)

© 1968 Warner Bros. Inc.; Seven Arts and Solar Productions, Inc.: 173 (lower left)

Nemo Warr, Detroit: 42

Gene Winfield, Canoga Park, California: 191 (bottom), 194 (bottom), 196 (top right)

Janet Woodard, Houston: 111 (bottom), 112

Eric Lloyd Wright, Los Angeles: 294, 296 (top right), 200, 203 (bottom left)

Michael Zens, New York City: 44 (top), 43 (bottom), 155

BIBLIOGRAPHY

Alloway, Lawrence. "Hi-way Culture: Man at the Wheel." *Arts Magazine* 41 (February 1967): 28–33.

Apollonio, Umbro. *Futurist Manifestos.* New York: Viking Press, 1973.

Banham, Reyner. "Industrial Design and Popular Art." *Civiltà delle Macchine* 6 (August 1955).

———. "The Machine Aesthetic." *Architectural Review* 117 (April 1955): 224–28.

———. *Theory and Design in the First Machine Age.* 2nd ed. New York: Praeger, 1967.

Baro, Gene. "Claes Oldenberg, or the Things of This World." *Art International* 10 (November 1966): 41–43.

Bentley, John. *Great American Automobiles: A Dramatic Account of their Achievements in Competition.* Englewood Cliffs, N.J.: Prentice-Hall, 1957.

Bergman, Par. "Modernolatria" et "Simultaneita." Stockholm: Bonnier, 1962.

Camfield, William A. "The Machinist Style of Francis Picabia." *Art Bulletin* 48 (September–December 1966): 309–22.

Clough, Rosa Trillo. *Futurism: The Story of a Modern Movement; A New Appraisal.* New York: Philosophical Library, 1961.

Crabb, A. Richard. *Birth of a Giant: The Men and Incidents that Gave America the Motorcar.* Philadelphia: Chilton Book Co., 1969.

Damann, George H. *Illustrated History of Ford: 1903–1970.* Glen Ellyn, Ill.: Crestline Publishing Co., 1971.

———. *Seventy Years of Chrysler.* Glen Ellyn, Ill.: Crestline Publishing Co., 1974.

Detroit Institute of Arts. *The Rouge: The Image of Industry in the Art of Charles Sheeler and Diego Rivera.* Detroit: Detroit Institute of Arts, 1978.

Dettelbach, Cynthia Golomb. *In the Driver's Seat: A Study of the Automobile in American Literature and Popular Culture.* Westport, Conn.: Greenwood Press, 1976.

Dorazio, Virginia Dortch. *Giacomo Balla.* New York: Wittenborn & Co., 1969.

Drudi Gambillo, Fiori Maria and Teresa. *Archivi del Futurismo.* Vols. 1 and 2. Rome: De Luca, 1958–62.

Fitch, James Marston. *Architecture and the Aesthetics of Plenty.* New York and London: Columbia University Press, 1961.

"Five Cars—Five Artists." *Art in America* 56 (May–June 1968): 92–93.

Flink, James J. *The Car Culture.* Cambridge, Mass.: M.I.T. Press, 1976.

Flint, R. W., ed. *Marinetti: Selected Writings.* New York: Farrar, Straus & Giroux, 1971.

Flint Institute of Arts. *Art and the Automobile.* Flint, Mich.: Flint Institute of Arts, 1978.

Frackman, Noel. "Tracking Frank Stella's Circuit Series." *Arts Magazine* 56 (April 1982): 134–37.

Frostick, Michael. *Advertising and the Motor-Car.* London: Lund Humphries, 1970.

Giacometti at the Salon d'Auto, Paris." *Paris Review* (1958).

Solomon R. Guggenheim Museum. *Richard Hamilton.* New York: Solomon R. Guggenheim Museum, 1973.

Gunnell, John A., ed. *Standard Catalogue of American Cars, 1946–1975.* Iola, Wisc.: Krause Publications, 1982.

Hamilton, Richard, and George Heard Hamilton, eds. *The Bride Stripped Bare by Her Bachelors, Even* (authorized typographic version). New York: Wittenborn & Co., 1960.

Hanson, Anne Coffin, ed. *The Futurist Imagination.* New Haven, Conn.: Yale University Art Gallery, 1983.

Haskell, Barbara. *H. C. Westermann.* New York: Whitney Museum of American Art, 1978.

Hendry, Maurice D. *Cadillac, Standard of the World: The Complete Seventy-Year History.* New York: Automobile Quarterly Publications, 1973.

Homer, William Innes. "Picabia's *Jeune Fille Americaine* dans l'état de nudité and her Friends." *Art Bulletin* 57 (March 1975): 110–15.

Hulten, K. G. Pontus. *The Machine (As Seen at the End of the Mechanical Age).* New York: Museum of Modern Art, 1968.

Institute of Contemporary Art. *Allan D'Arcangelo: Paintings 1963–70.* Philadelphia: Institute of Contemporary Art, University of Pennsylvania, 1971.

Karlstrom, Paul J. "Reflections on the Automobile in American Art." *Archives of American Art Journal* 20, no. 2 (1980): 18–25.

Kelder, Diane, ed. *Stuart Davis.* Documentary Monographs in Modern Art. New York: Praeger, 1971.

Kirby, Michael. *Futurist Performance.* New York: E. P. Dutton & Co., 1971.

Kirkpatrick, Diane. *Eduardo Paolozzi.* London: Studio Vista, 1970.

Kozloff, Max. "The Rivera Frescoes of Modern Industry at the Detroit Institute of Arts. Proletarian Art under Capitalist Patronage." *Artforum* 12 (November 1973): 58–64.

Léger, Fernand. *Functions of Painting.* New York: Viking Press, 1973.

Lewis, David L., ed. "The Automobile and American Culture." *Michigan Quarterly Review* (Fall 1980, Winter 1981): passim.

Lippard, Lucy R., ed. *Pop Art.* New York: Praeger, 1966.

Lord, Chip. *Ant Farm: Automerica.* New York: E. P. Dutton & Co., 1976.

Emily Lowe Gallery. *Art Around the Automobile.* Hempstead, N.Y.: Emily Lowe Gallery, Hofstra University, 1971.

Lynd, Robert S., and Helen Merrell. *Middletown.* New York: Harcourt, Brace & Co., 1929.

Maldonado, Tomás. "New Developments in Industry and the Teaching of Designers." *Quarterly Bulletin of the Hochschule für Gestaltung,* October 1958.

Martin, Marianne W. *Futurist Art and Theory, 1909–1915.* London: Oxford University Press, 1968.

Masteller, Richard N. *Auto as Icon.* Walla Walla, Wash.: The Donald Sheehan Gallery, Whitman College, 1979.

McCall, Walter P. *80 Years of Cadillac La Salle.* Sarasota, Fla.: Crestline Publishing Co., 1982.

Meisel, Louis K. *Photo-Realism.* New York: Harry N. Abrams, 1980.

Merkert, Jorn. "Pre-Fluxus Vostell." *Art and Artists* 8 (May 1973): 32–38.

Moderna Museet. *Raoul Hausmann.* Stockholm: Moderna Museet, 1967.

Morphet, Richard. *Richard Hamilton.* London: Tate Gallery, 1970.

Morse, A. Reynolds. *Salvador Dali, Pablo Picasso—Pablo Picasso, Salvador Dali: a Preliminary Study in their Similarities and Contrasts.* Cleveland: Salvador Dali Museum, 1973.

Nochlin, Linda. *Realism Now.* Poughkeepsie, N.Y.: Vassar College Art Gallery, 1968.

Norman, Dorothy. *Alfred Stieglitz: An American Seer.* New York: An Aperture Book, Random House, 1960.

O'Dougherty, Brian. *American Masters: The Voice and the Myth.* New York: Random House, 1973.

Papageorge, Tod. *Walker Evans and Robert Frank: A Study of Experience.* New Haven, Conn.: Yale University Art Gallery, 1981.

"The Photo-Realists: Twelve Interviews." *Art in America* 60 (November–December 1972)): 73–89.

Poulain, Herve. *L'Art et l'automobile.* Paris: Les clefs du temps, 1973.

Rae, John B. *The American Automobile.* Chicago: University of Chicago Press, 1965.

Ramelli, Agostino. *Le diverse et artificiose machine.* Paris, 1588.

Ratcliff, Carter. "Route 66 Revisited: The New Landscape Photography." *Art in America* 64 (January–February 1976): 86–90.

Roberts, Peter. *A Picture History of the Automobile.* London: Triune Books, 1973.

Rose, Barbara. *Claes Oldenburg.* New York: Museum of Modern Art, 1970.

Rosenstein, Harris. "Climbing Mt. Oldenburg." *Art News* 64 (February 1966): 21–25.

Rothschild, Emma. *Paradise Lost: The Decline of the Auto-Industrial Age.* New York: Random House, 1973.

Rubin, William Stanley. *Picasso in the Collection of the Museum of Modern Art.* New York: Museum of Modern Art, 1972.

Rudenstine, Angelica Zander. *The Guggenheim Museum Collection: Paintings 1880–1945.* New York: Solomon R. Guggenheim Museum, 1976.

Russell, John, and Suzi Gablik. *Pop Art Redefined.* New York: Praeger, 1969.

Schulze, Franz. "Chaos as Architecture." *Art in America* 58 (July–August 1970): 88–96.

Sears, Stephen W. *The Automobile in America.* New York: American Heritage Publishing Co., 1977.

Seitz, William C. "The Real and the Artificial: Painting of the New Environment." *Art in America* 60 (November–December 1972): 59–72.

Silk, Gerald D. "The Image of the Automobile in Modern Art." Ph.D. diss., Columbia University, 1976.

————. "Ed Kienholz's *Back Seat Dodge '38.*" *Arts Magazine* 52 (January 1978): 112–18.

Smithsonian Institution. *Sao Paolo 9.* Washington, D.C.: Smithsonian Institution Press, 1967.

Stein, Ralph. *The American Automobile.* New York: Random House, 1971.

Stern, Jane and Michael. *Auto Ads.* New York: Random House, 1978.

Swenson, G. R. "What is Pop Art?" Part I, *Art News* 7 (November 1963): 24–27, 61–65; Part II, *Art News* 10 (February 1964): 40–43, 62–66.

Szarkowski, John. *Mirrors and Windows: American Photography Since 1960.* New York: Museum of Modern Art, 1978.

Tashjian, Dickran. *Skyscraper Primitives: Dada and the American Avant-Garde, 1910–1925.* Middletown, Conn.: Wesleyan University Press, 1975.

————. *William Carlos Williams and the American Scene 1920–1940.* New York: Whitney Museum of American Art, 1968.

Tate Gallery. *Richard Hamilton.* London: Tate Gallery, 1970.

————. *Henry Moore to Gilbert and George: Modern British Art from the Tate Gallery.* London: Tate Gallery Publications, 1973.

————. *Eduardo Paolozzi.* London: Tate Gallery, 1971.

Tsujimoto, Karen. *Images of America.* Seattle, Wash.: University of Washington Press for San Francisco Museum of Modern Art, 1982.

Tubbs, D. B. *Art and the Automobile.* New York: Grosset & Dunlap, 1978.

Valturio, Roberto. *De re militari.* Verona: Johannes Nicolai, 1472.

Waldman, Diane. *John Chamberlain: A Retrospective Exhibition.* New York: Solomon R. Guggenheim Museum, 1971.

Whitney Museum of American Art. *Auto-Icons.* New York: Whitney Museum of American Art, 1979.

Zabel, Barbara. "Louis Lozowick and Urban Optimism of the 1920s." *Archives of American Art Journal* 14, no. 2 (1974): 17–22.

INDEX